F

THE
Working Parents
HANDBOOK

June Solnit Sale and Kit Kollenberg with Ellen Melinkoff,
the editors of the *UCLA Working Parents Newsletter*

A FIRESIDE BOOK Published by Simon & Schuster
New York London Toronto Sydney Tokyo Singapore

FIRESIDE
Rockefeller Center
1230 Avenue of the Americas
New York, NY 10020

FIRESIDE and colophon are registered trademarks
of Simon & Schuster Inc.

Designed by Bonni Leon-Berman

Manufactured in the United States of America

1   3   5   7   9   10   8   6   4   2

Library of Congress Cataloging-in-Publication Data
Sale, June S.
    The working parents handbook / June Solnit Sale and Kit Kollenberg
with Ellen Melinkoff.
    p.   cm.
    1. Working mothers—Life skills guides. 2. Parents—Life skills guides.
3. Work and family. I. Kollenberg, Kit. II. Melinkoff, Ellen. III. Title.
    HQ759.48.S25   1996
    646.7'0085'2—dc20   95-26176
                                                              CIP

ISBN 0-684-80237-6

Our sincere appreciation to Richard Parks, our wise and sensitive agent, and our loving acknowledgment to our partners and children: Sam, Laurie, Norman, Nancy, Josh, Peggy, Gary, Michael, Jeremy, and Alex

Contents

nine

ten

Introduction

THE UCLA WORKING *Parents Newsletter* has been offering practical advice, solutions, and ideas to working parents since 1989. Our six-page quarterly newsletters have been (according to the letters we've received) eagerly awaited by working parents all over the UCLA campus, as well as readers at companies such as McDonnell Douglas West, whose Employee Community Fund has helped underwrite the project.

When we began, we felt there was a need for the *Newsletter* despite the many parenting magazines at the newsstand. The magazines had long lead times that prevented them from tackling emerging issues. Further, their dependence on advertising revenue seemed to make them shy away from some topics. Could they give a thumbs-down to pull-up diapers when diaper companies paid the bills? We researched other parenting newsletters on the market and decided that there was nothing out there like the one we wanted to publish. The ones that existed were all too fluffy for our taste: too much white space and artwork and not enough content. Our vision was plenty of content, with no filler. We wanted each issue to be packed with information, advice, and helpful ideas that work. We had a point of view that was often different from those we were reading. And we knew that the best advice is clear and direct, not condescending or peppered with jargon.

Our goals are the same now as they were when we published the first issue of the *Newsletter:* to help working parents feel in control by understanding how to make the best of each situation they face and to help them with what will probably be the most difficult task of their lives: balancing two demanding roles.

After six years, we had a body of work that seemed destined to be collected in book format. So we went to work, thinking we were putting together a collection of our best articles. But the result, *The Working Parents Handbook*, has turned out to be much more than a binding up of our back issues. We have reexamined every word, every issue we've written about. We found that there were many important areas that we hadn't covered yet in the *Newsletter* that needed to be in the *Handbook* for it to be inclusive. We added extensively, updated, and, in some cases, rethought the topics.

Like the *Newsletter*, the *Handbook* is a mix of expected issues (finding child care, getting to work on time) and unexpected ones such as helping a child feel safe in an unsafe world (a significant issue for working parents who must be away from home for nine or more hours a day); feeling jealous of a caregiver—the one you feel so lucky to have found; maintaining friendships with non-moms.

As we started organizing the book, an overriding theme began to emerge: time. Your concerns as a working parent begin when you consider the best time to announce your pregnancy at work. Then there's how much time to take off. Followed by how to get to work on time. Using your sick or personal time for your child's pediatric appointments. And time to be alone.

So how do working parents cram thirty-six hours' worth of activity into twenty-four? How do you balance the demands of a nit-picking boss and a colicky baby? Whether you're part of a two-parent family or are a single parent, the demands on your time, your attention, and your energy are tremendous. Let's face it, working parents have two critical, challenging jobs. Two masters. Two Circes. How do you balance and perform them both to the best of your ability?

After all, it's not okay to be the "employee of the month" if you arrive home late at night with nothing left to give your kids—no energy, no attention, no oomph. It's also not okay to be "mother (or father) of the year" if you give so little attention to work that your job performance suffers.

We have always written about the real-life issues of working parents. Real life is an adoption coming through a month sooner than expected. Getting a baby to sleep through the night so you have the energy to do your job at nine in the morning. Waking to a toddler with a high fever the morning of your big regional meeting. Replacing a nanny who quits without notice. Worrying that your preschooler is spending more time with TV cartoons than with real friends. And finding a safe place for your ten-year-old on Veterans Day.

We feel that all working parents have a common bond. A partner in a big law firm, an assistant in a small dental office, a waitress at a busy fish house, a police officer—the basics are the same. Sick kids. Caregivers who won't work a minute past six, whether they're English nannies or a YMCA after-school program worker. Worrying about being there for your child while putting in exhausting eight-hour days on the job.

We begin with the issues that arise during pregnancy and progress to problems that emerge as your child grows older. We're not always talking about babies; we want this handbook to be as useful to parents of a five-year-old as to parents of a ten-year-old. Some issues are very age-specific (the first days in child care); others are long-term (limiting television watching).

In our years of working in child-care centers and in the community, we've talked with hundreds of working parents who have survived and thrived. The personal vignettes that are sprinkled throughout the book are from the many working parents we've talked with. We asked them to tell us stories about incidents in their lives that other working parents might learn from.

We've filled *The Working Parents Handbook* with advice and ideas that will help *you* handle, survive, and excel in both your jobs. To paraphrase Voltaire, you *can* have the best of both possible worlds.

The Time to Plan

Before Your Baby Is Born

Being Pregnant in the Workplace

ATTITUDES toward working mothers have changed drastically in the last few decades (although there are still pockets of unreconstructed thinking out there). Laws have changed. Expectations have changed. Life has changed. While today's prevailing attitudes, laws, and expectations may not be ideal—yet—there has been considerable movement in a more enlightened direction.

You may be lucky enough to have had others blaze the trail in your workplace and now you've inherited a thoughtful, compassionate situation that will help you to handle your increasingly complex life. There may still be some changes to be made. Maybe you don't think of yourself as the trailblazer type. Maybe you just haven't found any trails that needed blazing—until now, when you see the necessity for family-friendly improvements.

A generation ago, women sat out their pregnancies at home. They were expected to quit work when they pipopped their first waistband button. They disappeared from the office, the factory, the nurses' station, the cashier's desk, the classroom—usually for years, to stay home and raise their children. Adoptions, for the most part, were by mothers who stayed home.

Nowadays, if you stop working halfway through your pregnancy, people want to know why. Is there a medical reason? They'd accept nothing less. Vanna White kept turning those *Wheel of Fortune* letters until a few weeks before delivery. So unless you climb telephone poles for a living or your doctor has medical concerns, you'll probably work through most of your pregnancy. Also, you're likely to return to work fairly soon after delivery—maybe in six weeks, six months, or a year or two. Today's workforce, which is 57 percent women, is made up of a substantial number of working mothers: mothers of infants, toddlers, preschoolers, kindergartners, and so on.

In most workplaces, it's now acceptable to look pregnant, to be pregnant. There is no right time to stop working. It depends on the kind of work you do, your energy level, your health, and your finances.

Still, being visibly pregnant does distract people, and that's something you must face and deal with as you approach the midpoint of pregnancy. In an otherwise impersonal business situation, people will know something very personal about you. They may not know if you are married or not, have children already, or vote Republican or Democrat, but they do know this very personal thing about you. You lose a sense of anonymity. People may be looking you in the eye, but they've got your belly on their minds. They will have fleeting (or not so fleeting) thoughts about your health. Should you be standing so long? Are you comfortable in that chair? Would you like something to drink? These ministrations, while sincere, can divert attention from the task that brought you together in the first place: work. This attention is a mixed blessing. It's nice to be fussed over, but it's disconcerting to be treated as if you need some special assistance to carry on, especially if you feel fine. This is even more true if you're a private person and your pregnancy has thrust you into an unwanted limelight.

There are more than two hundred people in my office. I worked there for over three years before I became pregnant, and there had been several women who had babies during that time. I remember going to showers for them, and I will admit to asking a few innocuous questions while we were waiting for the elevator about when they were due or if they were hoping for a boy or a girl. But when I got pregnant, it seemed that every time I turned around somebody wanted to talk about me and my baby. One woman brought me her old baby clothes. People didn't just ask about names, they had very strong opinions. Our "girl name" was Katie and one woman told me it was too common—I should think of something else (we had a boy). People would tell me the latest studies on pregnancy that they'd read in magazines. They'd tell me I was having a girl because of the way I was carrying. I felt like Subject Number One. I'm sure it was the same for the women before me. At first, I was very self-conscious about all the attention, especially since I felt people were watching my weight! But I did learn to relax about it. Looking back, it felt like my fifteen minutes of fame.

There *is* a spotlight quality to being pregnant, which you may have already discovered. Your pregnancy will become a topic of conversation—with or without you around! Coworkers will comment in the elevator, "I hear Melinda is pregnant."

Having a baby has its communal aspects. It makes you part of the family of man in a way you weren't before. It may even make you wonder what people thought of you before you became a card-carrying breeder of the next generation. Were you just a meaningless blip? You may or may not agree with this concept—that being pregnant makes you a "real" member of society—but be assured that there will be people in your workplace who will now welcome the pregnant you as a new member of the club.

You will be showered with advice as well as attention. You will hear stories of other people's pregnancies—including amazingly personal information such as how many centimeters they were dilated when they got to the hospital or how their episiotomy went. (For some reason, this, and other intimate details, become part of casual conversation once you've joined the club. Brace yourself.) Self-appointed protectors of *your* unborn will watch your eating habits for you. They will want to make sure you're getting enough calcium. They may think you should swear off Diet Coke.

Here's the deal: The elders of the tribe have this elemental urge to pass along all the tribal wisdom to you through oral traditions. It's an ancient approach but one that has its place in the modern age. And it can be significant to a new mother, whose own family may not be close by to guide her through this important time. Now, you may be thinking that tribal elders aren't always knowledgeable or up-to-date. But there is also much common sense to be learned from most people who have raised families. Think of it as cultural anthropology. And remember, when you settle into your new-mother role in a few months, the spotlight will move on to someone else. A more newly pregnant woman will surface, and you will move one step to the left as you slowly work your way to tribal-elder status.

Consider also that your condition may stir up strong emotions in those around you, both at work and beyond. A pregnant woman can be very unsettling to other people. Older women who have grown children may envy you, wishing they could turn back the clock. Or they may be reminded of the fact that the world was not so accepting of working mothers when they were young, and they had to make some hard choices. Women who are struggling to conceive may see your pregnancy as too easily accomplished and a painful reminder of their failures. Men will have strong feelings, too. Your pregnancy may make them feel locked out of nature's wonder, unable to really understand what it means to give life.

Hovering above it all is the feeling that bringing a child into the world is truly wonderful. Everyone may wrestle with personal issues, but at the core of the experience is the sense that a new, wanted child is what it's all about. The concern, questions, and attention are all indicative of the primal need to be part of the continuum.

It's magic. And you're the magician. You'll have a magnetic, magical draw for the next few months even in the most staid of workplaces. There'll be those inquiries into your health, even a few well-meaning-but-unasked-for hands on your stomach. You will probably even unknowingly invite this behavior. Pregnant women often touch their own stomachs more than they did before, which may be taken as an invitation for others to pat you as well.

This is one of those I-can't-believe-I-did-it stories. A few days after I announced my pregnancy, I was in a very important meeting with three vice presidents and our company's legal counsel. All men. All suits. I was about three and a half months along. I spent the entire meeting stroking my stomach. At least, that's what I was told. One of the vps, with whom I'm on good terms, pulled me aside afterward and said, "If you're rubbing your belly like that now, what can we expect in four months?" I asked, "What do you mean?" And he demonstrated. I was mortified. I realized—but only at that moment—that I had been doing it. ("The Little

Mother in the Boardroom.") *Thank goodness he told me. I was very careful after that. It was important that I remain as professional as I had always been.*

Sooner or later, coworkers, customers, clients, and bosses will all know about your condition. Depending on the spirit of cooperation or competition in your workplace, your pregnancy may work to others' advantage. By subtly creating the impression that you are not working at peak efficiency or not as committed to the job as you were before, a coworker may manage to turn your condition to his/her advantage by seeming more efficient or committed. Neither of you may have changed in your productivity or passion for the job, but by commenting on how tired pregnant women get or how you must have a lot on your mind now, another worker can alter perceptions of your work. Of course, people who undermine coworkers don't need a pregnancy to do it. It is a lifelong methodology. A pregnant coworker is just a fresh opportunity.

> *It was so hard to keep my mouth shut at work about my pregnancy. I wanted to tell everyone immediately, but we decided to wait until I was four months along. I'm glad I did, hard as it was. It shortened the time I was pregnant, if you know what I mean. I was able to handle the low energy of those first few months by myself. I blamed a few bad days on the flu, and no one paid much attention. I think if they had known, there would have been a lot more said about it—the wrong kind of attention.*

This is not how it goes in every workplace, thank goodness, and it may seem, at first, to be an unnecessary downer to bring up these issues. But we feel that it's helpful to be aware of such Machiavellian possibilities so that you size up your particular situation before you announce your pregnancy, fret out loud about morning sickness, and so on. You may be able to be candid about your midafternoon fizzle or how hard it is to keep yourself from daydreaming about baby names. Or you may decide it's wiser not to reveal so much. You may find that acting just as you did before is what it takes to keep everything going the way you want it to go. Being the only, or the first, pregnant worker in a place is like being the first woman, or the first African American, in a particular situation. Fair or unfair, all eyes are on you.

If you are reading this in the first trimester of your pregnancy, when energy levels are traditionally lowest (with the exception of your last few weeks), you may have doubts about how long you can keep up your work pace. You may worry that you'll have to stop working before you really want to. You're pooped. All you do is work and sleep, work and sleep. If your energy continues in this downhill direction, you'll be comatose by the fifth month. Courage! Most women find a renewed energy level during the second trimester. You may not be at your prepregnancy levels of vigor, but you'll feel that more things are possible.

Planning Your Leave

When you tell your employer that you are pregnant, he or she will want to know what your plans are. You may have a very formal, distant relationship, or you may have a friendly, spill-over-into-private-life relationship. Either way, your boss will have immediate concerns about how your pregnancy will affect the workplace. How long will you be able to work? How long are you taking off? Who will do your work when you're gone? These are the bottom-line issues. Don't tell your employer that you're pregnant until you've thought through these issues thoroughly.

It's essential that your boss be told directly by you and be the first to know. Hearing "Did you know Sandy's pregnant?" from another employee can miff a boss. When you walk into that office an hour later with your carefully rehearsed "Guess what?," your employer may feel like the last one to be told, a little foolish, or left out of the loop and, as a result, not be as positive and helpful as might have been the case had your news gone there first. Bosses like to be "the first to know" everything. So in the spirit of enlightened self-interest, accord your employer that privilege.

One worker's maternity leave can have a ripple effect on coworkers. The new mother's work may have to be parceled out to others who may then feel put upon. They have their own work to do. A temporary replacement may be hired who may or may not be able to do your work efficiently. Your work may simply not get done for a few months, holding up others in their work. Before you announce your news, think through what these ripples might be and develop some plans for dealing with them.

Requesting a leave implies returning to work. Since you are not quitting your job, you are telling your employer that your plan is to come back to your position afterward. This can be a difficult thing to promise. You don't know what's ahead. After your baby is born, you may decide that you want to stay home for a much longer period of time than your job could reasonably be held for you. During your leave, you may rethink your job entirely, step back, and realize that you'd be happier looking for another position.

Most mothers (85 percent) return to the workplace after childbirth. Keep this statistic in mind. It may come in handy when you negotiate your leave plans with your employer. She may take to the idea of temporary arrangements (such as hiring a sub) better if she realizes the statistics are on "her" side.

An employer's hesitancy to believe that you'll return to work in a few months may be the result of an experience with another worker who requested a leave and then didn't return, leaving the company in a tight spot. You may suffer from her legacy. Or create a legacy of your own. Face it, you may have a change of heart. Women who were willing (eager!) to swear that they would be back at work in three months, who thought they wouldn't be able to bear being away from the stimulation of the workplace any longer, have been known to do a 180-degree turnaround. On the other hand, some mothers who imagined themselves loving every minute of their leave have discovered that they couldn't wait to be working again.

Talking with Other Working Parents in Your Workplace

The best place to be a working parent is usually where there are plenty of working parents around you. (The worst may be where you're the trailblazer, as in an office of singles or all men.) Not only do other working parents understand what you're going through, they also won't be oversolicitous or act as though there's something abnormal about having a baby. Later on, they will also empathize with your distracted state of mind the first few days your child is in a new child-care arrangement or your worry about your child having many ear infections.

Beginning now, when you are pregnant, consider people to seek out for parent-to-parent chats. In most workplaces, chatting with other workers who have similar jobs or job levels may be the wisest course. Talking too much about motherhood to both supervisors and subordinates can have side effects—just as talking about your love life or other personal issues can. To people of another job level, you may lose your sense of authority or seem like a complainer, but such ramifications are much less likely to come into play if you hold the same conversations with a coworker.

Ask coworker parents what it's really been like to juggle work with parenting. Remember to phrase your questions carefully, because you don't want to hear bloody war stories. You'll hear enough of them unbidden in the next few months, from folks who spot your stomach from a hundred feet away, rush to your side, and being their litanies of "You ain't seen nothin' yet." Don't set up situations in which you'll hear more than necessary. Try, "How did you do your leave?" and "How would you have done it differently?" The hindsight of others can be your foresight. You're after facts and good advice, mixed with only a few horror stories. Don't borrow trouble.

Along these same lines, seek out coworkers with generally upbeat attitudes. Some people moan and groan about everything, and they bring that bummer attitude toward their working-parent role. Perhaps a coworker was granted a six-month parental leave and feels she has been subtly penalized ever since. Hearing that, you might decide to request a shorter leave. But that coworker may have had a history of poor work habits. What she saw as being penalized about her leavetaking may have really been about her work in general. Proceed cautiously.

Find out how long other working parents took off for the birth or adoption of their children. Were they encouraged to take as much time as they needed? Or were they made to feel guilty?

Stopping Work

If you are having an uncomplicated pregnancy, the chief concerns that affect your decision of when you stop work will be your own financial needs and the needs of your job to run smoothly without you.

This may be a good point at which to remind yourself of a fact of life that will be with you for at least the next eighteen years—nothing's for sure. Always assume the best, the most normal, the most healthy path is ahead of you, but remember that life can turn on a dime. A healthy pregnancy can take on problems that require bedrest, or you may be set for a vaginal delivery and wind up with a cesarean. Either of these complications will change your leave plans considerably. As you make your arrangements, ask yourself how they could be modified if you had to stop working at seven months rather than eight, or if you had to recuperate from a C-section. Don't leave an important meeting for your last day at work or put off training your replacement for too long.

Since you can't know what is ahead, consider the wisdom of requesting as much time off as possible. You may have a medically routine delivery and a mellow baby and decide to return to work earlier than you'd planned (don't just show up unannounced, of course—there may be a temp there!). This approach may be more beneficial to your reputation as a devoted employee than asking for the minimum leave now and having to request more time after your baby is born. Of course, a longer leave request could be viewed as a lack of commitment on your part, proof that motherhood and career don't mix. So after carefully reflecting on your situation, you may decide that it's wiser to put in for a shorter leave—indicating your commitment to fulfilling your work obligations—and keep your fingers crossed.

> When we adopted Corey, I arranged six weeks of leave from my accumulated days. The problem was I didn't have a due date. We were adopting from Guatemala and were told to be on alert—but that it could take two years. When we got the word, I had a week to get my desk in order. Everyone at work was very helpful, but it was a burden on many people. And I never imagined that I would have a hard physical adjustment. After all, I wasn't recovering from childbirth, just a trip to Guatemala City. But Corey woke up several times a night for months and needed a lot of attention. I needed an extra two weeks off before I had the energy to face work.

There are companies that pay full or partial salaries to workers on pregnancy leave. If only every employer would! Most working women have a limited number of days designated for vacation, sick, or personal time that becomes the core, sometimes all, of their leave. Whatever else you take may be unpaid; you may get no extra paid days during your pregnancy leave, aside from disability benefits from the state. What you use up before the baby is born shortens the time you'll be able to spend at home afterward. You may be able to get a six-month leave approved, but only one month with a paycheck.

My maternity package (ha ha!) consisted entirely of my accumulated time: twelve days of vacation time, nine sick days, and two personal days. And the Fourth of July was in there. A little over a month. The rest was unpaid. I did get disability when my company days ran out. I went back to work when Maggie was seven weeks old, mainly out of economic necessity.

The Law

The laws that affect pregnancy and parental leave are not universal in application. They don't cover small employers, and certainly not the self-employed.

The federal Pregnancy Discrimination Act applies to employers with more than fifteen workers. It prohibits a worker from being fired simply because she is pregnant (which has been known to happen). It requires employers to treat a pregnant worker in the same manner in which they treat employees with temporarily disabling conditions, such as a broken arm or a heart attack. The act provides job security, but only to the same extent that an employer provides it to workers with other kinds of disabilities.

The period of disability is whatever your doctor says it is: usually four to six weeks following a vaginal birth or six to eight weeks after a cesarean birth. Technically, what's called maternity leave is usually covered by company time in some fashion (paid or unpaid leave, vacation days, sick days, etc.) and then, when that runs out, by disability benefits, which vary greatly from state to state. If you request more time beyond what's termed maternity leave (or your spouse requests time off), it is referred to as parental leave.

The law also requires employers to offer equal treatment in matters of vacation time, seniority, and sick leave. Most employers do not pay salaries during parental leaves, but some do continue to pay the employer's share of benefits, such as health insurance premiums. For example, IBM employees who are on unpaid parental leave are entitled to full employer-paid health coverage (which can last up to three years if the employee works part-time in the last two years of the leave). Du

Pont and AT&T offer full company-paid benefits for up to six months. Some companies that do not pay benefits will allow the employee to take over payments during the leave to ensure uninterrupted coverage. At Prudential Insurance, employees can prepay medical benefits for up to six months of leave.

Although parental leave is most commonly taken by the person actually having the baby, a growing number of companies are allowing new fathers some time off—unpaid, of course. A recent study at Du Pont showed that while 92 percent of parental and family leaves were taken by women, the number of fathers requesting them is increasing every year.

Referring to pregnancy and recovery from childbirth as a "disability" can have both positive and negative effects. On the one hand, doing so has made it possible to get the law passed and to demand that employers make some long-overdue changes. It also allows you to file a disability insurance claim and collect money for the last few weeks of your pregnancy and the first few weeks afterward. But at the same time, women are fighting the negative baggage that comes with the term "disabled." Depending on how things go for you, you may not feel disabled for more than a few days. But being saddled with the label, while it allows you a longer leave and guaranteed return to work, may have subtle undertones and ramifications.

The federal Family and Medical Leave Act, passed in 1993, applies to employers with more than fifty workers within a seventy-five-mile radius. Under this act, both male and female employees are guaranteed that they will be able to return to the same or equivalent jobs when they take up to twelve weeks off (in any twelve-month period) during the birth, adoption, or foster-care placement of a child—or, additionally, to care for a seriously sick child, spouse, or parent. During this period, the employer must maintain existing health coverage, seniority status, and benefits. However, the employee does not accrue benefits such as vacation days during the leave. To be covered by the law, an employee must have worked for the employer for at least one year. The up-to-twelve weeks of leave is unpaid, unless you make arrangements with your employer to use your vacation or sick time.

Employees are required to provide thirty days' notice before taking leave. Exceptions include situations of early delivery and pregnancy complications. In these cases, an employee is required to give as much notice as reasonably possible.

There is a big loophole in this law: Your employer has the right not to hold your old position for you if you are in the top 10 percent of the highest-paid employees in the company and to do so would, in the employer's opinion, cause severe financial consequences to the company. Your employer can also require you to use your paid sick and vacation time as part of the twelve weeks. This may, at first, seem like a disadvantage to the employer; why would she insist on your being paid rather than unpaid for part of the leave? Because otherwise you may decide to extend your time away by tacking on weeks, even months, of accrued paid vacation and sick days, thereby extending your time off beyond the time the employer feels the company can do without you. Under this law, if the employer so chooses, you can be limited to twelve weeks of leave.

Many states have more generous leave laws that offer greater or different protection than the federal laws. Further, certain unions may have reached collective-bargaining agreements that are more generous, requiring employers to provide longer paid or unpaid leaves.

One of your first tasks as a pregnant working woman should be to tally up all your accumulated time. If you were given a copy of the personnel manual when you were hired, dig it out. Or ask to see your employer's personnel policy in the employment manual. Don't ask specifically to see the pregnancy leave sections unless you have already announced your condition at work. We suggest reviewing the manual quietly before making your announcement. Make photocopies and study them at home.

What you want to know, both from the personnel manual and from applicable state laws, is the maximum number of weeks you're entitled to, if your employer must continue to contribute to your health benefits, and what job you are guaranteed when you return. Employer coverage of health benefits varies greatly from state to state. If you quit work rather than take a leave, you may lose your health benefits just when you need them most. For many women, this issue can be the overriding factor in determining whether they return to work or postpone formal resignation until after giving birth, then returning to work for a trial period.

I was employed by a small-city government for two years before I got pregnant. I got a fairly good maternity leave and my employer paid my health benefits while I was out. I had told my boss

I'd be back in two months, but during that time, we decided to move to another county. Just before I was scheduled to return, I called my supervisor and said I was going to have to quit rather than go back to work. The city has now threatened to sue me for the paid days and the health benefits during the maternity leave because I didn't return. I should have gone back to work for a few weeks, even if I had to commute sixty miles each way.

To get some perspective on the subject, we asked to see the union agreement for some of UCLA's service employees (the union is AFSCME, the American Federation of State, County and Municipal Employees). The relevant sections are included in Appendix A. We found it off-putting and cold, but typical in spirit of most other employee manuals. Concessions seem to be granted in a rather patronizing manner. When you compare this text to your own personnel manual, which is likely to be similar, you'll see that pregnancy issues are routinely dealt with in formal, impersonal terms. This is the way it is, and you're not alone.

Small Workplaces

If you work for an employer that is not covered by the same laws that apply to larger companies, your job may not be protected during your leave. That means it may not be there when you return. You'll have to negotiate your own leave, and how successful you will be depends on your employer's needs and attitudes, as well as the prevailing leave standards in your field. Before you announce your pregnancy, take the time to research what these standards are. If you are an office assistant in a two-person office, find out what comparable office workers in large companies get. If you're an accountant in a small firm, inquire about what large accounting firms have to say on the subject. Then you can approach your employer with a more authoritatively researched request.

An employer may view your request as the start of a negotiation. You ask for six months, he says he couldn't possibly spare you for more than two, you settle on four. You might want to request a longer leave than you hope to get, in order to "compromise." Agreeing to a shorter leave or returning to work earlier than you agreed to can only be viewed as in your favor. What a team player you are! Conversely, a request for a lengthy leave could be turned down with no bargaining at all.

For the most part, in a small workplace it is much harder to cover for a worker who is out on an extended leave than it is in a large workplace. A three-month leave may not be practical. Your employer (who may in fact be the only other person in the office) may not be able to be without your services for that long, and may need to find a replacement while you are on leave. The employer's first reaction may be to let you go and hire a permanent replacement, but you may be able to mount a winning argument that it took much longer than three months (or however long you plan to be away) for you to get up to speed when you started the job.

I work as a dental assistant. It's just the dentist and me; we've worked together for five years. When I announced to him that I was pregnant, he had the most amazing look on his face. As if I'd betrayed him! He's a very nice man, but he likes things very calm and routine. I could tell what he was thinking: how was this going to affect him? The next day he said very quietly that I could work as long as I was healthy but that he felt he'd have to replace me when I left. I didn't say much, but I did make some calls to temporary agencies. I showed him their brochures, told him how their temps are always filling in for maternity leaves. I reminded him how well we worked together, and that the three months would go by fast. He took a few days to think about it, but then he agreed. I think it made him feel good that I liked my job so much I was willing to fight to keep it.

The Informal Policy

In every workplace, there are two kinds of work policies: formal and informal. There's a difference between what's actually on the books and what situation you can really work out without putting your job or work climate in jeopardy.

The law is only half the picture when you start to make your plans; the "lay of the land" is equally important. This takes into consideration typical maternity leaves in your job in general, as well as your own employer's previous attitude and reaction to working mothers. Your boss's and your coworkers' reaction to your news will be highly colored by the experiences they've had with other new mothers. If your boss has a wife who went back to work a month after the births of all their babies, he'll have similar expectations for you. Take three months and you're automatically a slacker! On the other hand, his wife may have had a difficult delivery, a protracted recovery, and a colicky baby. To him, a three-month leave will seem reasonable. Female bosses bring their own histories. Those with children will—we hope—keep in mind how they struggled to do two jobs at once. Those without children may have no grasp of the nitty-gritty of having a baby. You can expect the same range of reactions from coworkers.

My supervisor has a two-year-old. His wife returned to her job when their baby was six weeks old, and it was very hard on both of them. She had no alternative. I remember it took several months for them to adjust to their new schedules. He was very sympathetic and really went to bat for me to see that I got a four-month leave, and that I wasn't hassled over it. He did it just because he's a nice guy, but it sure made me want to return his kindness with good work.

Sizing Up Your Employer's Parent-Friendliness

There are those wonderful companies out there that believe it is important to help employees fulfill their family responsibilities. They know it is in the company's interest: An enlightened approach to the demands of working parents makes for more satisfied, productive workers, less turnover, more profit. If you're employed by one of these companies, your adjustments in the next few months will be far less stressful than if you're in the pioneer role, educating your employer as you go along.

A shining example of an enlightened corporation is Fel-Pro (which makes car gaskets), in Illinois. Employees there may receive up to ten weeks' maternity leave at half or full pay and—with at least two years of service—extend that up to one year. Full benefits continue during the leave. Employees are also entitled to up to three months of family leave, at no pay, for an adoption or to care for a sick child or family member. Fel-Pro will contribute up to $2,500 in legal expenses during adoption proceedings and purchases a $1,000 treasury bond for all newborns of employees. The company has an on-site day-care center for forty children and sends trained caregivers to employees' homes to care for sick children and other dependents. For employees' children, there's a summer camp, tutoring, and scholarships. Employees themselves get flexible work hours and child-development seminars. Talk about a progressive company!

According to a recent study by the U.S. General Accounting Office, the watchword for family-friendly (and indeed simply employee-friendly) employers is *flexibility*. Flexibility means which hours, how many hours, range and quantity of benefits, and so on. The underlying understanding is that a worker who is allowed to tailor some aspects of work to meet individual needs will be better able to balance a complex life.

How to Identify a Family-Friendly Employer
A family-friendly employer need not have all of the following elements or programs in place, but it should have several of them.

1. *A corporate family policy.* The employer should recognize the importance of promoting family-friendly policies, and this begins with a formal, well-thought-out policy. In this arena, it's often true that "when companies are good, they are very, very good." For instance companies such as IBM and 3M have extremely detailed, carefully considered, and extensive programs and policies for their employees.

2. *A work/family committee and/or a manager for family affairs.* Such a manager has the full- or part-time assignment of overseeing working-parent issues, from child care to sick-leave policy.

This committee and/or manager should have the primary or sole purpose of addressing working-parent issues for employees at all levels of the company. Of course, different job categories may carry with them their own problems, and some companies are more enlightened in their policies toward one segment of their workforce than toward others. For example, executives may be allowed to unofficially leave for children's medical appointments, while assembly-line workers may have to clock in and out. Or, conversely, assembly workers may be able to use their accumulated time without specifying the reason for their two hours off, while executives, working hand-in-glove with a vice president, may have to explain their absences, however brief, in detail.

3. *Forums where family issues can be discussed, such as parenting seminars, prenatal education classes, and themed lunchtime brownbag discussions.*

4. *A progressive attitude toward work hours, which includes these possibilities:*

a. *Part-time work.* Family-oriented companies allow, as much as possible, for employees to work part-time for a period of time. This policy can come in very handy after the birth or adoption of a child, during summer-school vacations, or when a sick child needs long-term nursing at home. IBM's program permits employees to work part-time for these reasons for a minimum of six months and not longer than three years. Employees can return to full-time status at the end of any six-month period. New York State employees have a program that allows even more flexibility, in which they can return to full-time work at the start of any pay period. Some companies prorate benefits for part-time employees, while others offer full benefits.

b. *Job sharing.* In this arrangement, two workers share one job (and benefits) between them. They work half days or alternate days, dividing or sharing tasks. Job sharing can be difficult to arrange. It requires that two employees want to do it and that those employees be well matched for an equal division of the workload.

c. *Flexible work schedules.* Employers require workers to put in a certain number of hours in a pay period, but allow the employee to determine which hours they will be. Often employers require that certain "core hours" be covered. For example, everyone must be at work from 9:00 A.M. to 3:00 P.M. but each individual can decide how early, and subsequently how late, to work to put in an eight-hour day.

d. *Meal-break flexibility.* IBM offers this benefit in some of its offices, whereby employees can take from thirty minutes to two hours for lunch, as long as they work the required number of hours in a day. This policy allows parents to leave for a school play, for example, without faking a dental emergency.

5. *Benefits that meet differing needs of employees.*   Personnel people refer to this type of program as a smorgasbord approach, allowing employees to pick which benefits are most important to them and to avoid duplication. Let's say, for instance, that a family with two working parents is covered by two health plans but no dental plan. Customized benefits permit an employee to relinquish medical benefits already covered by a spouse's employer and add dental insurance and/or life insurance. Some employees receive a "health waiver" cash amount in their paychecks when they don't sign up for the company benefit—not the full cash value of the insurance premium, but a nice percentage.

6. *A flexible workplace.*   Employers permit employees to work at home or in satellite offices close to home. Telecommuting allows employees to work at home through computers, modems, phones, and faxes.

7. *Sick-child days.*   Parents may openly use their own sick time to tend to sick children or children's medical appointments. It's so much less stressful to be able to say you're coming in late because your toddler has a doctor's appointment for an ear infection than to say you've wrenched your back (again). Enlightened companies allow employees to use their sick time as they see fit. At Grumman Corporation, workers have five days of "paid absence allowance" each year. Hewlett-Packard has an even more progressive policy: it allows employees to combine vacation and sick time and use it at their own discretion.

8. *Help with child care.*   Some possibilities:

a. *Child-care programs.*   There are many ways in which an employer can provide child-care assistance to workers, including on-site or near-site child-care centers; resource and referral programs (see Chapter 3 for a full discussion); development of child-care resources; partial payment of child-care costs (paid either to parents or providers); participation in child-care consortiums with other employers; child-care programs for sick children; and emergency child-care programs.

b. *On-site/near-site child-care centers.*   These may be operated by the employer or by an independent child-care provider. Often-cited reasons for not choosing to operate centers or contract with independent centers are that they are too costly and that they unfairly distribute child-care benefits among employees, since usually only a portion of employee families can be enrolled (even though they can benefit the entire company in terms of morale). Other methods, such as subsidized child care for all employees, may be more equitable.

c. *Referral services.* Some companies provide information on child-care providers to employees through a designated employee or by contracting another organization. Honeywell offers a computerized referral service in partnership with the Greater Minneapolis Day Care Association. Parents can use the service to find out about available licensed providers in their areas. Work/Family Directions, Inc. is, for example, a nationwide information network with which many companies contract.

d. *Sick-child care.* Employers who realize that workers often have to stay home with sick children because their usual caregiver will only take care of them when they are well are beginning to consider sick-child care. The care of sick children may be at an on-site center, at hospital day-care centers, at specially designated areas of child-care centers, or by visiting nurses at home. Honeywell employees can choose among all these options.

e. *Emergency child care.* Different from sick-child care, emergency child care, such as that provided by Time Warner, is backup care when your usual provider is unavailable or when school is closed unexpectedly (as for snow or storm days).

f. *Employer-shared costs.* Then there are employers who pay part of child-care costs. This may be based on an employee's salary, a flat rate, or a percentage of actual costs. As an example, American Express employees are eligible for a subsidy of up to $35 a week for child care.

g. *Consortiums.* Some employers have too few employees to offer these kinds of benefits. It's not financially possible for them to hire someone to deal with family programs. Many such companies have found the solution is to join together in consortiums to open child-care centers for employees of all member companies, or, alternatively, to jointly hire a resource adviser. Consortiums can give employees in small companies access to child-care resources similar to those offered by large corporations.

h. *Tax benefits.* Under Section 129 of its code, Dependent Care Assistance, the IRS allows employees to set aside up to $5,000 a year in pretax salary for dependent care (child care or elder care). This amount is excluded from gross income, effectively reducing it by up to $5,000. When employees pay a child-care provider, they submit their receipts to the employer for reimbursement from this set-aside sum. Neither the set-aside money nor the reimbursement is considered taxable income. Both employees and employer can benefit. Employees reduce the amount of their taxable income, and the employer does not have to pay benefits on the set-aside amount. While working parents can take child-care deductions on their tax returns, such deductions are usually only beneficial to families earning less than $25,000 a year. In contrast, Dependent Care Assistance is a money saver at all income levels. The downside is that once designated, the money cannot be returned to the employee. It cannot be used for any other purpose and will continue to be deducted for the rest of the year. Further, since parents have to pay caregivers according to their agreed-upon schedule, they must pay out-of-pocket for the first month, until reimbursement is received. Many employers do not know about "Dep Care"; you may want to read up on it further and broach the subject yourself.

Gathering Information on Child-Care Possibilities

There are those stories about parents who—five minutes after their home pregnancy test comes out positive or they sign up for adoption—are on the phone to a sought-after day-care center or Lamaze teacher to get on the waiting list.

But pregnancy *is* the right time to explore available child-care possibilities in your life. You should find out what's really available in your area and what the rates are, and think about what kind of child-care arrangement you would be most comfortable with. And, if you choose to, it's a good time to get on a waiting list. We will go into a more detailed discussion about these issues in Chapter 3, when it's time to make decisions, but here is brief overview. We most often use the term *caregiver* rather than *family day-care provider, day-care teacher,* or *nanny*. We feel it is warmer and more encompassing. We use the term *she* since most caregivers are women, but we also want to acknowledge the fine male caregivers who choose to do this work.

Many parents who can afford it choose in-home child care for very young babies. This one-to-one arrangement is expensive. Whether your caregiver lives in your home or her own, you are paying a full-time employee. And, of course, your child will get full-time attention. A live-in caregiver will give you the most flexibility in terms of hours, but you might find the arrangements inhibiting, unless you have plenty of room for an extra person in your home.

In family day care, a caregiver cares for children in her home. Licensed day-care providers are usually licensed to care for no more than six children (although they may care for more, up to twelve, with a full-time aide). Of course, this regulation varies by state. Such care is less expensive than in-home care, since theoretically, you're sharing the cost with up to five other families. It's crucial to find the right match in family day care—namely, a caregiver who shares your values and with whom you will be able to share parenting duties. For those opting for out-of-home care, family day care is the arrangement of choice for most families with children under two.

Center-based care becomes the arrangement of choice as children get older. Most children in centers are two and a half to five years old, although some centers do take infants as young as six weeks. The physical size of these centers varies greatly, accommodating 15 to 250! Most have 60 to 100 children.

In shared-care situations, two families jointly hire a caregiver. The costs are much lower than costs for a single-child caregiver (though maybe not 50 percent less, since caring for two children is more work than caring for one), and your child has the opportunity to be with another child. Shared care can be in one family's home or alternate between the two families.

Many new parents are most comfortable having a grandparent or other relative taking care of their child. They feel they can count on a loving caregiver, one whose attitudes are familiar and comforting. But remember, even these familial arrangements must be carefully worked out in advance.

Support in the Months Ahead

As you adjust to your new role of parent, you need as much comfort and support as possible. If you're like most people, having a baby will change relationships, as well as attitudes, more than almost anything else that happens in your life. A new baby can heal old family wounds or cause new ones. It can bring friends closer together or drive a wedge between them.

If your parents and in-laws feel good about your pregnancy, they can be wonderfully helpful in the next few months. All those years of worrying that they'd never be grandparents are finally coming to an end. Their immortality is set (well, you know what we mean), and they will no longer despair that you'll never experience the greatest joy in life—two fewer things to worry about. On the other hand, exuberant grand-parents-to-be can offer too much unsolicited advice and act as if they own the baby.

Some new parents, those who have spent much of their adult lives holding their parents at arm's length, may discover a little bend in the elbow. Maybe it's because the focus in no longer set so squarely on them. They have (gladly) relinquished center stage to their newborn and find it pleasant to be a supporting player for a change. Much less pressure. And it can feel great to have so much love, appreciation, and adoration lavished on your baby.

In fact, when it's your turn, you might even find it comforting to have your mother around to answer urgent questions. Or a mother-in-law whose mission in life, for the time being, is to help you get some rest. Yes, a baby can indeed enhance family relationships.

And then there's the flip side. Your mother tries to help, but ends up making you feel incompetent. She doesn't let you take care of your own baby. She elbows you out of the way when she hears a cry from the crib (hey, what happened to her maternal feelings for *you?*). She tells you you're doing everything all wrong and refuses to understand that things have changed since she had her babies. She wants to sterilize every item in the house and bundles the baby up on a 90-degree day. When you try to tell her the new way of thinking is that a good scrubbing in hot water is enough for most equipment, and that babies shouldn't be any more bundled up than anyone else, she waves you away with a terse "I guess you read that in a book!" Is there any point in going on with the discussion? (Of course, new mothers are in a tender position emotionally and may not be able to deal with comments that might seem innocuous at another time.)

Still, she did raise a child to adulthood—she has something to offer. Tell yourself that she needs to feel important. Relax. Let her talk.

My mother-in-law, whom I love dearly, had a very strong reaction to my daughter's birth. It stirred up a lot of unresolved issues in her life. She was thrilled to have a grandchild and was so good with her. But it got her thinking about her life as a young mother, how much harder it was for women of her generation. She gave up a career as a teacher to stay home with her three children. She talked a lot about what drudgery taking care of a new baby was in her day. The sterilizing of bottles, the diapers. It was so much more work than it is today, with breastfeeding and disposable diapers, and so on. And she watched me go back to work after three months. I get to have my darling little baby and a career. She had to choose. It's been very painful for her. She is very happy for me, but down deep, she wishes she could have had the same choices.

One of the ways our society is stratified is that singles and childless couples have more in common and socialize more together than either group does with couples who have children. Until your baby is born, you're still in the childless-couple category, at least as far as a social life is concerned. You do what you want when you want. And you expect the same kind of flexibility from others.

We're not suggesting that you give up your old childless friends. But it's time to start thinking about cultivating friends with children. They don't have to have newborns—children under six or seven will do. These parents will understand rashes and 104-degree temperatures that come from nowhere, plus the dilemma of caring for a sick child while meeting a work deadline.

So where do you find *these* parents—these people who get more animated about the correct sleeping position for a baby than about the situation in the Middle East—who push strollers through the world, laden down with enough supplies to cross the Gobi Desert. We'll discuss in detail finding new friends in Chapter 2. For now, look around in your childbirth class. Many a great friendship has been forged between a pant and a blow. Approach your class with an open mind, and see what possibilities develop. Go for a snack after class. You might find "couple" friends or another mother or two with whom to share your common concerns.

There was this woman, Nina, in my Lamaze class who zeroed in on me and wouldn't leave me alone. We ran into each other in the market, so she knew I lived close to her. She thought because our babies were due within three weeks of each other that we should become bosom buddies. I didn't think we had anything in common. She was nothing like my friends. She made me promise that I'd call her when I delivered. She wanted to hear every detail. In those first few weeks after Sasha was born and her son was born, she called me a lot, and I slowly began to realize that we did have something major in common. She was the only person I knew who was worrying about her milk, the belly button healing, the color of her baby's poop. We were friends for several years, and I must say my life was much richer for Nina being in it. It was much easier being a new mom with another new mom to talk to.

Bye for Now

The last few days of work will be spent making sure things run smoothly in your absence. Work needs to be parceled out and explained. A temp may need training. And you need to decide if you want to receive work calls at home. Try to strike that middle ground between eager employee and exploited worker. After all, you're not on vacation, as other working parents will know well.

two

The New Working Mom

The Fourth Trimester

SOMETIME between the end of Chapter 1 and the start of this chapter, you've had your baby. We imagine that you've consulted the many birthing books for the big event, and now, as you take on your new role as "soon to be back to work" parent, we pick up the story.

(This might be a good time to define our concept of *family*, which is very broad. In terms of this book, we refer to family as at least one adult caring for at least one child. We use *spouse* and *partner* interchangeably throughout the book; neither term is limited to the legally married. In our minds, couples and families define themselves.)

New Role, New Thoughts

Talk to new, first-time mothers and one of the most frequent comments you hear is that they are overwhelmed with a sense of responsibility. They may have understood this notion of responsibility intellectually before but they didn't realize at a gut level what it's really like to have an infant totally dependent on them. These new parents may have jobs in which other people depend on them to save their lives, counsel them in difficult situations, or understand complex legal matters. But having a child is different. Isn't it?

I worked for five years as a paralegal in a legal aid office, then got my law degree and went back there to practice. It was always high-stress. People's lives depended on how well I did my job. When we decided to have a baby, I was thirty-five. I bought a few books on parenting to study up on, which is how I've always attacked anything new—study it. I expected that would help to get me through whatever I needed with a baby. I was home from the hospital only a few hours before my research failed me. My baby wouldn't stop crying. My milk hadn't come in. I thought I was starving her to death. I felt clumsy picking her up. My husband and I were hysterical. I don't remember anything at work ever coming close to being that scary. Here was this two-day-old baby whose life was in my hands. For the first few days, I was really worried that I would not be able to handle it. In my panic, I remember saying to my husband that maybe we should give her away. In two weeks, I wondered how I could ever have had those thoughts. . . .

Parenting is often called the most important job a person will ever have. Now you're probably starting to understand what that means. Suddenly you're someone else's lifeline. This parenting stuff seems like all you can handle. It's a full-time job—at least for you. You start to think in a new way about the working parents you know. How did Irene manage to go back to work at six weeks? How does Andrea handle her nursing career *and* three-year-old twins? And what about your cousin who teaches sixth grade and has three kids under age ten? How does she manage to be at work by eight o'clock every morning, ready to call the roll?

According to 9 to 5, National Association of Working Women, the average time that women take off for childbirth is eight weeks. How do they do it? Not just physically—how can they leave their children in the care of "strangers"? And—on the flip side—don't they ever need to be alone? Have you begun to wonder if you'll ever be that carefree, spur-of-the-moment, well-informed person you used to be?

Blame it on raging hormones. Blame it on lack of sleep. Blame it on your horoscope. Whatever you blame it on, just hold this thought: You *will* learn how to be a working parent. You will discover that not only can you work, but you can also get promoted, get raises and awards, *and* be a loving, attentive parent. And somehow, you'll still have time for a long soak in the tub with the latest issue of *People* magazine.

Maybe not this week. Maybe not soon. But someday.

Childbirth, especially a first birth, is traumatic to the body. You may be sent home from the hospital the day after, instead of resting there for days as your mother and grandmother probably did. But that doesn't mean the healing process is any faster. Recovery is the fourth trimester. It may take even longer than three months. The lack of sleep and disrupted sleep of the first few months certainly contribute to a slower healing process.

The timing of the typical final postpartum checkup, at six weeks, creates the impression that everything should be hunky-dory—that by then, you should be back to your perky, prepregnancy self. The reality is that at six weeks, you'll probably have twenty pounds left to lose, be exhausted and not the least bit interested in sex, and potentially have hot flashes, mood swings, breast problems, and hemorrhoids. Through all this, you're supposed to concentrate on work?

When you start feeling overwhelmed, remember how the first few weeks are on any job: all-consuming. You think about work every waking minute: while you brush your teeth, drive, watch TV. Your mind keeps switching back to the job at hand. You've surrendered your soul, your essence to it. You don't feel as though you have a life. You don't go out at night, or even read. Too exhausted, you come home. Eat dinner. Drop in your tracks.

Now, doesn't this sound familiar? Feeling exhausted? Going to bed after dinner? Surrendering your essence to this new commitment? You're starting this new motherhood job, and as with any new job, you're in that new-job mindset. Slowly you'll find a sense of balance, the exhaustion will lift, and you'll start daydreaming about non-baby-related things—just as you did after a few weeks in a new office or company.

Remember: You're on Maternity Leave

Perhaps those last few weeks of pregnancy went a little sluggishly. You got a lot less accomplished than you had planned. The lists—written or mental—of what you had to do before the baby was born didn't all get checked off. The work you took home was only partially tackled—and halfheartedly at that, not at all up to your usual exacting standards.

But you had a vision of the first few weeks postpartum: returned vigor. Free time while your baby naps. After all, don't newborns sleep most of the time? Twenty hours a day, they said. Awake four hours. Why, that sounds like a part-time, not a full-time, job. You have at least six weeks at home with this part-time job. A new list gets started.

Fantasies change into reality. Your baby seems to be nursing every twenty minutes. All you can think about is sleep. You promised to work on some reports, do some research. Now, suddenly, taking a shower is a major accomplishment.

These first few weeks are the time to sort through new feelings, get comfortable with your new role. They are also a time of great hormone-driven mood swings—the mother of all mood swings, so to speak. It may be hard to know what you're really feeling.

Accept a lower level of accomplishment. And a new body. No lists. No setups for failure. No playing by the old rules. Relax.

Unpredictable Changes

One of the major lessons of parenthood, as we've said, is that nothing is predictable anymore. And there's a corollary to that: namely, you may have to back out of commitments at the last minute. For example, when your baby spikes a fever.

Life for many working adults who don't have young children can be quite routine. They control their own schedules—when they get up, when they go to sleep, when they stay home, when they go out, when they talk on the phone. And if they're not the type to get sick very often, they probably accomplish most tasks—work-related and personal—around the time they planned to. Reports get turned in on time. Papers get graded promptly. Jobs get done according to schedule. They never cancel dinner plans.

A few years ago, I reconnected with a long-lost cousin. We hadn't seen each other in ten years. At that point, she and her husband had an eighteen-month-old girl. We didn't have children. We invited them for a Saturday night dinner, and I was really looking forward to seeing them. We spent the day sprucing up our apartment, and I cooked a very elaborate dinner. About five o'clock, my cousin called to say that her daughter had diarrhea, and they wouldn't be able to come. I was furious. It didn't seem like a good enough excuse to me. Couldn't the babysitter call her if there was a problem? I was so angry, I didn't want to see her for years.

Now I have two young children and I understand completely. I've had to do the same thing myself. When I have to cancel plans with other parents, they understand. But people who don't have children—well, they're like I was.

Here are a few of the unpredictable possibilities of the first few months of parenthood:

You have a C-section or other complications that will extend your recovery period.

You discover that your maternal instincts are much stronger than you ever thought they would be, and you decide you can't leave your baby until she is at least six months old.

You decide that your maternal instincts are not as strong as you thought they'd be, and you can't wait to get back to work.

Your hormonal swings are severe. Postpartum is kind of a comedown, like the day after a big party.

Your baby is born prematurely or has other complications that require him to stay in the hospital for several weeks or months. You are in an extremely difficult state of limbo.

Your adopted baby is born three weeks earlier than expected.

Your baby is born with special needs.

Your baby is colicky.

Your spouse is jealous of the baby.

Nursing is difficult—and constant.

Your mother, or mother-in-law, who is supposed to come and help you out for the first few days or weeks, gets sick.

A call from work has you worried about a crisis brewing there.

Things just aren't how you imagined they would be. As of now, there is no ultrasound machine for colicky babies, no EKG to measure maternal feelings. Not every C-section is predicted beforehand.

Now is the time to learn a new mantra:

Nothing is predictable; I'll do my best.
Nothing is predictable; I'll do my best.
Nothing is predictable; I'll do my best.

A Roller Coaster of Emotions

No matter how confident you feel about your child-care arrangements, expect wild emotions as your return to work approaches. The sense that your baby will be helpless out in the world without you can be overwhelming. The last few weeks at home, you may have started to feel bored—and boring. Out of the loop. Home alone with no adult companionship all day long. But suddenly, you start rewriting recent history: Maybe it wasn't so bad. Isn't this how nature meant it to be? You start getting this primal buzz: A baby should be nestled in his mother's arms, dawn to dusk. Are you ruining his life by going back to work? Will this make him a serial killer?

This is a tough time, emotionally and physically. There's no getting around it. No use sugarcoating it. But you won't always feel this way. You may cry all the way to work the first week, unable to get the image of your sweet baby out of your head . . . but maybe not the second week.

It's double-whammy time, since you'll probably be physically exhausted as you adjust to your new dual life. Your baby may not be sleeping through the night. A 2:00 A.M. feeding is a killer when you have to be at work at 8:30 A.M. Or your baby may wake up at 5:00 A.M., just when you really need an extra hour of sleep. This kind of broken sleep or too little sleep affects all aspects of your well-being.

It helps to reach out to supportive people at this crucial time. Talk with other mothers at work. They'll remember that first week. This is definitely not the time to revive the "Should you even be going back to work—it's just not right" debate that you may have had with your parents, in-laws, or other people in your life.

Your First Day Back at Work

Looking for child care is such a major part of returning to work that we have dedicated an entire chapter to it. If you are feeling especially anxious about making child-care arrangements, you may want to read Chapter 3 first.

Knowing your child has already experienced and, yes, survived, her first day in child care will make your own return to the job much easier. As we explain in the next chapter, a gradual adjustment—over a week or more, if possible—is best. And unless you've done a complete dress rehearsal, the first day you go back to work will still be decidedly hectic.

Plan your clothes the night before. (In fact, it's not a bad idea to plan wardrobe for the whole first week.) Include purse, shoes, jewelry, shade of lipstick—anything involving a decision. If you will be taking food (or bottles) for either you or your child, prepare it and/or pack it the night before. This should become your standard operating procedure, which will be covered in more detail in a later chapter.

Put gas in the car, a full tank. Or get change or tokens for the bus or train. Get up earlier than you think you need to.

I cried all the way to work the first morning back. I had to fix my makeup in the parking lot. I walked through the front door feeling like I had a two-ton weight on my back. I could see my old coworkers gathered at my desk. There was no sneaking in. Somehow, don't ask me how, I managed to force a smile on my face. Around nine-thirty, I realized that I hadn't worried about Jeremy for a whole hour. I got caught up in catching up and I forgot to worry. I felt really guilty. Like only my constant worry would get Jeremy through the day. I could leave him physically, but I was supposed to keep him in my thoughts. At one point, I had a long, panicky moment. He was so little. So defenseless. Suddenly, I had to be with him. And then my supervisor asked me to sit in on a conference. Another hour went by. Then a guilt pang. Gradually, over the first week, I started going two, three hours without getting misty.

If work permits, call the caregiver during the day to reassure yourself and to hear updates on your child's adjustment. No, Nicole is not crying forlornly in her crib, misery personified. She's in the caregiver's arms and they are in the backyard watching two older children play ball. Now . . . go back to work.

And call again later.

If you are lucky enough to have on-site or near-site child care, you can stop in and visit during the day. Even with a live-in caregiver or with a center or family day-care arrangement closer to home, you may consider taking a long lunch for the first few days so you can make a reassuring visit. Child-oriented caregivers will support your need.

Learning from Caregivers

Everyone expects to learn from a traditional, starched, and proper nanny, the kind who looks like she'd take care of the royals' children. Most parents would be putty in such hands.

But you don't have to be nanny to a crown prince to know some tricks of the trade. All experienced caregivers are walking encyclopedias of parenting information. Someone who has reared three kids of her own and taken care of dozens of others *knows things*. Someone who has been a nanny for twenty years *knows things*. Someone who runs a day-care center *knows things*.

Take advantage.

I'm the type that reads all the books. So when I had my son, I read Spock and Brazelton and Leach and probably another ten books. And I have a college degree. And I was thirty-three years old when I had my first baby. So I thought I should be able to manage. And I think I've done reasonably well. Mikey cried a lot, especially after I nursed him. I read up on burping and did everything the books said to.

But a lot of times, he didn't burp and remained miserable. One morning, the first week Mikey was at Lucy's home for child care, I brought him in still crying from his feeding. My burping hadn't helped. I was about to explain the situation to Lucy, but before I got out a word, she said, "This little honey needs a good burping." She took Mikey and lovingly placed him across her knees and burped him. It worked. The books never told me about that position. I used it all the time after that with great success. Lucy saw how relieved I was, how embarrassed for not knowing what to do myself. She didn't make me feel like a fool. As I left for work, she gave me a big, reassuring hug. We were working together. In many ways, she helped me to learn things that my mother, had she been alive, would have told me.

Can a Working Mother Still Breast-Feed?

Yes . . . and no. With a breast pump, theoretically, you can go off to a rest room at work, pump away, and store your milk in the lunchroom fridge. And there are *some* enlightened companies with designated areas for breast-pumping.

In real life, however, many new mothers find that the workplace isn't particularly conducive to pumping. It's difficult enough under ideal conditions, but worrying that a customer/mail clerk/vp—whoever—may burst in on you constitutes far-from-ideal conditions. If you do decide to try it, be assured that many have succeeded. And wear the right clothes (easy access, with front buttons or tops that pull up from the waist, in patterns that camouflage leaks).

A compromise you might try is to have your baby on the bottle during the day and to nurse in the early morning and after you come home. Your baby can adjust, especially if you've introduced a supplementary bottle early on. Many experts recommend starting this system at about three weeks of age and having someone other than you (your spouse, your mother) offer the bottle, so your baby doesn't pick up your scent at the same time and get fussy or confused. You also might need to experiment with different bottle nipples.

Your milk supply will adjust to this compromise. You may have a few uncomfortable moments at the beginning, but after a few days your milk will know when to be there and when to wait. Even after going back to work two months after delivery, many mothers find they can nurse for a year or more.

Mothers usually find nursing a lot more flexible than they were led to believe, and they are able to vary the amount of breast milk their babies receive from one day to the next. It's not a rigid use-it-or-lose-it proposition. Some mothers wean their babies only to decide, for whatever reason, to resume nursing, and they are usually able to produce milk again.

I went back to work at three months and wanted to continue nursing as long and as much as possible. Using a breast pump at work was out of the question. I discovered that I could nurse Emil in the morning and twice at night during the week and then return to full time on the weekends. Mondays were a little painful for me, and I would have to go into the rest room and manually pump out some of the extra milk just for relief. But other than that, it worked very well for another six months.

Your workplace may not be breast-pump-friendly simply because no new mother has made it an issue. It may simply be a matter of scoping out the place for an available, underutilized room and approaching the right person to make it available to pumpers. And why not ask for a small refrigerator while you're at it?

Transition Clothes

There are those stories—probably all publicity—of Demi Moore or Susan Sarandon back on the movie set a week after giving birth in their old size-six pants. Put this silly stuff out of your head. Your uterus is still the size of Rhode Island. Your breasts are a size or more larger than usual. It'll take a little time—and effort—to get back to prepregnancy shape.

If your return to work is scheduled at six or eight weeks or even twelve weeks after your baby's birth, you'll need some transition work clothes. Not full-blown maternity clothes. But parading back to work in that sleek suit you always loved because it fit so snugly yet let you move . . . well, maybe you'll beat the odds. But please, try it on before that first morning you're due back and be ready with an alternate outfit.

Most new mothers don't beat the odds (the nature of odds, we understand). Most new mothers need some time to get back in shape and into their old clothes. Transitional clothes are the answer to the first few weeks or months: elastic waistbands, a little stretch to the fabric, buttons in front, and some room to spare all around. The more washable items the better, since babies spit up beyond the edges of even a carefully placed burping diaper.

Whose Life Is It, Anyway?

The answer: your baby's. For the time being anyway. Right now, it may feel as though you don't have a life—that you've surrendered your control, your freedom, your personhood to this ravenous, cranky creature. You feel like a mere caretaker for the next generation.

It won't always be like this. Yes, you've made a lifetime commitment, but the commitment changes over the years. For a while, you may see all the things in your life as severely curtailed by parenthood. But one day—sooner than you know—you'll be looking at a fifteen-year-old and thinking how limited your time is together. Then you'll want to squeeze as much togetherness into the next three years as you can.

Now, of course, instead of playing peekaboo, you'd just like to go out to a long lunch (the kind waiters hate) with an old friend, dish the dirt, never mention terms like *dilation* . . . and not leak through your blouse. Or maybe stay up until three in the morning to finish a Tony Hillerman mystery. Wait. Your time will come.

When Your Spouse Goes Back to Work

More and more companies are allowing fathers time off for the birth of their babies. They are no longer expected to show up the day after the delivery with puffed-up chest and box of cigars, then get back to work after a few hearty, manly handshakes.

With luck and good planning, your spouse will have at least a few days off to be with you and the baby. Even so, he will probably go back to work before you do.

Having a baby means a tremendous change of lifestyle for couples. You may have spent your whole life together living parallel routines: squabbling over bathroom time in the morning, wolfing down stand-up breakfasts in the kitchen, rushing to work, collapsing after work, sharing war stories in the evening.

During your leave, you have nowhere to rush to and, worse than that, no one to talk to most weekdays. No customers to complain about, no big sales to chortle over, no students to comment on . . . no stories to tell. "And what did you do today, honey?" "Well . . . I nursed Emma and then I put her down, and before I got the bed made she wanted to nurse again. Then she fussed for a while and I had to rock her. Then we both fell asleep and then she nursed for a while. I started a load of laundry but I didn't get it in the dryer. . . ."

Well, you're a thrill and a half. You probably haven't washed your hair in a week, either. Or listened to the news. And you're grumpy. And fat.

It's not fair that he gets to go back to work and get all dressed up and look good and talk to real people and you don't. After all, didn't you decide to have this baby together? Didn't you pledge to share the work, share the joys? Aren't you supposed to have a career here? This feels suspiciously like how things were in the fifties.

It's probably only a temporary time warp. You'll be back to the nineties in the next few months. And while your spouse may enjoy his work, he's probably missing his baby quite a lot during the day. Patience. You haven't been zapped into June Cleaver's world.

Here's another take on the situation: You're feeling left out of the loop—the work-world loop. At the same time, your spouse may feel left out of the new-family loop. He *leaves* the really important stuff every workday, instead of going off to it. He might very well be a little jealous of your time at home.

Other Mothers

One surefire cure for postpartum blues—the low-level kind, anyway—is to find other new mothers to talk to. Even if you aren't the outgoing type. Even if you don't know any other new mothers. Talking to your own mother is fine, but you also need mothers who are going through the same things *now*.

Just when it's imperative to find other new parents, a lucky happenstance of fate kicks in. This basic law of parenting will help: It's easier to meet people when you have your child with you. The world will talk to parents, the newer the better, in a way it never would to singles or couples.

> *I lived in my neighborhood for six years before I had Aaron, and I hardly knew a soul. Nobody talked to me in the supermarket or in the park or in the elevator. Now I go out with my baby and everybody wants to stop and chat. That was the first time I really got to know people in the community. I'm not very outgoing, and I was kind of worried about being so isolated. Having a child ends the isolation. Suddenly, you're part of the community. I began feeling much more at ease talking to strangers.*

Go where other new mothers go—the park, the mall, the laundry room. Look around while you're waiting at the pediatrician's office. You've got plenty in common, such as chronic fatigue or sore nipples. That's enough to build a friendship on.

Meeting Other Parents

New parents need new-parent friends. Remember thinking how boring your old college roommate was after she had her firstborn? Suddenly, this person you lived with for four years in a cramped dorm room and who was your soulmate no longer had anything interesting to say. She wanted to talk and talk and talk about soy formula and fontanels. You thought the Fontanelles were near Turkey.

And now you are she! You need to find sympathetic souls. The parents of teenagers don't want to hear about thrush. Couples without children (by choice or not) don't want to hear about the croup. They don't appreciate the momentous occasion when a baby flips from stomach to back *all by herself* or a six-year-old reads her first book.

So where do you find this great new circle? Start with the other parents in your child's day-care arrangement.

My son started at Christopher Robin Nursery School when he was two and a half, and he soon found three or four other boys that he spent much of his day with. He would talk about them at home, and when I picked him up I made a point of checking out their parents. Sometimes it was a surprise. The parents seemed so different from what I'd expected. Not like people I knew at all. A few looked like kindred spirits. But everyone was in a rush to get in and get out. Very little eye contact.

One day, I asked my son if he would like to invite Jorge over to play on the weekend. After work, I went over to Jorge's dad and introduced myself as "Ryan's mom," a title I was still getting used to. I invited Jorge to go to the park with us on Saturday and offered to pick him up and take him home. It was really hard to make the first move. I am, by nature, a shy person, although I've found how hard it is to stay shy and still be a good parent! I think Jorge's dad was shyer. But he and his wife seemed so pleased with my overture.

Although you are making this overture because you want to establish friendships with other parents, you may be surprised to discover that there are other areas of common interest, and long-lasting friendships can develop.

There's no reason to wait until your child is walking and talking to suggest getting together with other parents you encounter. Even with young babies who may spend your joint family outing napping, parents of same-age children have plenty to chat about.

> *My three children are all adults now. They haven't seen their playmates from nursery school days for over twenty years. But my husband and I are still close friends with many of the other parents from their nursery-school days. The kids lost interest in one another after a few years, but we found lifelong friends.*

Parents with a computer and a modem can talk with other parents through on-line services such as America Online and Prodigy. By hitting a few keys, you can ask questions in parent forums/bulletin boards and read about parenting issues on your computer screen. We tuned into one discussion about how to handle a mother-in-law who has a different approach to crying. The mother-in-law felt babies should be left to cry it out or they would turn out "spoiled." The new mom solicited advice from other parents, who responded with thoughtful and encouraging messages. For parents who have few real-life friends who are parents, on-line parent forums can be a lifesaver.

three

Finding Child Care

It Takes Time to Make the Right Match

How Children Can Benefit from Child Care

LET'S start out on a positive note. In a recent study reported in *Working Mother* magazine, 85 percent of parents surveyed felt that child care had made their children more independent, and 75 percent thought their children had better social skills and learned to share from day care. We know that when you first arrange child care, it can be extremely stressful, so it may help to bear in mind that so many working parents have these positive feelings.

The majority of today's children attend some sort of child-care program before kindergarten. While kindergarten was once the time when children began learning social skills and group behavior, today's children are learning those things in preschool. The child who has been at home those first five years, if the environment has not been particularly stimulating, will have a little catching up to do. (Of course, this situation will level out in the first two or three years of school.)

Ask yourself how you would care for your child if you were able to stay home for a year or two. Be absolutely honest. What would your days together be like? Would you plan every day, all day, around your child? Would you give your child as much attention as a good caregiver would? A caregiver is paid to devote all her attention to the child(ren) in her charge. She is a professional. Even children as young as two months can thrive with *good* caregivers. And in good situations, babies, toddlers, and preschoolers can receive plenty of stimulation and love.

A generation or two ago, when more mothers stayed home with young children, there were usually plenty of opportunities for those mothers and children to find kindred spirits in the neighborhood during the workweek. Today's mother and child can lead a much more solitary life. There may be other young moms nearby, but most (according to the statistics) are at work. Many new parents don't have extended families to visit with. Home neighborhoods will probably not be filled with potential playmates. Coffee-klatching is dead. Moms who do decide to stay at home for a few years need to put all their energies into providing stimulating, varied daily lives for both their babies and themselves.

In child care, young children are in the thick of things. In family day care, infants start to observe how older children play around them. In a center's infant room, babies tune into one another. So let the socializing begin!

What Are Your Child's Needs?

During the weeks you spend at home after the birth of your baby, you will see your baby's temperament emerge. You will see if she needs a lot of time with feedings and whether she naps easily or needs help from you to fall asleep. Can she sleep anywhere, or do the conditions have to be optimal? Knowing your baby's needs will help guide you when it's time to ask questions of potential caregivers or to make child-care choices.

What kind of environment would you like your child to be in all day? You may want a place that is just like home and look for a caregiver whose home and lifestyle seem similar to yours. Or you may decide to seek out a complementary environment, so that your child will be exposed to another way of doing things. Parents who live in apartments may feel that a center with a yard is essential. A parent who is allergic to pets might choose a family day-care home with a big, friendly dog, so her child can have a dog experience.

Our apartment is neat as a pin, highly organized, minimalist design. We are always going to be neat freaks, but we feel it is im-

portant to let our daughter know, as early in life as possible, that there are many ways to run a home. So we selected a more re-laxed, casual environment. The caregiver has two children of her own, plus the three she cares for. Things don't get put away as fast there as they do in our house. The box of Cheerios stays on the kitchen table all day: beds don't always get made; there are toys left out in the yard. But the care is superb.

This kind of approach shouldn't be viewed as inconsistent, but rather a change of pace or environment that can be beneficial but is by no means necessary. Consistency of *parenting* is what's essential—going back and forth between two housekeeping styles is something a child can handle.

Child Care for Older Babies and Toddlers

Parents have a better sense of their children's personality and temperament at one year than at two months. How much attention does he need? Is he a picky eater? Does he need careful drawing out, or someone to keep him from becoming too rambunctious? If your child is entering his first child-care arrangement in later babyhood or as a toddler, the questions you ask potential caregivers and how you size up the arrangement may be slightly different from how you would evaluate a situation for a very young baby. Issues of safety change as babies become mobile. Always be alert to emerging issues.

Even if it's your six-week-old who will be going off to child care, you want the situation you've chosen to be one you'll be comfortable with for a long time. Therefore, you should consider questions that apply to some older babies and toddlers long before your baby is crawling.

Child Care for Children with Special Needs

While the term *special needs* encompasses dyslexia, attention-deficit disorder, and Down syndrome, as well as physical disabilities, the common link is that child care will be more difficult to find. Sometimes, however, resource and referral agencies can help with leads.

Be up-front with the caregiver you are considering. Tell her all you know about your child's limitations and the extra demands that will be made on a caregiver's time. She must feel comfortable with the arrangement, whether that entails giving medications or injections or working with the child during the day. A special-needs child requires a special caregiver. They are out there, but your search may be longer.

Searching for Child Care

Searching for child care is a very difficult process and can be heart-wrenching. In our effort to be thorough, we may make this process seem overwhelming.

We are especially uncomfortable with the idea that caregivers may be untrustworthy, and yet we know that the media has dramatically shown bad child-care situations. It has been our experience that most caregivers and programs genuinely care about the welfare of children and their families. Read over the following information and follow through on those issues that are most important to you.

We strongly believe that the most important part of a good child-care arrangement is the relationship among you, the caregiver, and your child.

Good child care is worth pursuing. Judy Bencivengo, outreach coordinator for UCLA Child Care Services and an expert on these matters, believes that the best child care is found by the most persistent shoppers. If you can traipse around to six stores looking for the perfect sofa, surely you can do some comparison shopping for child care.

Making a good child-care arrangement is one of the most important challenges for a new family. It will influence the quality of life your child will have in the crucial formative years, and it will affect how well you will be able to perform at work. *A parent with a good child-care arrangement is a parent who can concentrate at work.*

> *I had an unexpected C-section, and it took all of my eight-week leave for me to recuperate. I simply didn't have the energy for the all-out child-care search that I had planned. Before Melissa was born, I had made lists of possible caregivers to check out. I only got to a few before I had to be back at work. There was absolutely no way to extend my leave and keep my job. So I chose a woman who had a safe home and seemed to genuinely love children. But I just didn't feel great about it. She wasn't someone I would rave about. Then I realized that I had to make another decision: to keep Melissa there for her first two years or look for another*

family day-care home. I decided to make a switch. I had more en-
ergy when she was about four months old, and then I got out my
list and really started going through it. I found a caregiver I could
rave about, and Melissa has been there for a year and loves it.

The critical decision about finding a caregiver will take time to research and to make. It can't be done in the last few days before you return to work. Ideally, there should be plenty of time to investigate and
reflect on all the options available. You may need to get on a waiting
list before your baby is born or put in applications at several centers or
family day-care homes.

We feel strongly that if you are unable to find the right child care
before you go back to work, it is imperative to keep looking. Yes, we
agree that the fewer changes, the better, but children will survive and
adjust, especially if the change is for the better. Keep looking. (We discuss making changes in child care in Chapter 4.)

While making the first child-care arrangements for your baby is the
most difficult, the issues involved in choosing care will be similar as
your child grows. Selecting a kindergarten, day camp, or high school
calls for much of the same methodology—asking yourself and
prospective caregivers and schools the right questions. Today—and
five, ten, and fifteen years from now—it all comes down to whether
your child will be comfortable, safe, appreciated, and encouraged, and
whether you will be able to get information and feel a part of your
child's experience. The things you learn now, as you hire your first
caregiver, will come in handy over and over again.

There are many reasons why new parents are drawn to a particular
type of child care: geography, odd work hours, cultural background,
the age and/or temperament of their child, a glowing recommendation
from someone they trust. And cost. Child care almost always costs
more than parents want to pay, yet most child-care providers earn less
than they need to live comfortably. People who take care of children
are not fully appreciated, monetarily or otherwise, in our society. It is a
sad fact that caregivers are often personally subsidizing programs with
their low wages and lack of benefits.

Paying decent wages and benefits makes sense. It encourages a stable, contented workforce, which is a great advantage for children.
Good child care requires a high ratio of stable caregivers to children,
and that means money. Still, the cost of a child-care arrangement is

not always an indicator of quality of care. Families in one area may be paying the same amount for significantly different quality. Don't assume that a provider who is charging top dollar will provide the best care for your child. You still need to make a thorough investigation.

When you look for a child-care provider, you are, in essence, searching for someone to share your most crucial job with you. Quality child care is good parenting by a substitute parent. It's a home away from home. It involves much more than babysitting (which we define as the occasional watching of a child to make sure the child is safe). It is teaching, playing with, and nurturing children when parents are at work.

You're probably beginning to realize that entrusting your baby to someone else's hands brings up many concerns. Have I really judged this person accurately? What will go on when I'm not there? Will the caregiver become the most important person in my child's life? And how will we ever be able to afford it?

Of course, any definition of good parenting will be quite subjective. You may think that a good parent would never use a pacifier, while someone else would say that denying a pacifier is cruel. You may feel it is important to begin a no-snacking routine very early, while another parent may think that good nutrition is learned through eating whenever a person is hungry. The Supreme Court of Parenting has not ruled on these issues yet. But as we've said previously, what is important is consistency. A child who can sometimes have a pacifier and sometimes eat whenever hungry will have a harder time than a child whose caregiver and parents unite in setting rules.

You may already have your mind set on one type of arrangement and feel that there's no point in reading up on other options. You may be sure, for example, that you want an in-home caregiver. Or you're absolutely adamant against new babies in child-care centers. We urge you to read the pros and cons of all arrangements. There may be aspects of each that you haven't considered.

We will talk about quality caregiving throughout this chapter. These are the basics in a nutshell:

The major component in good care is the caregiver herself. A good caregiver (whether nanny, family day-care provider, preschool teacher, or grandmother):

- Has an understanding of young children and respect for each child as an individual
- Is friendly and cooperative
- Models behavior for children and parents
- Makes children feel secure
- Encourages children to make choices for themselves
- Uses positive ways to guide behavior
- Talks with children rather than to them
- Offers stimulating things to do
- Provides constant supervision
- Works closely with parents
- Adheres to health and safety standards

How to Find Caregivers

In the states that offer them, resource and referral (also called resource and information) agencies (*R&Rs*, in the child-care world) are the backbone of child-care networking. They are usually nonprofit agencies with full or partial government funding. The quickest way to find your community R&R is by calling the toll-free Child Care Aware Hotline, offered by the National Association of Child Care Resource and Referral Agencies: (800) 424-2246. This hotline will tell you the name and number of the R&R in your area. Also look in your local Yellow Pages under "Child Care" or call your city councilperson for the number of the resource agency in your area. You may also locate these agencies by calling departments of social services. How (and how extensively) they operate varies greatly from state to state. (If there's no R&R in your area, call the state agency that licenses or regulates child care and ask for information on providers in your area.)

Community R&Rs provide parents with free information on all regulated child-care centers and family day-care homes in their area. You tell them the zip codes in which you would consider child care, and they will give you leads in that area. It is essential to remember that these are just names and phone numbers—not recommendations or real referrals—despite the agency title. Furthermore, most R&Rs may not know if there are any openings available at the places they mention.

R&Rs can also answer questions about licensing regulations or registration, which vary from state to state. The licensing process generally focuses on health and safety issues. And while a license is one thing to consider when evaluating a caregiver, it certainly doesn't mean that the caregiver has been checked out for her loving, compassionate nature with children. That's your job!

Also remember that it may have been some time since a state evaluator has been to the site, if ever (some states only make visits when there is a complaint). Circumstances change. You should make your own health and safety check. Does it meet *your* standards?

Some R&Rs offer more ambitious community programs, going far beyond handing out phone numbers of caregivers. In Oakland, California, one of the oldest R&Rs in the country, Bananas, offers a wide range of support groups for both parents and providers, as well as lists of shared-care arrangements and family activities in the community. This can be an especially welcome resource for families who are having difficulty meeting other parents in their neighborhood.

If your company has its own R&R or contracts with an R&R service, you may find they offer more detailed assistance than community agencies. Some corporate programs ask detailed questions of parents and do much of the legwork for them.

A more personal source of caregiver leads is other parents in your neighborhood. Talk to friends and neighbors whose values you share. Do they know anyone who is wonderful with children? If you take your baby to a park where parents and young children congregate, approach some of the parents of preschoolers and ask them for suggestions. True, you don't know their values, but a family caregiver or center that anyone raves about is worth checking out—with a critical eye, of course.

Where you look for a child-care arrangement depends on attitudes in your area. In a small town, parents may post notices on bulletin boards and feel perfectly at ease calling numbers they find there, while parents in big cities would find that a potentially dangerous approach.

Here are a few sources of caregiver suggestions—to be used or not, depending on your particular situation:

- Other parents
- Community bulletin boards in grocery stores, launderettes
- Bulletin boards at work
- Workers in your doctor's office, clinic, or hospital
- Classified ads in the local or college paper

- Ads in the local parenting newspaper or magazine
- The Yellow Pages under "Child Care"
- Congregation members from your church or synagogue, or even from one that's nearby that you don't attend
- The secretary or other office workers in the neighborhood elementary school
- Colleges, especially junior or community colleges with early-childhood education, child development, or home-economics departments
- The Yellow Pages, under "In-home Care"
- Domestic-help agencies (see following section for suggestions on in-home care)

Types of Child Care

The basic types of child-care arrangements are family day care, center-based care, in-home (nanny) care, shared care, and care by relatives. The right one for you is the one that you are most comfortable with and can afford. But even if money isn't a factor, not all parents would choose the same type of arrangement.

The following sections address family day care and center-based care, occasionally intermingling the two. Then we'll talk about in-home and shared care.

Family Day Care

Family day care (often called family child care) is offered in a caregiver's home for a small group of children, often of mixed ages. Depending on state regulations, licensed or registered caregivers are usually limited to six children (sometimes they care for up to twelve children with a full-time aide). Many families choose this arrangement for the first few years, until their child is toilet-trained, and then move to center-based care. But some parents find a family day-care provider they like so much—who provides a good rapport and a stimulating environment—that their children stay in that situation until they're old enough for kindergarten. Even after that, the children may go back for after-school care.

If you choose this type of child care, your child will be in a family setting. Parents often cite a homey, noninstitutional atmosphere as a strong plus. In some homes, children may have interaction with only one adult (the caregiver) during the day, while in others, spouses, teenage children, and other visitors provide frequent occasions for socializing. There is no preferred arrangement for all children. A lot depends on the temperament of your child. Some children form intense one-to-one relationships with their caregivers and may show signs of discomfort when there is a flow of other people coming and going in the house. Other children enjoy the company of many people during the day.

When my son was seven months old, he began going to Mrs. Palacio's home while I worked. In many ways, I think the arrangement rounded out Sean's life. We lived in a fourth-floor apartment and he was an only child. Mrs. Palacio had three children of her own—the youngest was fifteen—and two of them lived at home. Her husband was a contractor, and he came home for lunch every day. She took care of four children at a time. She was older, almost my mother's age, and I liked her warm, instinctive way with the children. She didn't have an academic background in child development, but she loved children and she had great patience with them. At first, Sean just watched from her lap as all these people came and went to work and school. But as the months went by and he became mobile, he would toddle over when they sat down on the sofa. Everybody in the family knew all the children and their names. I liked that he was in the middle of all that commotion. In our home, it was pretty quiet.

Family day-care providers who are regulated must, in many states, have a plan for substitute care in case they are sick or otherwise unable to care for the children. In reality, there may not always be a backup provider. When you choose family day care, you will be relying pretty much on one person. Your sick days will probably depend on her (and your child's) sick days, and there will come a day when she is unable to care for your child. Discuss this issue with potential providers and people who are to serve as references. Another working parent can tell you if a particular provider has taken an excessive number of sick days.

To cover yourself, have your own backup plan. Who else could you call on at the last minute if your caregiver gets sick? A relative? Are there agencies in your area that provide last-minute in-home care? Call them now and get details. You might want to use them on a weekend as a test before you call them for weekday care. This contingency service will be expensive, but in an emergency, it might be financially feasible for one or two days—and worth it. Do you know someone who is staying home with her own child who might be able to help you out in a pinch (and we mean a real pinch), especially if you offer some sort of reciprocation plan, such as babysitting for her a few Saturday nights? All these alternatives hinge on one thing: your child's ability to adapt to change. Some children take a long time to settle into an environment, and for them substitute caregivers would not be feasible. If your child is like this, the only alternative may be for you or your spouse to stay home.

Most family day-care providers like to set work schedules just as everybody else does. They usually put in very long hours. A caregiver may have to get up very early, because Stacey arrives at seven, but Kyle may not arrive until nine, and both stay until six-thirty. That's a long day. When six-thirty comes around, the caregiver wants her workday to be over. A good relationship with your caregiver depends, in large part, on respecting her set hours.

That said, and depending on the caregiver, you may find that family day care provides a little leniency with regard to time that wouldn't be available in center-based care. If you are occasionally required to work late or have irregular hours, a family day-care provider *who is willing to accommodate your needs* is worth searching for. They are out there. But this is definitely an issue that should be discussed up front. Agreeing to pick up your child by 6:00 P.M. when you start the arrangement and then calling once a week or so asking, ever so sweetly, if your caregiver could watch Shawna another hour is neither professional nor considerate. Sure, everyone has an emergency. You may get a flat tire on the freeway . . . once. The caregiver, like the traffic cop, has probably heard every excuse in the book, and she probably has a sixth sense for when a parent is telling the truth. But if you do find a caregiver who will work longer hours, you should compensate her for it.

The daily routine in family day care can vary greatly, depending on the energy and personality of the provider. At its worst, caregiving is little more than caretaking—keeping children safe. At its best, it means planning activities that engage the children's interest, stimulating them without frustrating them. Television viewing is kept at a minimum, perhaps watching *Mr. Rogers' Neighborhood* while the children arrive in the morning or *Sesame Street* while the last child or two waits to be picked up. Children are free to move about. They are fed when hungry, and diapers are changed promptly.

A family day-care provider who is devoted to her work will have toys and equipment for all ages in her care. She will keep them in good repair, but they don't have to be new or fancy. She will know that playing with pots and pans at her feet in the kitchen is as good as it gets—at least in many toddlers' minds.

A good provider will have a definite rhythm to the day, which children can anticipate. It doesn't have to be a rigid 10:00–10:30 outside-play schedule. She may simply take the children outside first thing in the morning, then bring them inside for a midmorning snack when the time seems right.

She recognizes the importance of play and find ways to center the day around it. She knows that through play, children learn about their world. A good caregiver will think of the kitchen as a beginning lab course in math as she measures the flour for homemade biscuits. She recognizes that talking about pictures on the living room table can be a course in history. That in walks around the block, there is recognition of the seasons.

Another necessary component in a caregiver is responsiveness to a sense of partnership with parents. This is a shared task. You are both rearing this child, and consequently, you need to be in communication and accord. Search for a caregiver who willingly gives parents information about how the day went and who will listen to parents when they have things to discuss. As the months go by, this relationship can make or break an arrangement.

Getting the Basics by Phone

You can save a lot of time by asking potential caregivers key questions— eliminating gross mismatches without having to make time-consuming visits. Try calling during naptime or in the evening. In these calls, you are after both information and a sense of the provider's personality.

Here are some basics to cover:

Is there space available for your child? (The provider may already be caring for the maximum number of infants she's permitted, and may only be able to take a preschooler. No use going any further if you need care soon.)

How many children are there? What is the maximum cared for? How many are babies? How many come every day?

What are their ages?

Does she have children of her own?

What are her hours?

What neighborhood is she in?

What does she charge?

Don't make snap judgments. Remember that the person at the other end of the line *may* have five little ones doing all sorts of things to get her attention. Even a nurturing person can sound short on the phone if she's distracted.

If a phone conversation sounds promising, make arrangements to visit in person.

Visiting Family Day-Care Providers

Ideally, a first visit allows a parent to observe the arrangement carefully. Your objective is to draw conclusions to the general question "Is this a likely match?" Perhaps you can visit in the morning when all the children will be there and playing. If you can arrange it, don't take your own child on this first visit. You'll be better able to size up the environment and the caregiver without distraction.

Although you will probably be concerned with not taking too much of the caregiver's time, it is important to be thorough. Five minutes and a quick walk-through is not enough to make a thoughtful judgment—unless, of course, you get immediate vibes that this would not be a suitable arrangement. Instincts are very important. If you sense this is not the place for your child, trust that feeling and politely move on. You may need to visit several caregivers before finding one with whom you can make a solid arrangement.

As you observe the caregiver, you will get a sense of how she is with children. How does she (or he) handle discipline? Do the children seem happy and engaged in activity?

Watch how the caregiver interacts with the children. Does she respond to them individually? Cuddle and hold them? Does she get down to eye level with them? Does she enjoy her work? How do the children respond to her? Is there an easy familiarity here?

You'll also get a sense of her personality. Some caregivers are more outgoing than others. They may also be very relaxed and comfortable with children but a little reserved with or patronizing to parents. Some encourage parent questions, while others dismiss them.

Indications of problem care include physical discipline of any kind, verbal reprimands that hurt a child's feelings, signs of boredom, and lots of fighting among the children.

The right caregiver meets individual needs and preferences. You must feel a sense of rapport with her. Not only must she be capable of providing a safe and loving haven for your child, she must also give you the feeling that you can work and talk together.

My daughter's first caregiver was a very nice woman named Carla. She was about thirty and had two young children of her own, plus the three she took in. At first, I liked how friendly Carla was, always willing to talk and tell me how Harry behaved that day. But gradually, I started feeling like I couldn't get away. I wanted to spend five or ten minutes talking and leave. Carla would often ask me to have coffee. Sometimes she had a snack ready. How could I say no? What I first saw as chattiness became desperation for adult companionship. Finally, I just told her the truth: that I had to get home because I had a lot to do.

Although the family day-care provider has made an appointment with you, it is important to remember that her first responsibility is to the children. Your visit may be interrupted. She may have to stop several times to help a distraught child find a toy, to comfort a crying infant, or to change a diaper. If the children are ignored during your visit, you may logically wonder if your child will be ignored when the next prospective parent comes to call. A caregiver who puts these children first will put your child first, too.

If you like the caregiver, ask if there is an evening or weekend when you can visit again with your child. Find out the caregiver's plans for the next few years. Say something like "It's important to me to find a long-term arrangement, something that will be steady until my child is about two. Does that fit in with your plans?"

The Nitty-Gritty

When you are seriously considering a family day-care provider, there are nuts-and-bolts issues that need dealing with *before* you enter into an arrangement:

What is the fee? When is it due? Check or cash? (For tax purposes, you'll need a receipt for cash.) Are there extra fees?

What hours will she care for children?

What would happen if you had to work late? What would she charge?

What is the sick policy? Will she care for a child with the sniffles? A fever? Do you pay when your child is home sick for a day?

What is her backup plan in case she is sick or cannot work?

What about meals and snacks? Does she provide food or are you responsible for bringing it?

Who provides the diapers?

Do you pay when you go on vacation? When does she go on vacation?

What about holidays? Do you pay for Christmas and the rest?

What if you went away for a long period of time, like the whole summer?

Usually parents pay for space in the provider's home, whether their child is there or not. The provider cannot take in another child for the duration of your child's bout with chicken pox or camping trip. If you want your child to return, you may need to pay to hold the space.

You may be tempted to skip these details. They may seem unnecessary or too demanding. You may simply feel uncomfortable asking questions. But parents who don't ask questions up front learn the hard way that it's much trickier to get answers after you've established a relationship. At this point, you're asking a stranger if you have to pay her for Easter week when you know you'll be at your brother's house. Six months from now, you'd be asking someone you know well.

Some caregivers are very professional about these issues and will bring them up. They may even have a contract or printed list of policies. Others may be reticent, even though they, too, know that settling things up front is better. In many places, resource and referral agencies (R&Rs) provide checklists to guide the discussions. Some family day-care providers use written contracts (also available from R&Rs), while other prefer oral agreements. The most important thing is to clarify all points and to feel comfortable with them.

Requesting References

A prospective caregiver should not be insulted if you ask for references. Talking with other parents whose children she has cared for is an essential part of your evaluation. You can ask questions you couldn't ask the caregiver herself, and you can double-check answers to other questions. The caregiver may say she's only been sick one day in the past year. Do her references back this up? She may say that she encourages parents to ask about their children's days. Do these parents agree? Have there been any problems? How long do these parents plan to stay in this arrangement? If their children have gone on to other arrangements, why did they leave? How does this situation compare with other arrangements they've made? What did they like best about this caregiver? And what was the worst part of the arrangement?

Many people are uncomfortable with giving negative references. Listen for the tone of voice, as well as the words. Are you getting an enthusiastic or a cautious recommendation?

Center-Based Care

Center-based care is more formal and larger in scale than family day care. Child-care centers vary greatly in size. Small ones may take only fifteen children and very large ones up to two hundred and fifty. Most centers accommodate sixty to one hundred children.

Many centers do not take children under two (because of differing state licensing requirements for children below that age); others require a child to be toilet-trained. (Diapering is a time-consuming task when you add up the number of changes per child per day. Most children are toilet-trained by three and a half.) However, just because a program admits children on their second birthday doesn't automatically mean they offer the close care children this age require. A child who has recently turned two needs much more attention than a three- or four-year-old. He may find handling the many transitions in a typical day quite difficult.

The majority of children in centers are between two and a half and five years old. Some centers do take infants, but the ratio of child to caregiver in those cases is lower. At UCLA Child Care Services, for example, where the ratio is three to one, infants as young as two months old are cared for in a separate area from that of the older children. Infants stay there, looked after by specialized caregivers, until they are solid on their feet. The best of these infant rooms, which are worth searching for, are homey and nurturing.

Babies cannot be well cared for in large groups, no matter how promising the ratio of caregiver to infants may be. Twenty babies— even with twenty caregivers—would be far too stimulating and noisy an environment. When checking out infant-center care, look for small groups (a maximum of eight to ten babies) in separate spaces. Caregivers should do plenty of holding, carrying, and rocking. Babies are especially interested in other babies, and there needs to be enough space for this as well as playing, rolling, and crawling. Swings and walkers are not safe, and may be a way of substituting self-care for adult care. Babies need to be fed and diapered by individual need rather than on a schedule. Cribs or playpens are for napping, not confining an infant. Bottles and food from home should be identified for each baby and kept refrigerated and clean.

Toddlers also need specially designed environments that give them freedom to explore in a safe setting. They are beginning to participate in group activities such as listening to stories and singing, but since they can't sit for long periods of time, these group activities are limited. In such situations, children should be given the freedom not to participate. Generally, a good ratio of toddlers to caregivers is four to one.

Child-care centers have traditionally grouped children by age, two- and three-year-olds together; four- and five-year-olds in another group. Sometimes they are broken into even smaller groups. Children are "moved up" or "go over to the big side" when the time is right. Now some centers are changing to family groupings, where different-aged children are mixed. Instead of one teacher/caregiver being assigned all the young children and another all the older children, every teacher has some older and some younger children in her charge. The younger ones learn from the older ones, and the big kids enjoy helping little ones acquire new skills, such as building with blocks or catching balls.

Centers usually have very fixed hours. They will not take children before or after those hours. If you are late, you may be charged a fee, which may be very stiff to discourage tardiness. Or you may be asked to find another arrangement. Parents who must frequently work overtime may have difficulty with such an arrangement, unless they can arrange for someone else to pick up their children.

Depending on state regulations, center caregivers may be required to meet educational requirements in the field. While many outstanding caregivers have no formal degrees, new research indicates the importance of professional training. A good center will also have a low employee turnover. Unfortunately, child-care providers are so horribly underpaid that turnover is a common problem. Paying the best wages possible and creating a positive, rewarding work environment does help to counteract this problem.

With center-based care, your child will be around many more children than she will in family day care or, especially, in-home care. Children may also have several caregivers during the day, even though there may be one person who is primarily responsible for them. Similarly, a child may arrive at 7:30 A.M., while her primary caregiver doesn't arrive until 9:00 A.M. An arrangement that allows caregivers and parents to keep in touch is one in which caregivers' work hours include either drop-off or pickup hours.

A great advantage to center-based care is that the center doesn't close when just one caregiver is sick. You can be sure that except for announced holiday periods and when your own child is ill, you will always have child care. There may be days when a teacher is out sick and the director or a substitute takes over the group, but care will still be available in the same familiar setting.

The daily routine at a center is usually more defined than in family day care. A daily schedule may be posted. If not, ask for one. Babies won't have a schedule; toddlers will have a very flexible one. Because of the greater number of children, there may be more varied equipment and more space than either you or a family day-care provider can offer. But, of course, with more children come more germs! There's always a trade-off.

Important activities at child-care centers include art projects, music, science projects, story reading and telling, sand and water play, dress-up and housekeeping corners, and block corners.

I visited several preschool centers when I was looking for child care. At one, I noticed that the teachers spent a lot of time reprimanding the kids. They had them sitting in a circle for what seemed like an hour listening to stories. When any child started to get antsy and tried to get up, they were told to sit down. Those kids were bursting with energy, and they were being forced to sit still. These weren't happy kids. At another center, the children were busy working on art projects and playing with blocks, and the teachers pretty much let them work at their own pace as they kept close watch on them. When a child got bored and wanted to go to the doll corner, that was fine. The kids were thoroughly engaged in what they were doing and didn't need a lot of reprimanding. These were happy kids.

Some centers offer extracurricular activities for parents, including support groups, parenting classes, and family outings. These can be great ways to meet other parents with children the same age as yours who are grappling with similar issues. Other parents you meet at the center may live nearby, opening up opportunities for visiting, as well as exchanging babysitting.

Getting the Basics by Phone
Just as with family day-care providers, begin by making some phone calls to whittle out the mismatches. The first step to cutting down the list is to find out hours and space availability. Only visit those with hours that will fit in comfortably with your work schedule and with space when you want care to start. If a particular center has an especially good reputation in your area, it may have a waiting list. Get on it early.

How many children are at the center? What is the maximum number? What neighborhood is the center in? What does it charge? Is it affiliated with any organization (church, etc.)?

Visiting Centers
You will probably be meeting with the director of the center, who may not have direct charge of the children on a regular basis (but may when a teacher/caregiver is sick). She will be able to explain the center's philosophy and rules and answer your questions.

Then she will show you around the site and may invite you to wander around on your own. Find a chair—probably too small—and sit down in a classroom, giving yourself plenty of time to get a sense of the environment. Ask yourself, Is this an inviting place? If you were a child, would you want to spend your days here? Do the children seem happy? Do they look bored? Watch how limits are set and conflicts resolved. Are boys and girls treated the same?

How do the caregivers interact with the children? Are they encouraging constructive, imaginative play or would they rather sit under a tree and talk to one another? Do they get down on eye level and play with the kids? Do they offer children individual attention when they need it? Do they seem suited to the work?

The Nitty-Gritty

The nitty-gritty questions for centers are similar to those we suggested for family day-care providers:

What is the fee? When is it due? Check or cash? Are there extra fees?

How are late pickups handled? Is there a fee or other consequence?

What is the sick policy? Under what circumstances must you keep your child home?

What days will the center be closed? (Ask for a yearly calendar.)

Who provides diapers, food, drinks?

If you were away for a long period of time, would your child's space be held?

Are there any nonmonetary requirements for parents (such as participation in workdays or fundraising efforts)?

Are parents welcome at any time? (By law, in some states, they must be.)

How many children will be in your child's group?

Requesting References

Ask the director for the names and phone numbers of parents who have children in the center. When you ask about someone's experience at the center, be sure to listen for the level of enthusiasm in his or her voice. You may also want to check with your local R&R, even if you haven't been referred through that source, to find out if there have ever been any complaints about the center.

Criteria for Evaluating Family Day-Care Homes and Centers

Your intuitive sense of a good match must always come first. Yet, while the fanciest play yard or the most rigorously adhered-to diapering policy should not be the determining factor in selecting child care, there are still some objective criteria that must be evaluated.

Recent studies have shown that when a home or center pays attention to one health and safety concern, it is likely to pay attention across the board. Good homes and centers take their responsibilities seriously. When they take care to secure a safe play yard, they are likely to see to it that the indoor areas remain childproof as well. The same studies have shown that, conversely, when a home or center is remiss in one area, it is likely to be lacking in others.

Philosophy. Every caregiver has a philosophy on how to care for children, even if she doesn't call it that. How is separation handled? What are her thoughts on setting limits and discipline? The "right" answers to these questions are the ones that are in sync with yours.

How you ask questions will greatly influence the type of answers you get. "The TV isn't on much, is it?" will probably not elicit as much information as, "What are your feeling about having the TV on during the day?"

Ask plenty of "how" questions. How do you deal with fights over toys? How do you handle it when a child refuses to nap? How do you feel about thumb sucking? How do you handle crying?

Read between the lines. Are the responses rote, or does the caregiver take time to think about her answers? Some caregivers talk a jazzy line with parents but are very uninspired with children. Other times, as we've mentioned, the reverse is true.

Ratio of children to caregivers. A recent study by the Child Care and Family Project surveyed centers in Massachusetts, Virginia, and Georgia to see if they were in compliance with state-mandated ratios. Researchers found that one-quarter were out of compliance for infants and half for toddlers. This means that caregivers were caring for more children than they should have been.

The National Association for the Education of Young Children makes the following recommendations.

Recommended for Day-Care Centers

Child's Age	Staff/Child Ratio	Maximum Group Size
0–12 months	1:3–1:4	6–8
13–24 months	1:3–1:4	6–12
2 years	1:4–1:6	8–12
3 years	1:7–1:10	14–20
4 years	1:8–1:10	16–20
5 years	1:8–1:10	16–20
6–8 years	1:10–1:12	20–24

Safety, Health, and Cleanliness. All licensed facilities should have met basic safety requirements, which vary from state to state. Check with your local R&R or licensing agency, for the licensing requirements in your area. You can judge some of the basics for yourself, such as a resilient surface under climbing equipment. And remember that things may have changed at a day-care home or center since the evaluator came out with her checklist. Perhaps a remodeling project is now under way and construction equipment is carelessly left out during the day. Even if the yard was hazard-free six months ago, it might not be today. Heavy items may have been stored recently on top shelves, which makes for a very unsafe situation in an earthquake-prone area. Everything (cabinets, doors, electrical outlets) must be childproof and in good working order from day one of your involvement.

Find out what emergency plans the provider has made. Are there plans for fires, floods, earthquakes, hurricanes, tornadoes, power outages, and so on? Do caregivers know where the closest hospital emergency room is? Do the parents sign emergency-treatment forms? Do caregivers have cardiopulmonary (CPR) training?

Do all providers wash their hands—and children's hands—after every diaper change? The diapering table should be sanitized each time. You may not do this in your own home (although it is a good idea), but it is critical when there are many children using a diaper table, as it is a prime site for spreading disease. Does the caregiver use disposable gloves? If not, does she wash her hands thoroughly after every change?

For older children, toilets and handwashing sinks should be clean and accessible at all times. Do children wash their hands after using the toilet and before and after eating? Is there soap in the bathrooms?

Is drinking water always available?

Location. Ideally, a caregiver is on your route to work. Your morning routine already became complicated when you became a working parent, and it would be nice not to add extra miles to your daily route. Still, surveys show that some parents will drive ten to twenty miles out of their way for a child-care arrangement they feel is excellent.

Most experts feel that a caregiver should be close either to work or to home, rather than at a midpoint location that's impossible to get to quickly if there is an emergency.

If you commute to work by train or bus, a caregiver within walking distance of home makes the most sense. Lugging a baby and all that paraphernalia—plus your own purse, briefcase, lunch—on public transportation would be hellish.

A close-to-home caregiver may work best if there is someone nearby (a grandparent, neighbor, or friend) who can be available to your child if needed (for an earache or a sudden fever, for instance). It's important that this person be a stable and dependable backup. When a child develops a fever or other symptoms of illness, centers are likely to call parents and ask that the child be picked up early, which is when this backup person may need to be called upon to help. In family day care, indicative of its homier ways, a slightly sick child may be settled on a sofa in the living room until the end of the day (although the parent should be informed by phone).

Using a caregiver closer to your work will allow you extra time with your child as you commute to and from work. Of course, this option becomes more appealing when you no longer have to lug baby paraphernalia. This option also provides the added bonus that you can reach your child easily during your workday.

Environment. The physical setting should allow children to move around comfortably. Is parking easy and accessible? Is the yard inviting? Are there shade trees? A nearby park? Grass? No poisonous plants? Are the rooms light and airy or dark and gloomy? Imagine yourself crawling around the space, inside and outdoors. What would it feel like to be a crawler or a toddler two feet off the ground? Is this the kind of space you'd like to spend your days in? Are carpets and floors kept clean? Toys and play equipment are part of the environment. Are they accessible to the children, age-appropriate, clean, and unbroken? Would they hold children's interest?

Many aspects of an environment can be judged by the senses: the smells, sights, and sounds offer quick clues and instant reactions. The smell of cigarettes, poorly vented cooking odors, diapers, or strong antiseptic can be repellent—and cause for further thought.

In-Home Care

In-home care is, almost always, the most expensive type of caregiving. Not everyone can afford it. And not everyone who can afford it will choose it.

In-home care, one-to-one, is parentlike. This arrangement allows children to stay out of cold or rainy weather. It doesn't require you to bundle up and pack up a child early on a freezing morning for a trip to the caregiver. When the caregiver comes to your home or lives with you, children don't have to be awakened to get on the road.

But in-home care can also be the most unreliable type of care, both because many caregivers are dependent on public transportation and because so much depends on feelings of loyalty. Caregivers are isolated workers rather than part of a staff. And while the cost may be high to the parent, the salary is small to the worker. It's the parent-caregiver relationship that holds an in-home arrangement together or causes it to unravel. In any case, it can be volatile. To work well, both caregiver and parents have to be forthcoming and understanding.

Sometimes parents will hire an in-home caregiver who has a young child of her own whom she will be bringing to work with her regularly. A skilled caregiver should be able to look out for both your child and hers. Her child will provide yours with some companionship, even if they are two infants who eye each other tentatively from across a blanket on the rug. A caregiver with school-age children may want to bring them with her on school holidays and vacations. This can be a treat for younger children and sometimes a challenge for older ones.

In-home care runs the gamut from professionally trained, Mary Poppins–like nannies and au pairs to grandmas to people who just consider caring for your child a job. Once you've decided on in-home care, the big question is: live-in or live-out? The advantages of a live-in caregiver are that she can be available at odd times (depending on the arrangement you've worked out) and that you can observe how she interacts with your child in casual moments, even if she isn't caregiving just then.

For live-in arrangements to work well, you need at the very least a decent spare room and, at the best, a spare room and bath that is somewhat removed from the other bedrooms. It also takes the right temperament—of both parents and caregiver—to make such arrangements work well. Parents need to be able to genuinely welcome another person into their home. A live-in will not stay long if she gets bad vibes. For instance, you can't stop talking every time she walks in the room . . . and yet it won't work if you get too chummy with her, either. A successful arrangement falls somewhere in the middle. You must be able to feel that you can be yourself around the caregiver, first thing in the morning and last thing at night.

For years, I'd observed friends with live-in caregivers and how they treated them. Usually they hired someone with limited English and nothing in common with the family. Some had children of their own in their home country and they sent money there every week. They spent their lives taking care of other people's children, while never seeing their own. These women seemed like specters. Ghosts. The word slave *even came to mind. I never understood how someone who was expected to be an alert, loving caregiver could also be a person who could be shunted off to the spare room when her shift was over. It gave me the creeps.*

At first, I didn't want to hire a live-in helper because of this. But I work odd hours, sometimes two to ten, sometimes nine to five, and a live-in seemed to make the most sense. I'm a single mother, and I couldn't afford an agency nanny, so I started interviewing caregivers from other countries who agreed to work for less than the going agency rate. I interviewed ten of them until I found one who I felt I would be able to develop some sort of relationship with. I wanted a live-in person who would talk with me even though we had to struggle with her bad English and my bad Spanish. I wanted someone who would be a person, who would be free to share stories and experiences. I wanted her to feel relaxed in my home, to think of it as her home. I found that person in Martina.

We suggest that you take time to consider whether a live-in caregiver would work out for you. It means having someone who is not family living with your family. The rich, of course, have always done it—think of *Upstairs, Downstairs.* But that kind of setup, with many servants, allowed for live-in servants to have their own life, just in a different part of the house (or manor). The nanny was just one of many hired helpers. And frankly, the Downstairs life always seemed more lively than the Upstairs.

In today's reality, the nanny is usually the only live-in help. If she doesn't participate in the family's life, what else is there for her? We know of too many nannies who are expected to fix a dinner plate and eat on their beds away from the family, nannies who don't even have a separate room but sleep on a cot in the nursery.

There will, we know, be some of you who couldn't imagine having a nanny at the dinner table, who have definite ideas on the role of hired help. *It's simply not done*, you might shudder. *And what would we talk about?* It's funny how au pairs seem to be welcomed at the dinner table, though. In fact, agencies require that an au pair be "considered a regular member of the family."

Still, we recognize that many nannies may prefer to retreat to their rooms before dinner. They've put in a long day, and to eat with the family would just feel like another hour or two of work. Many would prefer to curl up, even on a bed, and eat in front of a TV.

Our advice is that before you hire a live-in nanny, make sure you can offer a decent living situation, that you are able to welcome her as a human being and not that specter who is both there and not there. If you prefer that she take her meals separately from the family, make sure she has a pleasant room environment and other opportunities for social interaction. If you can't offer these things, maybe you need a live-out caregiver who rings the doorbell after breakfast and leaves before dinner.

A professionally trained nanny will understand the relationship between nanny and family, probably even better than you do. She'll help you find the balance. But if you're the caregiver's first or second family, she may have trouble sensing things. You'll have to struggle together.

Au pairs are young women (and sometimes young men) who live with a family to care for the children, not as a long-term career but as a break in their schooling or usual work. Traditionally, au pairs come from Europe, but these days, many are from the United States. They take the job to get away from home for a while, maybe to see another part of the country or world. For someone from a small town, being an au pair can offer a way to live in a city like New York or Chicago in a protected environment.

Au pairs can be delightful, though temporary, additions to a household. They are young and energetic and often well educated and eager to learn about the country or your locality. They'll also provide you with an opportunity to learn about their home countries. Often families form close bonds that extend far beyond the au pair's return home; there may be visits back and forth, meetings with the au pair's parents, home stays in Switzerland, or the like.

Foreign au pairs (the official ones) are all from Western Europe and are placed with American families by agencies under the auspices of the U.S. Information Agency (call 202-619-4700 for a list), which grants them permission to work here for up to one year under a J-1 visa. This one-year limit is a decided drawback. It may sound like a long time now, but before you go the au pair route, remember that you will be looking for another caregiver in a year, perhaps when your child is only about sixteen months old. Government regulations also place limits on foreign au pair activities during the year, including no more than forty-five hours' work a week, no housework, two weeks of paid vacation, and a $500 education stipend. You pay a weekly stipend of $115 regardless of how many children are in their care. But to estimate the true cost, figure in at least $3,000–$4,000 in program fees over the course of the year.

Finding In-Home Care

You can begin your search by making the same sort of inquiries we mentioned for finding family day care. As usual, a personal reference can offer a sense of security.

Parents often also respond to or place classified ads. If you decide to do this, proceed with caution. Spend plenty of time on the phone with all callers before inviting one over for a home interview.

The most expensive way to find in-home care is to use an agency. Nanny agencies vary tremendously. Some are highly professional and refer only well-qualified applicants who have been carefully screened. Others are far more cavalier about whom they refer—perhaps anyone who walks through their doors. Use caution in your dealings with agencies. Some provide training and do fingerprint checks and so on.

Others are simply clearinghouses for employment. Check very carefully what services are provided for your agency fee and how long the organization has been operating. Check agency references, too.

Agencies may charge an up-front consultation fee, plus more on placement. This may be a flat fee or a percentage (10 percent is typical in many areas) of the first year's salary. Good agencies earn their money. The screening is thorough, and they offer a neutral venue for interviews.

Interviewing In-Home Caregivers

Without underestimating the need for a good relationship between parents and both family day-care and center-care caregivers, a higher level of rapport is required when someone comes into your home every day, and it's even more critical when that someone is going to live there. Even if you like someone instantly, allow a little time to be certain. Some people make a great first impression but don't sustain it.

The interview will probably be nerve racking for all concerned. The caregiver, eager to make a good impression, may not seem as warm and spontaneous as she is in less-tense situations. You, eager to make the right choice, may not seem as warm and spontaneous as you usually are, either. All the more reason to proceed slowly.

Find out what kind of caregiving experience she's had. Why did she leave? Has she cared for children your child's age? Has she had first-aid and CPR training for children?

Discussions of discipline issues are paramount, even if you have a newborn. Look ahead to when your child is a toddler. How would the caregiver handle typical situations: tantrums, hitting, biting? As your child grows, the two of you must be in harmony on these matters. You've probably read enough on child rearing by now to know what your basic philosophy is, even if you haven't put it into practice yet.

If you want the caregiver to do any housework, now is the time to spell out your expectations. Do you want the beds made, the laundry done, the floor vacuumed? Or do you want her to devote herself entirely to your child? Parents vary widely on what extra work they expect. The key is always to talk about it in the interview.

How much housework you expect the caregiver to do should depend on the ages and number of children to be cared for. Remember that her primary task is to be with your child, not to sit your child in a playpen in the living room while she cleans the bathrooms. Sure, it would be grand to come home to a spotless house, but it takes a thoughtful assessment (and periodic reassessment) to make sure your delight in a freshly mopped kitchen floor comes after your secure knowledge that your child is well cared for.

If possible, ask the caregiver you would like to hire if she would care for your child for a few hours to see how things go. Pay her for her time. You might want to be in another part of the house or apartment while she is there—close enough to evaluate the care, but not so close as to inhibit or influence it.

With foreign au pairs (or even ones from another state) referred by agencies, you will have to rely on the agency's judgment and a phone call to the prospective caregiver, no matter how far away she lives. The phone call is especially important with au pairs who are not native English speakers, so you can evaluate their fluency yourself. The agency may be relying on a report from a recruitment office in Europe or on the fact that the au pair checked "fluent" on her application. A ten-minute call will confirm not only her aptitude at English, but also some general information that could be important to you.

Checking References

Unless you or someone close to you knows the reference givers personally, your call should have dual purposes. You want the truth from a real reference. You want the truth from a real reference. You also want to ferret out false information from fake references.

First, ask how long the arrangement was for. Why did it end? How did the reference giver's child adjust to the caregiver in question? There are formula answers that make the caregiver sound 100 percent perfect, and there are real-life answers that reflect what really goes on in a caregiving arrangement.

Criminal records: The courthouse in your county can tell you if someone has had any civil or criminal convictions there. Some states provide centralized criminal information, which, of course, is much better. You will need the person's name, date of birth, and Social Security number.

A promising new service in California called Trustline allows interested parties to run a thorough criminal record search. It's expensive

($85) but may be worth it for your peace of mind. Check with your local department of social services or R&R to find out if a similar service is available in your state.

Driving records: Each state maintains records through its department of motor vehicles. To check for driving violations and license suspensions, you'll need the person's name, date of birth, address, and license number.

In-Home Care Makes You an Employer

While politicians and wannabe politicos scurry to pay back taxes for nannies they hired ten years ago, every parent who has in-home child care should take the law seriously—not just so you don't get outed when you're nominated to the Cabinet, but because it is the right thing to do. Of course, being upstanding is also a pain in the neck. Bookkeeping up the wazoo. First you need to apply for an employer identification number, using Form SS-4. You must pay Social Security and Medicare taxes (FICA) if you pay cash wages of more than $50 to any employee in a calendar quarter and must file Form 942 (Employer's Quarterly Tax Return for Household Employees) quarterly and Form W-2 (Wage and Tax Statement) yearly.

You must also pay Federal Unemployment Tax (FUTA) if you pay cash wages of more than $1,000 in a calendar year, filing Form 940 or 940-EZ (Employer's Annual Federal Unemployment Tax Return) at the end of the year.

You are also required to withhold federal income tax if your employee asks you to do so, completing Form W-4 (Employee's Withholding Allowance Certificate) to be filed quarterly. You are also responsible for filing any state-mandated forms.

The IRS publishes a booklet, #926, to guide you through all this mumbo jumbo, but you may also want to double-check everything with a tax adviser.

Additionally, there is the issue of insurance. Your homeowners' policy may already cover you. If not, you can buy a workers' compensation policy for your caregiver, which will cover you if she is hurt on the job. Health insurance is in such a state of flux as we write this book that we hesitate to say anything more about it than our own belief that all workers need health insurance.

If you want your caregiver to chauffeur your child, be sure she has a valid driver's license and is covered by car insurance, either yours or hers. International driver's licenses are valid in the United States, but not all insurance carriers accept them for coverage. Take a test drive with the caregiver to see if she seems as though she'll be able to get around safely. Can she drive safely in *your* neighborhood? A small-town driver may be overwhelmed by big-city traffic. If she has her own car, check her insurance, seat belts, and tires. You may want to invest in another car seat to be installed in her car while she is in your employ.

Ask to see written proof of a recent tuberculosis test (many agencies do this for you). Sometimes a positive test may result from other causes (for example, in many Asian countries, vaccinations are given that result in a positive skin test, so X rays may be required to confirm a prospective caregiver's status).

And, of course, there is the question of whether the caregiver is in the country legally and how you feel about it. If your caregiver does not have a green card, which authorizes her to both live and work in the United States, you may have trouble down the line with those pesky Senate confirmation hearings. And, under existing Immigration and Naturalization Service laws, you could be fined or jailed for hiring an undocumented worker.

If there is someone you want to hire who does not have a green card, you can help her by participating in a sponsorship program. This can take from five to fifteen years, and you are not supposed to hire the person until the application is granted. You should know that this is a complicated process and requires the help of an immigration attorney.

Your Agreement with an In-Home Caregiver
If you work with an agency, it will provide forms detailing what you and the caregiver agree to. Otherwise, make up your own agreement and have both parties sign and date it. It's essential that there be no misunderstanding. Include these issues:

- Days and hours of employment
- Payment: amount, when paid, method of payment (cash, check), overtime pay, pay for extra chores, payment for which holidays, sick time, vacation
- What food and amenities you will provide
- Working conditions: phone privileges, visitors when you are and aren't there, TV and radio usage

- Notice required by both parties to end arrangement (two weeks is customary, but you may feel that you'd need three or four weeks to find a replacement)

Scheduling the Day

Well before your in-home caregiver begins her first day with your child, start thinking about how you want those days to be structured. Begin by writing down your typical schedule with your child. There may be a logical starting point, but since your baby will be developing rapidly, the schedule will have to be altered to meet changing needs.

When you discuss the schedule with the caregiver, ask for her input. Does this seem practical to her? Ask her to try it for a few days, and make sure she feels that she can bring up any problems she has with it. She may want to take your baby for a walk in the stroller right after you leave, because it seems to calm the baby down. Or she may feel that a walk is better just before lunch, even though you've said to take a walk midmorning. Both of you must be willing to try new things and see how your child reacts. Thoughtful planning should also go into a preschooler's schedule.

Explain how you like your child's food prepared and the best time for feedings. Show her where the toys are. Explain your feelings on television viewing. Have her watch as you change a diaper, explaining as you do it how your infant likes to be changed. Talk about naptimes. Show her where all the emergency supplies are kept. Inform her of the places in the neighborhood you feel it is safe for her to go on outings with your child. Ask her to leave a written note and phone message whenever she goes anywhere during the day.

Classes for Your Caregiver

To make absolutely sure that your in-home caregiver knows CPR and has a basic understanding of child development, consider signing her up for a class (if she's agreeable). It may be worth the $25, $100, or more for peace of mind. When you add up the cost of child care for a year, even a high-priced class is a minor expense.

Caregivers can take the same classes that parents do, or you can sign her up for a class that focuses exclusively on caregiver issues. The American Red Cross and many Ys, as well as private companies, offer such courses. Besides the mechanics of CPR, first aid, and safety and medical basics, there are classes that involve caregivers in discussions of what they and the children in their care are going through. It can be both a source of vital information and a social and emotional outlet.

For instance, you may not be able to get to a mommy-and-me class, but your caregiver might. Your child will have a great opportunity to socialize (which is important at even three months!), and your caregiver can benefit from the adult socializing as well as the new information she'll receive. Call around in your area to find out if there are some mommy-and-me classes that might embrace caregivers. She'd probably feel more comfortable under those circumstances than if she's the only non-mom in the circle.

Shared Care

In shared-care arrangements, typically, two families will hire a caregiver together to take care of their children in one or both of the families' homes. Sometimes, with children beyond infancy, three or four families may share care.

In the case of infants, the main reason for choosing shared care is to reduce costs. Parents may imagine that this option will cut their child care costs in half. Not so fast. A caregiver should be paid more for caring for two children than for one. You will save money, but not as much as 50 percent.

Not only is shared care an economical advantage, it is also a way to offer the stimulating presence of another child, which is a great plus. An eighteen-month-old who spends his day with another toddler will have a much richer experience than one who is alone with a caregiver all day. Such an arrangement also enriches the caregiver's day.

Sometimes shared care is rotated back and forth between the two families. Other times, everyone agrees that one of the homes should be used exclusively. The advantages of the care being in your home: your child doesn't have to be bundled up in inclement weather and has all his own clothes and toys around. The disadvantage: considerable wear and tear on your home.

Shared care works best when the two families know each other in advance or have spent time talking about common values. This arrangement calls for a relaxed friendship where issues can be discussed easily, beginning with how to compensate the family whose home is getting greater use, how to provide food for the children and caregiver, and how to buy and replace toys and equipment.

The dynamic that makes shared care work is that both families are satisfied with the caregiver. To ensure this, both families should prepare for and interview all serious prospects.

Typically in such situations, one family decides to end the arrangement before the other family is ready. It may be because of dissatisfaction with the caregiver or simply because another arrangement seems preferable. Perhaps, for instance, one set of parents wants to expose their child to more children. One of the up-front issues for the participating families should be how much notice is required to withdraw from the arrangement. The remaining family may look for a replacement family or may opt for another kind of care. You must also agree on what kind of notice to give the caregiver when the time comes. A contract signed by both families and the caregiver can help avoid misunderstandings.

If your child will be cared for in another family's home, it is important to assess the health and safety of that home just as you would a family day-care provider's home.

Sit down with the other parents to work out the ground rules. How will you pay the caregiver? If one child is sick (a day, a week, or longer), how would that affect things? How about insurance? What if you have different opinions on how the caregiver is doing? What kinds of toys or equipment will be available? Who is responsible for providing them and replacing broken ones? A written agreement can spell out all the necessary issues. Both families should review their homeowners' or renters' insurance to see if the coverage includes situations that may arise in shared care. Realize that difficulties can arise. The visiting child may damage an expensive sofa, the caregiver may damage it, or someone might get physically hurt.

A variation on shared care for older children—parent-organized summer camp—is discussed in Chapter 11.

When a Relative Is the Caregiver

When your mother, mother-in-law, aunt, or sister cares for your child, there is a level of trust that can never be reached with nonrelative care.

Having a relative provide care may also drive you crazy in a way nonrelative care wouldn't. At its best, relative care can be the highlight of a child's life, a time of being fawned over by a grandmother or other doting relative. At its worst, it can bring up all sorts of unresolved issues between mother and daughter, siblings, and so on.

Before you ask your mother, mother-in-law, or other relative to care for your child, take a long hard look at your relationship. Has it been one of open discussion or long-festering grudges? Can you tease each other? Can you take each other's criticisms? Will she be able to accept you as the final authority with your child? Or will she undermine you?

Between any two generations, there will be different schools of parenting. Each generation does things in a new way. And with newfangled notions, there is usually a rejection of the old. Not so long ago, breastfeeding was discouraged. The experts told mothers not to. Of course, this seems unthinkable now. Today's grandmothers may have kept their children bundled up when they had a fever and may have been admonished that a strictly adhered-to schedule was essential. Others might have been reading Spock from the get-go. In any case, there used to be a lot more drudgery involved in being a new mother than there is today. These sharp differences can be discussed in an evenhanded, almost anthropological manner—or they can be used as cannon fodder. Can the two of you reconcile these inevitable generational differences?

Does your relative *really* want to take on this responsibility? Or is she agreeing to do it under duress and family obligation? You may think this is the most logical, most fulfilling way she could possibly spend her sunset years; she may have other ideas. This arrangement may meet your needs beautifully, but does it meet hers? Some grandparents will find taking care of their grandchildren full- or part-time to be a thoroughly rewarding experience. An honor. A thrill. They don't feel exhausted or in the least hemmed in. They love it.

Other grandparents may not be quite so thrilled. But they may not feel they can speak frankly. You have pressed your case forcefully, pushed a few guilt buttons. But this is a decision that must be made freely.

My mother works at Penney's and has for fifteen years. She's in the linen department and doesn't make much money. My husband and I decided we'd much rather have her caring for Heather than hiring a stranger. We told her we'd pay her what she makes at Penney's. We thought it would be easier on her, not having to stand all day long. We thought she'd jump at the chance to be with her granddaughter all day instead of having that grind at work. But she turned us down. She said she liked it there—and the benefits. Liked all her coworkers, and would be lonely at

home with a baby. At first I thought she was crazy, but now I real-
ize that she was right. This wasn't the job for her, even though
she was the grandmother.

Before you propose a caregiving arrangement, observe how your relative is around you and your child. Does she make you feel good about
your parenting abilities? Or do you feel subtly put down or shunted
aside, like a know-nothing in the presence of a great authority? Ask
yourself if you agree on the important issues: feeding and cuddling on
demand, scheduling (or not), napping, discipline. We repeat again our
philosophy: A young child needs consistency in approach.

Before you start, discuss how long you anticipate this arrangement
lasting. Perhaps you'd like your relative to care for your baby until he's
walking. Or talking. Then you might want to explore family day care
or a center. Tell her now. If you wait until the first steps or first words,
she may see your plans as a criticism of her caregiving. Of course at
this point, you may not know how long you'd hope to continue the
arrangement. Still, it's better to discuss it up front. Mention the possibilities—that you would like to explore centers after a year or two, or
whatever is in the back of your mind.

While grandparent care is usually never just a matter of being
cheaper, the economics can be very appealing. Maybe you wouldn't
have to pay your mother-in-law the prevailing rate. Maybe she'd decline any attempts to pay her at all. "It's my grandchild! I couldn't
charge." Again, is what she is saying what she really means? Are there
other ways to compensate her or show your appreciation? Could you
hire someone to do the cleaning in her home as a way of lessening her
workload?

A relative may seem like a simple solution to child care, but this
arrangement is as complex as the others and requires just as much
planning.

four

Let the Caring Begin

FINDING child care is just the beginning. Once you've found the caregiver, you must also adjust to, maintain, and—occasionally—change the arrangement.

Leaving Instructions and Important Information

All caregivers—even grandparents—should have written information and instructions to refer to when needed. You should request this information from centers and licensed family day-care providers. If you find any child-care arrangement in which the caregiver does not ask you to fill out detailed forms, you should see to it that the caregiver has the information on pages 90–91 in legible, written form and that it is kept *up-to-date*.

If you have retained an in-home caregiver, make sure the instructions are in an accessible place. Remind her periodically where they are and what information is specified in them. Some parents put their child's info on three-by-five-inch cards or in a small notebook; such methods work well for both in-home and out-of-home care.

Don't overwhelm the caregiver with so many unnecessary instructions that she may start to think you find her less than competent. You might head the list with a softening phrase: "Ben's habits: He likes his

IMPORTANT INFORMATION FOR CAREGIVERS

Child's full name _____

Mother's name _____

Mother's employer and phone _____

_____

Father's name _____

Father's employer and phone _____

_____

Other phone numbers:

Fire department/paramedics _____

Police _____

Poison control center _____

Child's doctor: name, address, and phone

_____

Nearest hospital: name, address, and phone _____

_____

Close neighbors (if possible)

name/number _____

name/number _____

Relatives

name/number _____

name/number _____

Friends

name/number _____

name/number _____

School or preschool _____

Taxi (if caregiver has no available car) _____

Child's height and weight _____

Health-plan member number _____

Allergies _____

Health history

_____

_____

_____

apple juice diluted in half. He naps best in a dark room. He likes to get out of the crib the moment he wakes up." Such a tone is much more suggestive than an instructive tone: "Make sure you take Ben out of his crib the moment he wakes up."

Phrases such as "she likes" or "he seems to prefer" are great ways to couch your requests. You're not saying, "I want you to feed Ben at 11:30 A.M. sharp," but rather, "Ben seems to prefer eating at about 11:30." Nobody likes unnecessary orders. Nobody likes orders that could have been requests.

There will also be times when you need to leave temporary instructions. For in-home caregivers, leave them on the kitchen table or fix them on the fridge door with a magnet, then make sure she knows they're there. Some centers have bulletin boards or keep instructions in a notebook. You may worry that in the early-morning flurry of activity, your antibiotic instructions will be forgotten. You can help impress upon the caregiver the importance of such instructions by writing (even better, typing) them out and handing them over with a serious demeanor.

Anytime your child must be given a medication, leave written instructions: "1 teaspoon at 11:00 A.M. and 1 teaspoon at 3:00 P.M." Make notes clear and unambiguous. In some states, there are laws that require caregivers to initial and record the time whenever prescription medication is given. Some caregivers will not give nonprescription medications, not even aspirin, without written permission from the child's health professional. In these cases, they're protecting themselves from liability, which can be necessary, even if the parent writes a note requesting the administration of medication.

Written permission for emergency medical treatment is essential. Hospital emergency rooms demand it.

Preparing for That First Goodbye

One of the most important ways to make the transition from your care to caregiver care is to do it gradually. If you are due back at work on July 15 and, after a hearty round of welcome-backs, are expected to put in a full day of work as if you've never been away, you should begin child care *before* July 15. Unless you have absolutely no other way of doing it, you should be getting your child adjusted to his new caregiver well before your big day. Even a few hours will help if that's absolutely all you can manage. Ideally, allow a full week or more for the transition.

Here's the reason from the parent point of view: If you've eased your child into his new situation the week before, you already know he can handle it. You have enough to worry about; that first day back at work is a killer. Knowing your child is on his sixth day in child care will go a long way in lifting a very heavy burden from your shoulders, allowing you to focus on your job.

Whether you've chosen a center, family day-care provider, nanny, or relative, the transition begins with your baby's spending a few hours with both you and the new caregiver. On the first day, spend an hour or two chatting together, explaining your baby's idiosyncrasies and your ideas on parenting. This will, of course, be easier with a nanny, for whose undivided attention you are paying, than for a child-care-center teacher or even a family day-care provider, who can't devote 100 percent of her attention to you. You may be able to talk only in piecemeal fashion, but your baby will be spending a stress-free, hour or two in her new environment.

Here is your chance to talk about how your baby likes to be diapered; that you've found he needs a lot of soothing and talking to on the diaper table or is edgy to get off, so it's better to change him as quickly as possible. This is important information for the caregiver. Point out that your son needs a lot of time with his bottle and needs to be held in a certain position after he finishes. Show how you put your baby down to nap. These little nuggets of information help your caregiver create a sense of continuity between your child's two worlds.

If your child is older, there are many different points for the caregiver to learn. Jeffrey loves apples, but they have to be peeled. Hates eggs. Needs his bunny at naptime. Is slow to accept new situations. Loves the book *Goodnight Moon*.

As you talk through these introductory days, your child will be absorbing his new surroundings. Even a two-month-old is sensing new smells, new sounds, the pattern of lights on the ceiling, the new caregiver's voice. There are many things to which he must acclimate himself in his new daytime home.

After a day or two of short visits while you are there, leave your child alone for an hour or two with his new caregiver. Courage! Say goodbye and assure him that you will be back soon. Whether he is six weeks or four years old, always, always say goodbye. Never sneak out on a child. Even a baby will feel abandoned. It's preferable to leave when your child is awake, but it you must leave when she is sleeping, leave something of yours to remind her of you and/or home. It could be a favorite cloth book or a photo of you tied to the crib.

After you say goodbye, leave. Do a couple of quick errands and come back to pick him up with a reassuring "Mommy came back to pick you up, just as I said I would," or "Mommy always comes back." Again, this message is an essential litany for preschoolers as well as infants. Repeat this message until your child seems to feel confident that you will be back (and maybe even awhile beyond that point). Your child may need only a few days to really believe that you will keep your promise to return . . . or she may need to be reassured for weeks.

Over the next few days, increase the time you leave your child with the caregiver. Same goodbye; same "Hello, I'm back." Then leave for a full day. A pretend workday. This may be the longest he's ever been away from you. And you from him. It's much easier to wrestle with the guilt the week before you go back to work, when no boss, no client, no coworker, no customer is tugging at your sleeve for attention.

> *The first full day Carlos was in family day care, I could not think about anything else. Thank goodness I didn't have to be at work. I brought him over around eight-thirty and went grocery shopping. As soon as I got the groceries put away, I called and Mrs. Kazanjian said he was sleeping and just fine. I went to the cleaner's and as soon as I got home, I called again. Carlos was in Mrs. Kazanjian's lap watching the older kids play. I went to the mall to look at suits in my new size. I called at one o'clock. Carlos had just finished a bottle and was in her arms. I went to the gas station to fill up the tank. I decided to be strong and didn't call!*

Whew! Now that you've been away from your child for a full day and know in your heart that both of you can do it, it's time to go back to work.

And All the Goodbyes That Follow

No matter where you say goodbye—at your front door as your nanny takes over or in a family day-care home or center—allow ample time for farewells. This is not the time to rush. A hurried goodbye will hang over you like a dark cloud all day.

As you hand over your baby, verbalize what's happening: "I'm handing you to Katie now, and I'll be back later." Take time to walk an older child to his cubby and talk about the things he'll be doing during the day. Remind him that you'll be thinking about him and will be back to pick him up, as you always are.

When you say goodbye, reassure your child that you will come back at the end of the day. Say it loud and clear. Let your child know that the separation is hard for you too but that you must go to work. Start preparing for the leavetaking in the car, train, or bus. Talk about the interesting things he will probably do that day. Mention something that you have to do.

Until your child is very relaxed with the child-care arrangement, set aside a few minutes (maybe even fifteen minutes) for the separation. This is not so you can struggle with your indecision. The actual goodbye should be at the end of the fifteen minutes, not the beginning!

Overlap care for a few minutes. Help your child get adjusted to her new surroundings or her nanny. Chat with the caregiver. Try to get your child involved in an activity. But remember, never sneak out.

When it's time to leave, make it warm but firm. It's crucial not to give mixed signals. Don't let your child see you wavering, coming back in for a few more minutes, or peeking through the window. Once you've made a move to leave, follow through with it.

Starting when your child is a baby, remind him that you will be thinking about him during the day and imagining what he is doing. He'll sense the warmth behind your words, and when he becomes verbal, you'll already have established a cozy routine. Tell him how you will be looking forward to picking him up and hearing about all the things he did during your time apart, stories he heard, who was angry, who was sad.

There are also ways to leave your child with reminders of you during the day. You can put snapshots in his cubby, or little drawings in his lunch box, something that will remind him of how much you love him. Do something silly, like cut a sandwich with a heart-shaped cookie cutter.

Asking permission to leave is asking for trouble: "Is it okay for Mommy to go now?" If he were to say no, you'd be stuck.

Bribing your child not to cry when you leave is also problematic. No candy bars. You'll pay for it down the line—and the price will be more than the cost of a Snickers bar. You'll be encouraging endless manipulative scenarios. Once children begin to think this is how the game is played, they'll always expect compensation. When you go out at night or to the doctor's, you'll be expected to deliver a bribe.

Establish a goodbye routine, a little ritual that is special to both of you. You may whisper in each other's ears, "I love you gobs and heaps." Or, "I will think about you every time I blink."

You might begin the routine before you leave home with a few goodbyes (note the key word *few*, as it could easily get out-of-hand) to special possessions. "Goodbye Mr. Teddy; Goodbye, Samantha the cat; Goodbye, rosebush."

Routines such as waving goodbye from a window or reading part of a favorite book help a child learn that this is the sign that Mom's going to leave.

Adjusting to Child Care

Here are two extremes for children's behavior when they enter child care or switch arrangements:

1. They are barely in the door when they spy a toy, wiggle in excitement, and hardly acknowledge your goodbye.

2. They cry. And cry. And cry. For days. Refuse to eat. Or sleep. So you quit your job and never work again.

Your child's behavior will probably fall somewhere between these extremes: some apprehension; some crying. But since you've taken great pains to find a good caregiver, your child adjusts. Even thrives.

The concept of adjustment is not limited to how a child separates from you in the morning. It affects a child twenty-four hours a day, at home or at the caregiver's.

Fear and anxiety can be expressed through many different behaviors, depending on the age of the child:

- Being fussy and cranky
- Refusing to let you leave
- Throwing tantrums
- Regressing in toilet training
- Refusing to eat
- Eating everything in sight
- Sleeping more
- Sleeping less
- Having bad dreams

- Showing hostility toward parents
- Showing hostility toward caregiver
- Showing hostility toward other children

Although there are always exceptions, babies generally adapt better to new situations at a younger age. If you have to return to work quickly, you may be comforted to know that from six weeks to three months, it tends to be relatively easy for a baby to accept a new caregiver. It's still much easier for a infant of three or four months to adjust to new surroundings than a six- to ten-month old, at which age they are starting to differentiate between themselves and others. With increasing awareness, they tend to care more about who is caring for them when it isn't you. This awareness may express itself in fussiness at naptime, crying when you leave, irritability, or behavior that tests your limits.

Of course, if your baby cries when you leave, it doesn't mean she hates being with the caregiver. And it certainly doesn't mean she'll cry all day until you return. Crying is how children express feelings of sadness, anger, and disappointment.

Chistopher cried and cried when I left. He'd turn red. I wondered what happened after I left. After one of these really painful good-byes, Mrs. Latham suggested that I wait a minute and tiptoe back and stand on the porch to listen. I did, and Christopher had stopped crying completely. I could hear the other kids playing, but no crying.

Babies, as well as older children, also cry when their mothers pick them up at the end of the day. They've had a long day, too. When you return, your child can be himself again, let his hair down. And the relief this releases can often be expressed in tears.

Another possibility may be that your child clings tightly to the caregiver just as she'd held on to you a few hours before. Has she forsaken you already? Your worst fears confirmed! Don't panic—this doesn't mean she's found another mother. It's her way of handling the overwhelming emotions of seeing you again. If she doesn't want you to take her from the caregiver's arms, wait for an indication on her part that she is ready to make this transition. Give her a big smile, let her hear your voice. But don't force her out of the caregiver's arms the moment you appear. Chat a moment with the caregiver. Develop a small ritual between you and your child for this time, a special greeting that you two share only then, such as rubbing noses or kissing her on the forehead.

Security Objects

The new smells and sounds of child care can be overwhelming to a young child. She needs some sense of home. One way to ease things is to bring along her favorite blanket or cuddly toy. Her new environment will not be totally foreign if she has a comfort object to hold on to or just to smell occasionally during the day. She may also be calmed by a memento of you—a piece of a scarf you've worn or something else that has your familiar scent on it—pinned to her sweater or tied to her crib.

When a toddler or preschooler starts a new arrangement, put a family picture or two in his cubby or lunch box. When he starts missing you during the day, he will find a photo reassuring. We know of one center that keeps a Polaroid camera on hand to take pictures of parents before they leave that first morning. The new child gets to keep the snapshot with him all day for as many days as he needs.

And don't forget to phone and talk to your child.

Maintaining a Good Relationship
with Your Caregiver

You have it in your power to make or break a caregiving arrangement. Our suggestions for keeping things running smoothly:

Don't take advantage. Deliver and pick up your child within the specified hours. Don't refer to anything as an emergency unless it really is. Don't ask your caregiver to do extra chores unless you pay for them. If you ask, don't be upset if she says no.

A caregiver may not always tell you when she is irked over your late arrival. She may build up resentment to the point that one day you may push her too far, causing her to quit on the spot. Be diligent about keeping your end of the bargain, and remember that a good caregiving situation is a two-way street.

Pay on time. Don't ask if your caregiver can wait until Monday or give partial payments. Don't bring a check if the agreement is for cash.

She may need money for the weekend. Likewise, centers have payrolls to meet. If you have a financial emergency, make arrangements prior to when payment is due. Paying the caregiver is as important as paying the rent or mortgage or car payment. It keeps you working.

Bring the agreed-upon supplies. If you're supposed to keep a stack of diapers on hand (the usual arrangement of most family day-care providers and many centers), don't put your caregiver in the position of having to borrow a diaper from another child's pile and then having to remember to return it whenever you get around to resupplying. Most caregivers require at least one change of clothes for infants, toddlers, and preschoolers. Replace the changes (sheets and blankets, if necessary) you take home to wash and make sure the spare clothes and blankets are appropriate to the season.

If you are required to bring all or part of your child's food and drink, make sure you pack plenty. Overpack in the beginning, then ask your new caregiver for an evaluation of how much you should send with your child. Since some children eat less than usual until they are adjusted to a new setting, she may not have an accurate idea for the first few weeks. If she is frequently having to raid her own cupboards to get your child through the day, she will not be happy.

Show respect. Don't talk down to your caregiver. Ask about her family. Give her a holiday gift. Find out when her birthday is. If she's from another state or country, ask about her life there. Family day care in particular means being part of someone's existing family. Take time to get to know other family members.

Express your appreciation on a regular basis. If your caregiver makes the effort to have your child freshly diapered for you at pickup time, thank her. After you have settled in, tell her that you're glad she is taking care of your child. Comment on positive things your child has been doing or has learned with her. Talk out problems. Don't let things fester.

Feeling Jealous of Your Caregiver

At some point during the first few years, the thought will probably occur to you that a child in child care spends more time with the caregiver than with her own family. Sure, if you count sleeping hours, you're together more. But if you stick to daytime hours, the caregiver wins. *Wins* is right, you mutter. As you adjust to the demands of being a working parent, feelings of resentment may creep in. After all, the caregiver, not you, is enjoying all your child's finest moments. She gets to play with her in the morning and when she's fresh from her nap—the times of the day when she's most engaging, least apt to get fretful. You get her at the end of the day, when she's ready to pop—and frequently does. The caregiver may be witnessing her first smile, her first step. You might miss these events—as well as all the endearing non-events in her life. Bummer.

Don't drive yourself nuts here. The first time you see your child take a step—*that's* her first step. The first time she smiles at you—*that's* her first smile. Remember, unless you pull a Joan Crawford, you'll always be number one. Even if she cries when you try to take her from the caregiver's arms.

The jealousy factor often comes out at the end of the workday, when a parent arrives to pick up her child. A child who, rather than eagerly rushing into a parent's arms, wails at the idea of leaving the caregiver's embrace, can appear to have chosen a new mom. Remind yourself that this a stressful, confusing time of the day for your child. Transitions are hard, especially for a tired child who has been trying to "behave" all day.

Feeling jealous of a caregiver is common, and these feelings can surface as long as your child is in child care. A three-year-old may say, "You don't read that story the right way. Marta knows how to read it." Or "I like the way Alison braids my hair better."

As long as people have different talents and children can talk, they will, sooner or later, point out something that their caregiver does better than you do. The possibilities are endless: ties shoes faster, plays Candyland better, juggles better, reads better stories, doesn't watch boring news shows on TV, doesn't insist on eating yucky foods just because they're good for you.

Now let's put this green-eyed monster in perspective. Would you feel good about a caregiver who didn't have any good qualities, one who was just so-so in everything that had to do with taking care of your child? Suppose she read stories in a monotone; braided hair sloppily before a trip to the park. Remind yourself that your child benefits from a caregiver's talents.

There may come the day your child says in a fit of pique, "I wish Mrs. Beasley was my mommy." He knows just how to wound . . . deeply. Keep your cool. He is venting his frustration at you. Tell him, in as reasoned a voice as possible, "I'm your mom for life." Follow this up with a little reassurance of how much you love him and will always love him, even when he is feeling this way about you. Even mention that you are so pleased that he likes Mrs. Beasley. Your unconditional love, your pledge to always be there for him may be what he's really looking for in the first place. Then find a cozy spot and read *Runaway Bunny* together.

A child who points out the ways the caregiver is "better" than you are (more fun, more energetic, more athletic, and so on) may need a gentle reminder that people have different abilities. Realizing this and recognizing its value is an important life lesson.

Recognizing a Match That Doesn't Work

There are cut-and-dried grounds for ending a caregiving arrangement immediately, such as signs of emotional instability, substance abuse, and neglectful or abusive behavior.

Then there are the less clear-cut situations. Your child may suddenly start complaining about his caregiver, the one to whom he'd seemed so bonded. He may announce that he's not going to see her anymore. That he doesn't like it there. Or that "she's mean." A child who has displayed all signs of adjusting to, and thriving in, a day-care arrangement may one day—seemingly out of the blue—balk at it. It doesn't mean he's being mistreated. It does mean, however, that you need to explore the reason behind it, first to rule out mistreatment and then to straighten out issues between the caregiver and your child. Perhaps she is forcing your child to drink more milk than he wants to (well-meaning but not effective), and it has become a serious bone of contention between them.

This attitude change toward the caregiver may occur at those peak stranger-anxiety stages of development, roughly eight to eighteen months. If it's garden-variety stranger anxiety, you may need to spend more time in the mornings working through the separation process, just as you did in the first few weeks. Your child may need some security objects (bunnies, teddy bears) with him during the day, or extra assurance that you'll pick him up on time. Or he might need a brief phone call during the day.

Make time to sit down with the caregiver and discuss the changes in your child's attitude. Ask her if she's noticed what upsets him. Express your support for her caregiving ability. If there is something going on at home that might be contributing to the situation, share it with her. You may want to point out that your child's anxiety may just be a reaction to being away from home. Some children think that if they make a big enough fuss, Mom will stay home.

In a different scenario, your child may seem perfectly content in day care, but something is gnawing at you. You've started thinking that you no longer want this person, or this center, caring for your child.

It is important here to distinguish between a general sense of anxiety you would have no matter who took care of your child and one that is directly linked to this specific caregiver. You will always worry about what is going on when you are not there. Are the caregiver's safety standards on a par with your own? Does she leave your child unattended? Does she swear she isn't doing something you know she is doing? Is she loving enough?

Do you have specific reasons for doubting this caregiver's suitability? It may take some thinking to pinpoint the source of your doubts. Maybe, when you picked your child up one cool, clammy day, you found her barefoot in the yard. Maybe the caregiver uses the TV as a babysitter. Maybe you've found the yard gate open a few times at the center. Or you noticed that at pickup time, the children are just waiting for their parents, not engaged in activity. Or that the caregiver doesn't consistently tell you enough about your child's day.

Sometimes there are enough small things that bother you to build into one big thing. You don't feel comfortable ending the arrangement because of these little things, but when something comes along that you can use as an excuse, you latch on to it. Blow up. Fire a nanny or, child on hip, storm out of a family care provider or center, never to darken the door again.

Unfortunately, when a parent blows up, the explosion may take place in front of the child, who will be quite confused and extremely upset. Two people whom he loves are fighting—and about him. If this happens, it is crucial, once you've calmed down, to make it as clear as possible that the anger was caused by many things—not just one incident—and that the child is not to blame.

The first six or seven months that our nanny Cynthia took care of my daughter, I thought she was a dream. Then little things started to bother me. She forgot to refrigerate the medicine one day. I had to keep reminding her to change Katie's diaper; she was usually soaking wet when I got home from work. And Cynthia's room was a mess, a real mess. And she seemed to be on the phone much too much. Then she'd be sweet and cuddly with Katie, and I'd feel bad for being so picky. One day, I came home and found Katie in her crib crying, soaked through. I called out to Cynthia and she didn't answer. I grabbed Katie and ran from room to room. I had this moment where I thought Cynthia wasn't there. I found her talking on the phone, lost in conversation. She looked panicked when she saw me. I went into a rage. Katie started screaming. I called her an incompetent menace and I fired her on the spot. Katie didn't know what was happening, but she was frantic. I paid Cynthia off. I gave her two weeks' pay. I had the presence of mind to get all my keys back. I said, "I just want you away from my child." Katie was still crying.

There was no way I could explain to my daughter what had happened. I'm not sure I knew myself. But her beloved Cynthia never came back. Now I wish I'd had a little employer-employee conference before I blew up. It was a very bad scene. Very bad.

Our advice: Don't make a decision to change caregivers in haste—but don't ignore your doubts, either.

Spotting an Abusive Caregiver

Verbal and emotional abuse can be subtle. And it can be subjective. One person's gruffness can be another person's abuse. What's acceptable varies from personality to personality and from culture to culture. Some people have loud voices that can be scary to children who are accustomed to soft ones at home. Our American way can seem gruff and overbearing to people from some cultures. Still other cultures may appear harsh to us. Any assessment of abuse must begin with a thoughtful evaluation of the cultural attitudes and expectations of the people involved.

True verbal abuse is humiliating and deprecating. A verbally abusive adult takes away all of a child's power in a desperate attempt to sustain total control. Tone of voice is as hurtful as the words themselves: shouting, hissing, jeering, critical, sarcastic, flippant, demeaning. Even teasing can take a toll. A toddler may sense verbal abuse without understanding the words, because the message is clear. Both toddlers and older children can be wounded and lose self-esteem.

There are signs that a caregiver may be neglectful or abusive. An infant who is unusually clingy or fussy may be under- or overstimulated during the day. In older children, nightmares, loss of toileting skills, sudden overeating or loss of appetite, or a new tenseness may signal problems in child care—or it may have some other cause.

Parents who are concerned about the quality of care their child is receiving when they are not around must make every effort to investigate the situation, fairly and without hysterics—but also without delay. A thorough conversation with the caregiver's references before hiring her may weed out applicants who have displayed suspicious behavior in the past.

Vary your routine. Come home unexpectedly in the middle of the day or arrive at the center or family day-care home at an atypical hour. Do this more than once. Ask a friend to pop in. Ask other parents at the center or family day-care home if their children seem to be showing signs of stress. Of course, this must be done with great tact and discretion. Unsubstantiated and groundless accusations have a way of taking on a life of their own.

A child who is old enough to talk may tell you about problems, although perhaps not in words. There will always be some kind of change when something troubling is happening. If you suspect problems, evaluate your child's behavior before talking with her directly. When you do ask her questions, be very careful not to lead too strongly. Don't put words in her mouth. Young children may simply tell adults what they think they want to hear.

As we've said before, ending a relationship calls for notice, two weeks at least. But if you've decided to end an arrangement because you feel your child has not been properly cared for, you may not want your child to remain with the caregiver for those two weeks. It may be better to make a clean break. Still, offering two weeks' severance pay (unless your contract states otherwise or there are extenuating circumstances) and any back vacation pay is the honorable thing to do.

If, for some reason, you are asked to write a letter of reference for a caregiver you have dismissed, it's safest to stick to the facts: that she cared for your children from what date to what date. Include your phone number and hold off on any frank discussions until someone phones you for details. If you pull out of a center, be clear with the director about your concerns with the caregiver. Talk to the resource and referral agency that gave you the caregiver's name in the first place. If you suspect that there has been any abuse in a day-care arrangement, you must, by law, report it to your local social service agency.

When Your Child Is Too Sick to Go to Child Care

There may be children out there who have never spiked a fever, never had that goopy stuff running out of their noses, never had an ear infection. But we've never met them. Young children get sick. The average child gets five to eight colds a year. Young children get sick no matter how isolated they are and no matter how fastidious their care.

Now that you know what's ahead of you, plan in advance for how you'll deal with the fateful morning (which just may fall on the day of your big presentation) when your child has his first ear infection. When a child wakes up with a headache, a fever, or a pain in the ear, parents—particularly the brutally honest kind—will admit that concern for their child's well-being is mixed with worries about missing work. If they could only will their child better (dry that nose up, drive that fever down) and get back to the office.

All working parents with young children need sick-care information and specific alternative plans. Before your child develops symptoms, find out what your caregiver's sick policy is and what your employer's policy is, then line up alternate care.

Family day-care providers and centers have many different guidelines for when to keep children home. UCLA Child Care Services developed its own guidelines with the advice of parents and physicians. We use them as a frame of reference, although your caregiver may have other standards, either stricter or looser.

At UCLA, parents are instructed to keep their children home if any of the following conditions are present:

- A fever of 102 degrees F (39C) or higher (rectally: 103 degrees F or 39.6 C)
- Diarrhea (loose, bad-smelling stools, very liquidy, more than three stools a day)

- Vomiting
- Eye infection (discharge from eyes)
- Persistent hacking or congested cough with sore (very red or blistery) throat
- A thin, nasal discharge in combination with any of the above symptoms if it is unusual for that particular child
- Unidentified skin rash, impetigo, or ringworm
- Difficulty in breathing
- Sore throat with fever

The weather is another factor in deciding whether to keep children home. Even the few minutes out of a heated house and into a pouring rain can compound your child's misery.

By the time symptoms of most childhood illnesses are apparent, they have already passed through one of the most contagious stages, which means that spreading germs from child to child is inevitable. Enlightened day-care providers realize that they cannot stop the flow of little beasties wafting in the air. They also know that rigorously adhering to healthful procedures cuts down on these germs and viruses enormously. Still, they must conform to state regulations for accepting sick children and are subject to monitoring in this area. Let's hope that in the near future, the focus will shift from containing the contagion to concern for the comfort of the mildly sick child and whether caregivers can provide the extra comfort required to tend a sick child's needs.

Parents must be as enlightened as they expect caregivers to be. While they don't want caregivers to act as though their little dumpling has the plague, they must also put the child's needs first. A sick child may need to be home and in his own bed. There is no "good time" for a child to get sick—well, maybe Friday night, so she has two days to dry up or cool down.

While just a few years ago pediatricians were telling parents to keep children home for the duration of a cold or ear infection, recommendations have since changed. The American Academy of Pediatrics, the American Public Health Association, and the National Association for the Education of Young Children have all gone on record in favor of permitting mildly ill children to return to child care. *Mildly ill*, in pediatric terms, usually means a mild respiratory illness without a fever, or an ear infection that's being treated with antibiotics.

So, mildly ill children past the contagious stage can go off to child care, providing there is adequate staffing to offer comfort and special attention when needed.

Of course, contagion goes both ways: another reason for keeping sick children away from other kids. A child just getting over an illness has a weakened immune system and may be better off away from other children who might have something else to pass along. In the long run, your child may miss fewer days if he stays home until he's fully recovered.

One way to judge the situation (beyond the ear thermometer) is to evaluate your child's behavior and temperament. Is he acting like himself? If he's acting lethargic or irritable, he may need a parent to take care of him until his condition improves. Temperaments of sick children vary: some are docile, others cranky and demanding. One way to understand your child's "sick" personality is to fill in these blanks: When my child is sick, he acts_____but when he is well, he acts_____. The cranky, demanding ones need more attention than usual (more than the caregiver can give), which probably means parental care or one-on-one care from a relative.

Sick-Child Care: The Choices

Even the best of parents have been known to send off a slightly, "may be coming down with something" child to child care, praying all the way to work that they don't get a call during the day. After all, sometimes a symptom does go away on its own. Maybe this time you'll get lucky.

But let's face it: the best place for a truly sick child is at home snuggled in bed. The second-best place is at another familiar place: Grandma's house or the neighbor's living room sofa.

If you can't stay home with your child, who might be able to? This is not a rhetorical question. You must answer it. If you do think of someone (better if it's more than one), call that person now and say that you are planning ahead. "If Evan had a cold and a fever and it was cold out and I had a big day at work, do you think you could come over and take care of him?"

Sick-child care is not something that most employers deal with willingly. There are a few really enlightened companies—and then there are most companies, where the employee herself has to call in sick.

The most forward-thinking companies are realizing that when they do something to help employees with sick children, it works wonders for job productivity. The average working parent loses five workdays a year to take care of sick children. Companies lose over $3 billion a year in this country because of working parents staying home to deal with child-care emergencies. Slooooooowly, employers are starting to do something about it.

A few progressive approaches:

In New York City: Fourteen companies have come together to offer care for sick children of their employees. Run by Child Care, Inc., a nonprofit resource and referral agency, the program places specially trained aides in employees' homes to care for sick children at home. The bill is sent to the employers, whose policies vary as to how much of the cost they absorb themselves.

At 3M in Minnesota: Employees are entitled to partial payment for up to ten days a year of in-home care for mildly ill children.

There are also child-care centers that specialize in caring for sick children. Check with your R&R or start calling on your own. And some regular child-care centers have separate sick rooms as part of their facilities. Thirty-two states permit this.

Another solution is special sick-care rooms in hospital pediatric wings. These rooms are set aside for mildly ill children who are brought in before work and picked up at the end of the workday. While this solution offers more highly trained caregivers, the downside is that it is in a hospital, and even though the rooms are decorated to be warm and inviting, there are still those hospital vibes around, and it is a strange environment for your child.

Once you've read the proverbial writing on the wall (that says, *There's no way you're going to work today*), you might as well get into a frame of mind that allows you to make the best of the situation. After all, your child may sleep much of the day, so you can get some work done or treat yourself to a long session with a new novel. Or reorganize your kitchen drawers.

In families with two working parents, the needs of a sick child may automatically fall to one parent. This might make sense: one of the two may be able to take the time off or work at home that day. In other cases, this assumption may need to be examined or reworked so that both parents share the responsibility. For example, parents may be able to each work half a day. (See Chapter 12 for a more complete discussion of sharing responsibilities.)

Toddlers and older children may need some special props to get them through a sick spell, and you may not be able to get out to the store once your little one gets sick, so it's always wise to put aside a few treats for the inevitable: a new videotape, puzzles, books, but beware of making staying home too much fun! Maybe this is the time to relax a few rules: lighten the limits on TV, for example. Or offer a special food for sick days—but make it a *real* treat. There are middle-aged adults out there still griping about their mother's milk toast.

Nine to Five for Working Parents

WORKING parents are almost forced to have split personalities. It's a struggle to be both good worker and good parent and to keep your mind on whatever role you're playing at the moment. How to concentrate at work, how to balance both roles, how to get work done, and still be an attentive parent—these are the concerns of all working parents.

Missing Your Baby

It begins as he is wheeled away from the delivery table to the hospital nursery. Do those nurses really know what they're doing? Wouldn't your baby be better off cradled in your arms? You'll see him in a little while . . . but you want to see him, touch him, hold him now.

And yet, right from that first separation, the missing is tempered with other considerations. Exhaustion and the need to sleep can be as powerful as separation anxiety. Through all the years of being a parent, the feelings of missing your child and needing to be alone are intertwined like a double helix. For working parents trying to do two jobs well and still feel like real people, these conflicting emotions can be exceptionally draining.

Separation is part of parenting even if you don't have to go back to work. As you will discover in the first few weeks, you can be pushing a grocery cart down the aisle, enjoying an hour alone in the supermarket, and suddenly you have this panic attack. Is your baby okay? Warm enough? Breathing? You consider abandoning your cart and rushing home to check on your baby's well-being. But you fight the impulse and head for the produce section.

> *After three weeks of nursing every two hours, I was going stir-crazy. Thank goodness my pediatrician said it was okay to start my baby on a supplementary bottle. My husband came home one day from work and I practically ran past him, shouting something about warming the bottle in the fridge and I'd be back in two hours. Where was I off to in such a hurry? I'm almost embarrassed to admit that I just wandered around the shopping mall. But I needed that nothing outing so much. It convinced me that I was still the same person. It told me that I could have time alone. And yet, half the time I was wandering from store to store, I was worrying about Ivy.*

These feelings, which take you by surprise in the beginning, become a regular part of parenthood. The missing and the panic—we have to be honest—never totally go away.

In some circumstances, a teenager can seem as tender, innocent, and in need of protection as a newborn.

> *When my two sons were sixteen and nineteen, they went on a four-day backpacking trip to Yosemite. They were experienced backpackers and so were the two friends they went with. But I felt the same panic I did when they were much younger.*

A sense of panic comes from not knowing every detail in our children's lives. We want to negotiate their way in the world. We want to protect them. Intervene. And it's hard to do when you're not right at their side.

As you return to work—whether it's at six weeks or six months—prepare for a case of the "some other woman's takin' care of my baby" blues that goes with missing your child while you're at work. Which leads us to another popular lament: *Why did I have a baby if I'm never with her?*

We've identified the two extremes that working mothers use to handle their emotions:

Denial. You shut out all thoughts, all references, all talk about your child. Or any child for that matter, if you could manage it. No mementos on your desk. No photograph of Alex at two months, Kristen taking her first steps, Shonda in her darling Halloween costume. The only way you can function is to go into complete denial while you're at work. If you let yourself gaze at your sweet little baby's picture and think about how adorable he looks when he's in his crib . . . well, you'll simply lose it. Like an alcoholic with a sip of wine. No emotional control. You'll feel the urge to rush to your child's side and clutch him to your breast in finest Greek-tragedy fashion. You may or may not act on this impulse. Even if you remain at your desk—which you probably will—you'll have a hard time concentrating on the task at hand. Better to purge all those thoughts.

> *When Laurie was four months old, I had to take a three-day business trip to Chicago. We live outside Pittsburgh. My husband and I decided that he would work short days while I was gone and spend more time with our baby. I had the ideal solution to a not-so-ideal situation, but it wasn't enough. I went into an emotional tailspin on the flight to Chicago. I started seeing Laurie's face in my head, and I let myself wallow in my misery over being away from her. I realized that the only way I was going to get through the next few days was to block out all emotion. I saw a baby her age in the hotel, and it drove me crazy. I was able to call home and check in but when I hung up, I went back to work immediately. I had the emotions of a robot. I didn't have to make another business trip until she was eighteen months, and that time, I was able to allow myself some mothering thoughts.*

The saturation approach. Photos cover the desktop. There are more in the top drawer. Framed snapshots on the walls. The term *shrine* comes to mind. You love to talk about your baby during the day, work her into conversations whenever you can. You need to feel connected all the time. If it can't be physical, then verbal and visual will have to do. When you think about your child, see his picture, you don't feel so far away.

• • •

So which do you do? Deny or saturate? Maybe—let's hope—you can strive for a midpoint between the two extremes. A framed snapshot or two, an occasional amusing anecdote about your little one's latest antics, and then back to work. But if you find comfort only toward one of these poles, then accept it. It works for you.

If you are not a classic denier type, there are techniques that some working parents swear by to get themselves through the long days:

Try visualizing your child's day in child care. Positive images. Imagine her playing with building blocks or chasing another child. Think of her as she plays with all the equipment you don't have available at home.

Take a security object to work. The standard piece of advice for handling children's separation is to send them off with a favorite stuffed animal or blanket to remind them of home. Who says parents can't use security objects, too? Take something with your baby's scent on it, such as a sweater or small blanket.

Set aside specific times to think about your child. Give yourself permission to daydream during your breaks or at lunch. Then you'll have something immediate to look forward to. You don't have to shut out thoughts for eight hours. Every two hours allow yourself a little baby fix.

A common source of worry for working parents is whether you've given the caregiver enough information, directions, etc. to take care of any eventuality. Did you remember to tell her to give your child his medicine at ten o'clock and again at two? She does know that the antibiotic needs refrigerating, doesn't she? Should you call and remind her? Will that insult her? Did you pack enough food? Does she know your work number is in a different area code? Did you remember to write it down on the form? Maybe there's an emergency right this minute and she can't reach you. Maybe the electricity will go out and the phone won't work. And on and on. A separated parent can work herself into a tizzy rather quickly. When you're on a roll, you can find all sorts of things to worry about—the caregiver's husband was using cleaning fluid this morning—did he remember to put it away in a safe place? Stop it!

Being a Parent During Working Hours

There is no way you will get your child from birth to high school graduation without having some emergency that wrenches you away from work. Sooner or later, the caregiver will call and tell you that your baby seems to have an earache. One day you'll have to register your son for kindergarten at 9:00 A.M. Or your twelve-year-old daughter, home alone on Presidents' Day, thinks she hears a prowler, and none of the neighbors are home to check on her.

Welcome to the world of the working parent. Nose to the grindstone, yes, but an ear to the phone at the same time. Even when you're someone's employee, employer, client, consultant—you're *always, always* someone's parent.

The parent part of you may have to go into a daytime dormancy state in order to get the job done every day. It is still there, however, ready to spring into action at a moment's notice. But when there's no earache, dental appointment, or getting accustomed to a new caregiver, you can back-burner the parent stuff. The longer you're a parent, the more you'll get the hang of this back-burner thing.

How fully you can devote yourself to your work will always depend in large measure on how good you feel about your child's caregiver or school situation. Trust in the caregiver and a sense of a good school environment makes it easier to put the worrying thoughts out of your head for long periods at a time. But the first day your child starts child care—or even junior high—well, you might as well forget trying not to worry, at least until you sense your child has settled in.

And then . . . BAM! Your toddler starts to vomit. Or summer vacation starts. Or your seventh-grader doesn't call exactly at 3:20 P.M. the way she's supposed to. Realize that there will be times when you have to leave in the middle of the workday or go into work late because you need to care for your child. You're expected to be in two places at once. How stressful this is depends on how family-friendly your work environment is—particularly how many coworker parents have paved the way.

If you can use your own sick time when it's your child who's really sick—and not have to lie about it—that's a significant stress reducer. If you can arrange to take three hours off one morning to attend a holiday recital without having to fake a doctor's appointment or medical emergency, you'll feel much more at ease with your dual responsibilities.

All workers need some flexibility in their work schedules. Everyone has to deal occasionally with a root canal or a cable guy who won't work weekends. Working parents need even more flexibility—flexibility for two people. Or three. Or more.

If your work situation is not as accommodating as it should be for a working parent, there may be ways to loosen things up a bit. For some of you, this means explaining your needs to a corporate-level decision maker; for others, you must simply deal with your immediate boss. Depending on your employer or supervisor, you could:

Point out that a brief call to your child when he gets home from school puts your mind at ease and makes you much more productive for the rest of the workday.

Explain clearly that you will occasionally need to be taking your child to the doctor and that, since you've never abused your medical time off, you don't want to start lying about your condition or whereabouts.

Quote from newspaper or magazine articles that say that workplaces that are family-friendly have more productive workers.

There may be times when you hear, "Can you work late to get the proposal finished tonight?" Before you were a parent, you didn't want to say yes any more than you do now, but you might have agreed. Now you can't: you've got a caregiver who charges a dollar a minute after six o'clock. But maybe you could take work home? Come in a little early? A counterproposal, even a weak one, will be better received than a flat refusal. When the burdens of being a good worker and a good parent are in conflict, the basic tack with either boss or client should be, *How can we solve this together?*

As your child gets older, explain to him about the nature of your work, and about work in general. This should include what is and isn't acceptable or possible in terms of contact during the day. For some office workers, an occasional, brief call for reassurance is no problem at all. For others, phone calls are impossible except at break times and for emergencies. Set up a system that works for both your roles. For example, explain to your child that it's easier for you to talk on the phone between noon and one o'clock, when most coworkers have gone out to lunch.

Plan your phone calls home or to the caregiver. If you don't have privacy at your desk, you might be better off springing for the call from a pay phone. Of course, the pay phone should be located in a quiet, out-of-traffic location. Scout around. Time your breaks for when there's the least competition for phone use. Maybe a cellular phone is the answer. It's expensive, but it allows you to call from any private spot (your car, a stairwell, outside the building) whenever you can make time for it.

Carrying a beeper is a less expensive way for your spouse, child, and caregiver to reach you in an emergency. You'll be reassured that it will go off if there is a problem, which beats sitting in a meeting or dealing with customers, wondering how things are going. In this case, no news is truly good news.

Making the Most of Your Lunch Breaks

To a working parent, the lunch hour can mean a chance to pick up a carton of diapers, baby food, or medicine, so you don't have to stop on the way home. Or it can provide an opportunity to take your child to the pediatrician. The term *lunch break* is really a misnomer for working parents: there's little time for lunch and no break from work/stress/pressure. A few suggestions to ease the load:

Take lunch from home and eat at your desk, so you can make personal calls or (honest!) relax a little.

Order from catalogs. From JCPenney to J. Crew, you can get a lot of shopping done with a minimum of effort. Order your clothes, your child's clothes, gifts.

Make shopping lists and plan meals ahead. Plan several meals at one time.

Call your mother and chat.

Check your home answering machine for messages and return calls during lunch, rather than doing it when you could be spending time with your child.

Take the Sunday paper or *The New Yorker*—or any similarly daunting but treasured reading—and keep it at work, making your way through in bits and pieces during the week.

Get out! Are there any errands you usually do from home that could be done near your office? Is there a cleaner near the office that's convenient for midday drop-offs and pickups? Can you switch to a pharmacy near work and get prescriptions filled at lunch? If you have a refrigerator at work, you can pick up a few perishable essentials at lunch and keep them cool until it's time to go home.

Is there a park nearby? A rooftop garden? A quiet spot near a fountain? Go there and meditate.

Networking with Other Parents at Work

We've said it before: Other parents at work can be a great source of empathy, sympathy, and good advice (plus, you can cover for one another). Anyone with a child older than yours can tell you stories about how she has handled a work/parent conflict that you can learn from. Other parents can point out which supervisors are sympathetic, and which are coldhearted.

Coworkers who are parents can offer emotional support on tough days when parenting worries become overwhelming—like when you know the caregiver just isn't right and you have to make a change. Or when the caregiver calls to tell you that your toddler has a slight fever, and she's got him sleeping on her bed until the end of the day. Or when your ten-year-old calls from a friend's house (an after-school no-no in your family). Or when your ten-year-old doesn't call at all.

You need a pat on the shoulder from someone who's been through these situations—and survived. A commiserator. A pepper-upper. In the past, you may not have made friendly overtures to fellow parents in your workplace. They may live far away or have a very different personal style or politics. True, you may not have had much to chat about before, but you've got a great deal in common now. Parenthood is a strong common bond.

Suggest to other parents that you get together regularly. Wednesdays at noon, for example. It can be informal and cheap (a special table in the lunchroom) or an organized treat (lunch out). You can spend time chatting about parenting and kids and exchanging advice and anecdotes. Or you can bring in experts to talk about relevant issues. You might approach your employer about doing this as a company perk.

If you work in a large company or agency, ask your human resources department for a list of other parents in your company who live in your zip code. This may take some prodding. Get together with them for carpooling, a babysitting co-op, or play dates among children of similar ages.

When You Absolutely, Positively Have to Take Your Child to Work

Taking your child to work with you should be a last-ditch act of desperation even if:

- You can close the door to your office
- She naps most of the day
- Other parents at your workplace do it
- She promises to play with her Lego set quietly on the floor next to your desk

Sure, it *sounds* as though it might work. Dream on. We think the only reason to take a child to work is that you've exhausted all other possibilities and not going to work would be calamitous, or, rather, *more* calamitous, because a child in the workplace could be a calamity waiting to happen.

Here's one possible scenario. Bosses, coworkers, and clients may know, intellectually, that you're a parent, but it's a lot different to actually see you in that role. In other words, it's one thing to hear stories about your new baby. It's quite another to watch you diapering and burping. Or dealing with a temper tantrum. In fact, it's more than they need to know about you. It's too . . . graphic. It detracts from your image as a worker. You are much more effective, as an employer and as an employee, if you present a consistent, unwavering image of a serious worker. Not a mommy. Not a daddy. Memories of you with a burping rag on your left shoulder will linger. This may apply only to traditional, hard-charger, corporate-ladder workplaces where working women worry about a mommy track. And it's probably less risky to bring in older children. But ministrations to babies are clearly problematic. This is an unfortunate scenario, but applicable to some environments.

I have come to the conclusion that stockbrokers can be mothers—just not to do the mothering in public. At least not in the office. I brought my four-month-old baby to work on what I thought would be a quiet day (the markets were closed). Everyone gathered around and they were all saying nice things about Jessie. Then Jessie started fussing, and I had to give her a little juice. Then I burped her. I just went into my Mommy thing, forgetting that I had an audience—two of the senior partners. I started to get the distinct feeling that this was all too graphic for them. Never again. It's okay to have snapshots of Jessie on my desk, but not Jessie.

Another reason to leave your child at home: You won't get as much work done. Very few parents can fully get over the feeling that at any minute, their baby will cry, their toddler will wail, their kindergartner will want to sit on their lap. Any minute the calm could be pierced, which makes concentrating doubly difficult. So you shift into Mommy mode.

If, however, you must take your child to the office, in spite of all our warnings, we have some suggestions:

Make it abundantly clear to all bosses, coworkers, customers, and clients that this is an emergency situation—that you haven't done this cavalierly.

Don't stay for the whole day, even with a young baby. Sleeping at home is different from sleeping in a strange room. There are strange lights and strange sounds that are difficult for your baby to tolerate.

Take plenty for your child to do. Old favorites and a few surprises, but all of a solitary nature. Try coloring books. Reading books. Hand-held games. Floor toys that don't ring, bing, or clang.

Don't dump your anxiety on your child. It's not fair, and it will ruin any chance you have of getting through the day.

Accept that your child is not going to be perfect. She will want your attention frequently. Very frequently. She will ask, "Why are you doing that?" and "What's this for?" She will announce, "I have to go to the bathroom" and "I'm bored" and "I'm thirsty" and "How much longer?"

Go into the office only long enough to pull together work that can be done at home.

Handling Veterans Day and Other Holidays That You Don't Get Off

With the possible exception of schoolteachers, most working parents face the problem of what to do about child care on days when they have to work, and school (even preschool) is closed. Those three-day weekends can be less than a treat when you have no child care for the third day and it's not a holiday for you. And what if the day-care center closes for the long Thanksgiving weekend but you have to work that Friday?

Most workers get six holidays a year. Some get more. Children get the most. These problem days need advance planning. You can't plan child care for the day after Thanksgiving while stuffing the turkey.

Most schools and preschools hand out school-year calendars in September. That's the best time to mark off all the days the school will be closed, and develop Plan B. Using a school calendar is essential to accurate planning, since many schools close on nonholidays as well. There are early dismissal days and shortened days (which have two different time schedules) and "pupil-free days," during which teachers and other staff meet to discuss administrative issues.

For these days, here are a few Plan B suggestions:

If there's a child-care resource and referral agency in your area (check the Yellow Pages), call for leads on child-care services that might be open (see Chapter 3).

Grandparents, friends, or relatives may be pressed into service if approached in the appropriate manner and with plenty of notice. Remember, turning to these individuals at the last minute may not get the response you hope for. After all, they'd rather be thought of as a first solution than a last resort.

Check with other parents who may have the day off. (Hmmm, doesn't Sonya's mother teach sixth grade?) They may welcome a friend their children could play with—especially if you offer to reciprocate on a Saturday night.

Are there responsible teens or college students in the neighborhood who are also home from school and looking to make some spending money?

Some community groups such as YM/YWCAs, YM/YWHAs, JCCs, recreation and park departments, church groups, and private day camps provide day care for school holidays. Some offer one-day care for Veterans Day and similar holidays, along with one- and two-week sessions for school vacations.

Some child-care providers you've employed previously may welcome a six-year-old alum for the day (for a fee, of course). And family day-care providers might also enjoy seeing how much a favorite toddler has grown.

Our final suggestion takes some organizing: Since there are several of these pesky school holidays a year, put together a group of reliable parents who can rotate care in their homes. That way, you'll only have to stay home one day.

Before you make arrangements, assess how well your child will be able to adapt to the change you are setting up. If you send your child off to a strange place, with teachers and children he doesn't know, will he be able to handle it? Some children can; some can't. Here's a tip: Sometimes a strange place does not seem so daunting if a child is accompanied by a best friend from his regular child care.

Stopping Work at the End of the Day

Before you had a baby, you could call home at six o'clock and tell your spouse, "Honey, I'm on a roll here, can you zap a Lean Cuisine for dinner? I'll be home around nine." Well, honey, those days are over.

Yes, you may have to work late occasionally. But you cannot put in those workaholic hours on a regular basis without compromising your role as a parent. Once you become a parent, it is imperative to get a balance going. Sure, someone else can take care of your child while you put in twelve-hour days, day after day: your spouse, the world's greatest nanny; the family day-care provider who likes a little overtime money.

But it doesn't make it okay. You can put in *some* late nights. You can go on business trips *occasionally*. But there's got to be time for your child. As a group, flight-attendant mothers have always had to deal with nontraditional working hours.

I've been a flight attendant for ten years, so I have the seniority built up to get the work schedule I want. There's no way I can work nine to five and still fly, though. Now that I'm a mom, what seems to work best is to work a two- or three-day route, and then I'm off for three or four days. When I'm home, I'm really home with my child, who's now three. I think we spend more time together than if I had an office job.

In some professions (the law, nursing), ten- to twelve-hours days are routine. They are expected. If that's the norm where you work, we can't pretend that it's not going to be stressful. You simply may not have any say in the number of hours you have to put in. But you may find creative ways to put in the time, such as taking work home, getting a home fax and modem or other equipment so you can work at home, splitting shifts arranged with your spouse, going back to the office late at night, working Sunday mornings, and so on.

Now is the time to work toward a balance in life. Children and workaholics don't mix. Remember the day the O.J. Simpson trial ground to a halt when prosecutor/single mom Marcia Clark stood up in court and said she couldn't work late? Sorry, judge, I've got to get home to my kids. She said it to the world. You can, too.

When You Work at Home

These are some of the problems that arise for parents who work at home:

A baby crying in the middle of a conference call.

A toddler pulling on your leg as you're modeming a letter.

A child of any age who doesn't understand the nature of work, the need for concentration, or why you can't stop everything and play catch or find Rufus the teddy bear. Most kids fall into this category.

Serious work—work you have to do to earn a living—cannot be done full-time while you have children at home. You can get *some* work done with a child in the house, but not forty hours' worth.

Working at home offers flexibility. It eliminates commuting. It means a relaxed dress code. But it is not a substitute for child care. Early infancy is the easiest time to work with a child at home, when they sleep as much as they're ever going to. For the first few months, you probably can put in a few to several productive hours a day, especially if you can choose the hours so you work around your baby's schedule. But there are exceptions here, too. You may be too tired to be effective, or your baby may not be sleeping through the night, so until you get your required REMs without interruption, you're a zombie.

Your next-best chance for a decent work-inducing environment is way down the road—namely, when all your children are in school full-time—and even then you'll only have that luxury during school days.

Many parents work at home because that's always been the nature of the job, not because they are now changing arrangements to meet their new responsibilities. If you've been working at a desk in the spare room, on the dining room table, or in the garage, you will probably want to continue. Having a child around will call for some adjustments, but perhaps only some fine tuning. If you work at the dining room table, you will, at some point, have to childproof your work area.

Even if you work at home, you'll still need some kind of child-care arrangement, although maybe not for as many hours as you would if you commuted to work. The question is, Do you find someone to come to your house, or do you take your child to a caregiver and then return home to work? To make this decision, you have to ask another question: How big is your house? If you're sitting at the computer in the corner of the bedroom and can hear everything that's going on in the rest of the house, you need to take your child to the caregiver and work alone. You may also be able to divide up your work: do the light-weight work with your child around. Then hire a caregiver so you can tackle the serious stuff.

If the house is arranged so that you can go off to your workplace in the basement, attic, or some other separate area and not be disturbed, then you've really got a fighting chance.

Working at home while your older children are on the premises, with or without a caregiver on the scene, requires firmness. You must be willing to say resolutely that you cannot be disturbed, and ask for cooperation. This kind of setup is very tempting for most kids. You're right there. What can be the harm of asking for help finding the purple crayon? You should draw up a detailed list of what constitutes a real emergency, then stick to it.

The same resolve is necessary with a caregiver in the house, who must accept the fact that when you are in your work area, you are not available to her or the children. The same criteria should apply as if you were working in a downtown office. It may sound hardhearted, but it's the only way you'll get any work done. A perfect example of this fact is that parents who work at home find that their productivity suffers during school vacations. Children answer the phone in less-than-businesslike manner. They yell, "Harry hit me" into the mouthpiece when you're talking to a client. They want lunch just as you're really cooking with ideas.

I've worked at home for years, sitting at my computer. It works fine during the school year. But I noticed that every June, I started to go into a mini-depression. Then I realized that it was caused by an upcoming summer vacation that my two kids would have and I wouldn't. They'd be home and underfoot, and I'd be screaming at them to be quiet. My output dropped. The tension was thick. I finally accepted the inevitable, that my productivity would drop from the third week in June until Labor Day. I've set special, lowered work goals for summer.

six

Nine to Five for Children Under Five

HOW your child's day goes is important to both of you. Of course, you want the best for your child in these critical early years. But the bonus that comes with a good child-care arrangement is peace of mind, which is exactly what's necessary to get work done.

Your Baby Missing You

Life, beginning with that moment when you were whisked off to the nursery without Mom and Dad, is a series of separations. We deal with it all our lives, but the painful issue of separation takes center stage when a child is getting settled in a first child-care arrangement. Both parent and child feel it intensely. Perhaps this is the time to think more broadly about separation and to find the positive elements mixed in with the pain.

Separation is not only about being apart from each other. It is also an essential link in the process of letting go of one thing and moving on to something else. This moving from one thing to another evokes a mixture of sadness and longing for the old and anticipation of the new.

When a child is separated from a parent, it can be miserable for him. But it is also a learning experience. The children of working parents learn very early essential truths of life: that they are okay when their parents aren't around; that their parents always come back; that the world is a relatively predictable place.

Learning to accept and deal with separation from loving parents is one of the major challenges—then accomplishments—of a young child. He learns trust: trust in others, trust in his parents for returning, and trust in himself that he can handle it. Separation can result in growth. It allows your child to learn about himself.

How a child handles separation depends on both temperament and the way you manage the leavetaking. Some children will have a tough time no matter how rigorously parents follow the slow steps discussed in Chapter 4. This first real separation—the workday separation— is important for both of you. It is the first step toward independence and freedom—for both of you.

Learning About Your Child's Day: Tuning In to Cues

Your infant can't tell you how his day was. You will have to rely on the caregiver's information and your child's behavior for clues. Is he content? This may be hard to evaluate, because pickup time usually coincides with the fussiest time of the day. Most children are at their whiniest, cryingest, neediest around five or six in the afternoon. Ask yourself, does he seem more distressed than usual *at that time of day?* Additionally, does your infant physically seem to be in good condition? Does he have a recurring diaper rash? Is he appropriately dressed?

Toddlers will begin to master a few words that can convey their feelings. And even when you can't understand their words, you can sense their tone. Toddlers can also tell you a lot by their behavior. How did she act on the way to the caregiver? How outgoing and relaxed is she in general these days?

Is your infant relaxed, hyper, angry, or worn out when you pick him up? Is he calm or anxious, unable to tolerate any waiting? If he's old enough, try putting some words out there and see if he picks up on them. They will reassure him that you know what he is going through. "You've had a long day. Linda said that Jake was grabbing your favorite truck all day. I bet it was hard." Be on the lookout for consistent behavioral clues that indicate more than just an occasional bad day. Preschoolers will often be able to express their feelings about the day.

If a child has a healthy home life, he should be willing and eager to attend child care.

If the cues you are picking up tell you that your child is not relaxed and not making the adjustment to child care—not even slowly—discuss this with the caregiver. If you can, spend some time there to see if you can sense what the problem is. Talk with the caregiver about your child's reactions, without seeming to place the blame on her.

Of course, children are always taking their cues from their parents. In order for them to feel good about child care, they must sense that their parents are pleased with the arrangement. Be upbeat and supportive. Sometimes parents need to make an extra effort to convince a child that the caregiver is okay. This may call for bringing up the caregiver's name in the evenings and on weekends and mentioning the good things about the day-care facility (swings, lots of blocks, good friends, and so on). Yet, even in this situation, parents must walk a fine line, both being supportive of the caregiver and creating an environment in which a child feels comfortable to express concerns about the caregiver.

When a Caregiver Speaks Another Language

The children of working parents often spend their days with caregivers who do not speak the same language as their parents. Whether your child is being cared for by a Spanish-speaking nanny or a grandmother who prefers Russian to English, you may worry that being exposed to two languages will be confusing to your child. How can a two-year-old distinguish English words from Spanish ones?

What does it mean for young children to be brought up hearing two languages during the course of an average day? How can they possibly understand? They don't really understand English yet, and they're being bombarded with Russian or Spanish.

They *do* understand. It's one of life's little miracles. Children are not the worse for it, either. Because they are acquiring two languages at the same time, it may appear that their language development is slower than those children raised in monolingual homes. But—and this is important—they catch up, and then they have the great advantage of knowing two languages.

Being bilingual is a great plus in life. And even if children forget much of the second language as it fades from disuse, they retain a heightened ability to acquire foreign languages, as well as a general command over communication skills. It is important to remember that those early years spent separating out two languages can actually help refine a child's mind skills as life goes on.

The important issue is consistency. Each person in a child's life should speak one language to the child, not bounce back and forth. This aids language acquisition. A father who speaks French at the breakfast table and English at dinner can easily confuse a young child. When a caregiver speaks Spanish all day long and parents speak English the rest of the time, the child's mind can sort out and absorb the syntax and vocabulary of both languages, learning the grammatical rules of each. Yes, believe it or not, all those irregular verbs and idiomatic expressions you struggled with in high school are routinely absorbed by your young child.

This process works in Switzerland, where nannies often speak a different language with their charges than parents do. In this country, we could be as linguistically inclined as the Swiss.

Parents who hire a caregiver who is not fluent in English may instinctively hope the caregiver will speak to their child in her native language as little as possible, so as not to confuse the child. Forget the confusion issue. What would be more harmful is a quiet environment. The taciturn caregiver is a problem, no matter what the language, because being talked to is essential to healthy development. Encourage a caregiver to converse with your children in her own language. Parents who make the effort to converse (even a little) in the caregiver's language are creating an environment that encourages a child to try it himself, as well as demonstrating to a child how to reach out to people.

Yet there *is* a serious issue concerning caregivers who are not fluent in the parents' language; namely, how parents can communicate information to that caregiver. How do you talk about schedules and how would you like her to react to crying or tantrums? How do you explain how to use the appliances, what to do in an emergency, and how to contact you at work? How does she tell you about your child's day?

In many areas of the country, a significant percentage of in-home child caregivers are not fluent in English. You may discover that many applicants you come across may have limited English proficiency. While how much English and how well it is spoken are not indicators of how nurturing a caregiver is, they will clearly affect your interaction with her.

And, of course, interaction between parent and caregiver is essential. Imagine coming home from work to your one-year-old child. You've been apart for ten hours. She lights up when she sees you. She seems content. You want to know what she did all day. Will your caregiver be able to tell you that she had a fussy morning and that she's starting to like spinach and that she slept for three hours instead of two?

If you call home to say that you're stuck in a traffic jam and will be a half hour late, will your caregiver understand? When your baby has a fever or other symptoms of illness, will your caregiver be able to discuss the situation with you so that together you can decide if you should leave work early? These are common scenarios for working parents. They can't be dealt with by knowing a few basics in another language. Booklets may work for house cleaning but not for child care—"How to talk to your babysitter in Spanish" won't cut it.

Before hiring a caregiver, imagine handling these situations with her. Are you comfortable with how you think things might go? We don't mean to suggest that you need a native English speaker or even a caregiver who is completely fluent in your language. If you interview someone whose English is limited, but otherwise you think this would be a good match, take some extra time to talk with her. Can you carry on a conversation about your child and what your expectations are? If not, this is not the right caregiver for your family—unless you want to take on the added burden of learning her language, immediately.

What Makes a Good Preschool?

Should preschools push playing or reading? We'll answer this one up front: playing.

You might remember the Steve Martin movie *Parenthood* in which a character has his four-year-old daughter reading Kafka . . . while the other children are playing outside. He puffs up his chest as she picks the square root of 8,694 from a card covered with the correct number of dots . . . while the other children are playing outside. Although she may seem a "superkid," Daddy's little whiz kid is not a happy child. While the other kids are chasing each other and playing Little League, this little girl is busy getting "on track," as her father calls it.

Superbabies, the hurried child, hothousing children—it's called a lot of things. We call it pushing preschoolers to perform—rather than to learn—because that's what they're really doing.

Of course, parents have the best intentions. They worry that their children are a reflection of them. And working parents, especially, feel the need to show that they are still good parents—even though they are working. Somehow, they feel that a four-year-old who reads is proof that they aren't neglecting their parental responsibilities.

Another reason parents push preschoolers (and older children, too) is their own feelings of inadequacy. Every generation of parents wants more for their children than they had themselves. Our country's history is that of immigrants with only rudimentary educations and little understanding of English who managed to put their children through college. Parents have dreamed of a Vassar or Harvard education as the key to a better life ever since such institutions were founded.

But the pushing used to begin later in childhood. Prepping for Harvard started well into the elementary-school years. The prekindergarten years were spent playing with neighborhood children. These days, parents are urged to enroll their three-year-olds in preschools that promise to have them reading in two months, or they sign up for an at-home enrichment program that has children doing division by dots. But these parents are being sold a bill of goods.

Enrichment *is* great, but division by dots is not enrichment. And ask yourself, does a three-year-old really need to be computer-literate? Playing Connect Four with a friend is real enrichment. Reach back into your memory; remember learning to read. For some children, it is a joyful experience. For others, a stressful one. Remember those reading groups? The frustration at not being able to "sound it out"? If you want to give your preschoolers a boost in life, the best way is to read to them yourself. Show pleasure in your own reading.

Studies back us up. There is no evidence that a child who learns to read and do math earlier does any better in the long run. Giving kids a headstart in life is, of course, a nice notion, but forcing them to learn just doesn't do it. In fact, the pressure is more likely to turn them into stressed-out kids. Children who are pushed tend to burn out rather than blossom. Pediatricians are witnessing more children who, because they're stimulated and pressured, develop headaches, stomachaches, sleeping disorders, and even chest pains.

Further, forcing children to read at an earlier age than their natural inclination suggests leads to poor motivation a few years down the line in other aspects of learning. In third grade, when reading skills are expected of everyone, a pushed child may be one who can follow instructions and complete tasks, but is merely going through the motions of learning, because he simply thinks of it as performing. Reading should be exciting. There *are* three-year-olds who are ready to read, and these children will read on their own, whether you teach them or not. They'll pick up a soup can and study the label. They'll ask what the street signs say. This curiosity is important to them; it comes from within. And, yes, those children do learn before their peers. But by the third grade, all reading skills have pretty much equaled out, regardless of how early a child starts.

Most children aren't ready to read at three. In fact, most children aren't ready to read until they are six or seven. Europeans, even the Japanese (who are hardly slouches in the academic department), don't begin reading instruction until age seven.

Sometimes parents push preschool academics because they're trying to prepare their children for later life—they know so-so classroom skills and a lackluster approach to learning gets a child nowhere. True, it's a competitive world out there, and it's getting more competitive for every succeeding generation. Parents do need to be thinking about the big picture. But reading programs for three-year-olds are not the solution.

The preschool years are for play. That's how children learn. Asking a young child to sit still and hold a pencil for an hour is too difficult. It's not natural for children at that age. There are more age-appropriate ways of learning.

> *I was very pleased with my son's preschool. I didn't want them pushing reading, and they didn't. I assumed that meant they wouldn't be learning anything "academic." I realized how wrong I was when my son named all the planets in the solar system and pointed them out in a mural the group had painted. And he could identify at least twenty different dinosaurs by silhouette. All this without reading. It was presented as fun and interesting. There were no academic demands placed on kids. No tests. It was, I'm embarrassed to say, quite a revelation to me that reading wasn't a prerequisite for learning.*

A preschooler's job is to play. Activities should be geared to their mental and physical development. Fantasy play, costumes, block play, storytelling and storymaking, learning to deal with other children, swinging on monkey bars—these are the activities that should fill up the preschool years.

During these years, children learn to relate to people, to develop their imagination, to discover the world and the different people in it. These are the years when they learn to test reality and experiment with relationships. These are important skills that apply to the rest of their lives. Waiting until your children are at a suitable age to learn specific skills does not mean lowering your expectations. Find programs that meet your child's current developmental needs.

Of course, you will encounter the occasional parent who brags that her four-year-old is fighting for the op/ed page at the breakfast table. You will be tempted by slickly packaged "educational" products in toy stores as you reach for a game of ring toss or a book you can read to your child. Hold this thought: Current thinking in pediatric circles says, "Play, don't push."

Reading to your child about pandas is enrichment of the first order. It's imparting information and loving at the same time. The most important task, after all, is to help your child love learning.

Making Changes in Child Care

Most experts would agree that the fewer changes in child-care arrangements, the better, but if a child-care arrangement is not working out and cannot be improved, then we believe that it's imperative to make a change and find something that will work for both your child and you.

Here are some common reasons why parents change arrangements:

Changed mind. You've changed your mind about the caregiver. It may be that the caregiver is not the person that you thought you were hiring. Maybe you didn't pick up on some clues you should have, or maybe there are elements that were only noticeable over time. Now you see that she doesn't really tune in to your child. Or that she makes assumptions, rather than listening to what you are really saying to her.

Different job. You've changed job or hours. The new job is in the other direction, or you have to work hours that are in conflict with the caregiver's or center's hours.

Better arrangement. You've found an arrangement that is better, costs less, or is closer to home.

Wrong facility. You've realized that the preschool you'd chosen is too academic and too stressful.

Of course, sometimes it's the caregiver who ends the arrangement: she moves away, on to another line of work, and so on. Similarly, a center may close down. Or it may be that it's simply time to move on. A caregiver may have been the most loving, nurturing, stable person you could have asked for. She may have given your child an extraordinarily strong grounding. But you still feel somehow that your child needs a change.

You may want your child to be exposed to more children during the day. Or just to new children. Your child may be the oldest in a group and you'd prefer more peer interaction. You may simply sense a boredom your child can't express by herself. Yup, it's time to move on.

Now you face two tasks: saying goodbye to the old and hello to the new. Separation again. Even if you and the caregiver have a businesslike relationship rather than a personal one, the issues here are human ones.

Saying goodbye to a long-term caregiver, one with whom you and your child have developed strong relationships, requires timing and sensitivity. Also remember that the relationship goes two ways. Your caregiver has developed an attachment to your child as well.

How much notice should you give? Hopefully, you have discussed this eventuality in your interviews (because it's always an eventuality, even if your child stays until the day before kindergarten starts). At most centers, you have a written document to refer to.

Some family day-care providers would like to have children with them until kindergarten. Others prefer a younger group. Some caregivers will take your moving on as a criticism, no matter how tactfully you present it. (That early interview was a good time to say that you were planning to put your child in a center after she was toilet-trained.) It can be perceived as a slap in the face, a signal that the caregiver or center is not doing a good job. For this reason, it can be very hurtful.

Even without a formal agreement, the minimum notice you should give is two weeks. Although it would be so much easier (and very tempting) to end the arrangement on a Friday as you walk out the door (preferably without turning around to see her face), you just can't handle it that way unless there's a compelling reason to end the relationship quickly.

Children need time to process this drastic change. Going from a nanny or family day-care home to a center is a major life occurrence for a young child. The most common mistake parents make is to make this a sudden change, announcing on the way home on a Friday, "By the way, you're not going back to Susie's house on Monday."

In a well-meaning but totally wrong effort to avoid a messy situation (their child pitching a fit, refusing to leave, crying hysterically), many parents save the big news until they are out the door for the last time or at breakfast on Sunday. Then they make it too casual or offhand. Most caregivers have sad stories to tell about the children who "disappeared" over the weekend with only a curt, uncomfortable phone call from the parents. It is *not* easier for a child to make a sudden change. They need a chance for emotional closure on this very important segment of life.

On the other hand, some parents can also go to the opposite extreme—informing a child too soon, even as they are first mulling over the idea of a change. Announcing it a month or two before the actual change is much too soon. Waiting that long with such knowledge is excruciating to a child.

When you should tell your child about your intentions depends on your child's age and temperament. Some children will need more preparation than others. Make an agreement with the caregiver as to when to tell your child. Two or three days before your child's last day is workable. If your child is old enough to understand your discussion with the caregiver, he is also old enough to be off playing or otherwise engaged when you bring the subject up.

Your child will need an explanation for the change. Use phrases such as "Now that you're bigger," "Now it's time," or "Mommy's new job is way in the other direction." It explains that the change is due to outside forces, rather than fostering a loss of confidence in the caregiver. Realize that a child should have memories to treasure.

A one- to two-year-old will not fully understand what is going on, but a two- to three-year-old will. Still, even babies need to hear your explanation. Yes! Use the same words and the same loving, comforting tone. They will pick up the vibes, and you will be getting practice in how to soothe your growing child during transitions.

While you tell your child that she will be going to a different place during the day, emphasize that Mommy and Daddy will be there always. Let her know that you know this is hard for her. "We're not going to Blanca's school anymore, but she still loves you." Even with babies, say things out loud.

Avoid saying, however, the new place will be better. Your child will wonder what was wrong with the old place. Even if you are making a change because you have lost confidence in the caregiver, your child doesn't need to be clued in.

Both parents and caregivers must work hard to make the child's transition as smooth as possible. Allow your child to express any strong emotions he feels. The thought of being separated from someone who has always been there for him, held him, cuddled him, fed him is traumatic. Don't diminish it. Acknowledge to him how important his last caregiver has been. How much she loves him. How happy you've been that she's been able to care for him while you worked. Putting down Susie in an attempt to move your child beyond his grief—and it is grief—isn't wise. While affirming your good feelings about the caregiver, talk about the outside influences in life that make the change a necessary or good idea. Tactfully weave in a few references to the new arrangement.

Before that last goodbye, take a few snapshots of the caregiver and the other kids so that your child will have something to hang on to. A small party is not always possible, but if it is, it's a nice way to wrap things up. Often, children will ask, "Can I come back and visit?" If they don't, parents should ask the question for them, in their presence. A child may not feel the need for a visit once she's settled into her new arrangement, but until then, it feels comforting to know that she can see someone she loves again. Write down your child's name and phone number (although, of course, the caregiver already has it in her files), so your child can give it to her. Your child will then be assured that the caregiver will know where to find her. Ask for the caregiver's number in return and give it to your child to keep so she feels a tangible connection.

Once the goodbye is over (whew!), follow up with a note thanking the caregiver for what she's meant to you and your child. Ask your child to decorate it with a few drawings from her memories of her days there. This small gesture will give the caregiver something to remember your child by and to tuck into her portfolio to show the next family.

If you decide to change arrangements for some positive reason—a job transfer to another city, for example—offer to write a glowing reference of the caregiver. Help her find another family to take your place. Such consideration can be the best thank-you of all.

Saying Hello Again

The first few days in the new child-care arrangement call for the same strategies you used in getting your child accustomed to her first day-care environment. The adjustment time may be compressed this time, because your child's already been through it once; you probably won't need a week, but then again you might, depending on your child's temperament and the time it takes for her to form new attachments.

Regardless of timing, you do need to go through the same easing-in approach. The new setup may be similar to the current one: nanny to nanny, for instance, or family day care to family day care. But a change from one type of structure to another is a big deal for children. A child accustomed to being the center of attention or one who is one of only five or six will need support in adjusting to a centerful of playmates.

If you can manage time off from work, take your child to the new setting for a short visit before the first full day. Your preliminary visit and the subsequent time you spend at the new place should be focused on helping your child understand the new routines and where everything is. You'll also want to help your child make a strong connection with the new primary caregiver, as well as help her spot a few hot prospects for friends.

For the first few days, encourage your child to talk about the change. What differences does she notice? Don't dismiss her longings for the old place. Let her talk about it all she needs to, but subtly bring up exciting aspects of the new place. Help your child to understand the role *hellos* and *goodbyes* play in life.

seven

Nine to Five for Children Over Five

SO FAR we've gone into great detail about child care for younger children, but older children also have important needs that affect how they spend their days. The issues and ages vary greatly, ranging from a kindergartner, who may still need a nap, to a ten-year-old about to enter junior high.

Before- and After-School Care

I was so lucky to find the perfect after-school arrangement for my daughter Emma. A woman a few blocks from her elementary school did after-school care. That's all; no all-day care. She had six kids she picked up at the schoolyard in the afternoon, first- to fourth-graders, and they all walked home with her. She gave them a snack at her dining table and then they had free play for forty-five minutes to let off steam. Then she settled them back down at the table for "homework time." That was a half hour. Then she read them a book or told stories. She was a gem. When we moved to another neighborhood, I couldn't find anything like that. Emma went to a program at the Y. They picked the kids up in a van and took them to the Y. It wasn't homey, but they were very good about allowing the kids to play first and then do home-

137

work. And they had special classes, like ballet, that Emma could go to some of the days. Each place seemed to have good things going for it.

With few exceptions, children need to be supervised before and after school until sometime in early junior high or late middle school. We know that doesn't always happen in real life. There are many eight- and nine-year-olds who are dropped off early in the morning at school or who spend the late afternoons alone at home. But most really aren't ready. They don't have the emotional maturity or judgment for self-care at that age. Of course, there are those especially self-confident kids who are mature for their age and seem to be able to handle the latchkey life. But you can't be too sure, even about them. (See "Home Alone" in Chapter 10 for a further discussion on this issue.)

When parents are polled regarding what is most important to them about after-school care, the biggest issues are safety and supervision. They want someone keeping their children out of trouble and trouble away from them. *Safety* usually means being protected from unsavory characters and traffic, but it can also include substance issues such as alcohol, cigarettes, and marijuana. Studies have shown lower substance abuse among children who attend after-school programs.

Keeping children safe until their parents get off work is not enough of a mandate for any program. While meeting the needs of working parents, after-school programs can also be very beneficial to the children enrolled. They offer companionship, stimulation, and counseling. Kids aren't in protective custody. After-school programs should be more than safe havens and places to do homework; they should also be fun and flexible places for children to unwind after a full day in the classroom.

The majority of before- and after-school care in this country is offered at Ys, JCCs, and on-school sites. Of course, the enthusiastic support of the principal is an essential ingredient in programs on school campuses. Other providers include Boys Clubs and Girls Clubs of America, PTAs, Camp Fire Girls and Boys, the Salvation Army, churches, temples, and other community groups.

Another frequent after-school arrangement is family day care. Almost 24 percent of school-age children are cared for in a family day-care facility. Some providers take care of infants, preschoolers, and older children, while others offer only after-school care.

Some child-care centers have created special programs for children over five. If you are considering such a program, make sure that the staff recognizes the different needs of an older group of children. Centers shouldn't just incorporate older kids into their preschoolers' activities.

We question programs where staff demands that children get to their homework the moment they arrive. The regular school day is structured and rule-based. We like programs that welcome children with a snack and encourage them to play (outside, if weather permits) for a while to work off the excess energy of the school day. Then they can get down to homework.

The best after-school programs try to minimize the structure and rules as much as possible, without sacrificing opportunities for children to participate in a variety of activities (arts and crafts, music, games, sports). They have a planned schedule that is age-appropriate. School-age children need to have some say in how they want to spend their late afternoons. The 4:00–4:30 basketball, 4:30–5:00 crafts-project schedule is too rigid. Older children need greater opportunities to develop independence. After-school programs call for attentive, well-chosen staff who understand that in this age group, children need more flexibility and motivation than do preschoolers.

Care for your kindergartner can be the most difficult to find. Because of the short school day, you need programs that are longer and can take up the slack. Not every after-school program accommodates the special needs of the kindergartners, so you may find yourself with more limited choices than when your child begins first grade.

While some school districts have ambitious, well-run after-school programs, many offer little more than supervised playground time. And often they're not so supervised. If your child is not checked in by an adult at three o'clock and you aren't required to sign him out at six, there isn't enough supervision. The free-floating basketball game, run by many "parks & rec" departments with a coach who may or may not even know which children are there, is problematic. It *may* work for older children, but not for younger students. A safe program has paperwork, medical release forms, and sign-out sheets near the door.

Toward the end of elementary school, children are in that neither-fish-nor-fowl group. They are tired of the long days in an institutional setting. Their idea of a good time has switched from "playing" to "hanging out." You know you've turned that corner when you say, quite innocently, "Did you play with Brandon?" and you are informed that playing is for babies. The best programs for these older children are not referred to as child care. They have names like *Teen Club*, even if the kids who participate are barely preteens. And even if such a "club" is part of a program that serves younger children, the children in it will demand to be treated differently.

Your preteen may be dead-set against going to an after-school program. She may feel the programs in your area don't meet the needs of kids her age and she may be right. Or she may be feeling the need to move on to another plateau. But you know she can't be left alone. Perhaps a more informal arrangement is called for. If your child is champing at the proverbial bit, her peers probably are, too. Call around to a few parents and see if they are facing the same problem. You may be able to hire a college student to watch over three or four children for the same or less money than you were paying for a program. (See the discussion of shared care in Chapter 3 for more on this subject.)

Matching a School to Your Child's Needs

In a departure from the situation that prevailed a generation ago, when going to public school meant going to the neighborhood school, many of today's public school systems offer their students options through magnet programs, child-care permits, and special requests. For some families, the choice may be broader, offering public, parochial, or private alternatives. There is no longer a single right school for all children.

How do you pick the right school? The same issues apply to making this decision as apply to finding a caregiver for a young child: safety, comfort, and stimulation. Here again, your decision will be based on both instinct and research. Parents concerned about getting accepted into popular elementary schools may need to begin their search very early.

Schools differ immensely. Some are very competitive academically. Some place a great deal of emphasis on sports. Others don't have an adequate playground. Some are very traditional, while others are progressive. You want the right school for *your* child.

Finding the right school for their children demands that parents put in the time to research the possibilities. Visit the schools you are considering—then visit them again.

Don't go by reputation, either good or bad. Some schools are coasting on reputations that were earned decades ago and no longer reflect actual performance. Other schools are carrying the burden of a generation-old bad rep, when in fact they've improved considerably. Parents may often rule out schools based on hearsay, without setting a single foot on campus. Other parents have been known to sign a child up for a school sight unseen.

All the parents I would talk to about good public schools in our area would all say the same thing: "I hear Lincoln Street School is great." I noticed that real estate agents would say "Lincoln Street School" in their ads. Wow! A free public school that was special. We didn't live in the district, but I found out that the school took twenty kindergartners a year who lived outside its boundaries. I rushed and got permission to withdraw from the school my daughter was supposed to go to down the street. I was twentieth on the list, and she started kindergarten the following fall. The first time I visited the school was her first day of class.

When I would tell people that I got Nancy into Lincoln Street they would ooh and ahh. How lucky. But I never liked the school. The principal that everyone said was so great had left two years before. The new principal was a self-serving martinet. The school was still lost in the 1950s, when it got its sterling reputation. I think it's been coasting ever since. The teachers were mediocre. The equipment was nothing special. At the end of kindergarten, Nancy transferred to the magnet school we had visited before signing up. I learned my lesson.

While school staffs don't particularly like disruption of the school day, they know that parents and prospective students will want to check out the campus in person. They are accustomed to families calling to request visits. So do it.

Here are some things to look for: Is there creative noise (the sounds of children who are busy and involved in their activities)? You won't hear this every moment of the school day, since teachers also need to give direct instructions, but if there's only direct teaching, there are probably a lot of bored kids. You want to see children working together. If the only action is between teacher and students, it can be very monotonous.

Ask yourself how you feel walking around the campus. You *know* when it feels good. Size up the teachers' attitudes. Are they engaged in what they are doing or only going through the motions? Ask the principal if any teachers have gotten individual classroom grants. Teachers apply for these themselves, and it can be a strong indicator of teacher involvement and commitment.

Both teachers and administrators should be willing to discuss the curriculum and explain why they've made the choices they have. Ask how they follow state guidelines. Do they use basic texts for teaching reading, or do they use other literature? Don't rule out a school simply because they use traditional texts and math methods. If the teachers are inspired, even traditional texts are okay. (Well, maybe not *Silas Marner.*)

While traditional methods, thoughtfully taught, can be effective, schools must also be wholeheartedly preparing children for the twenty-first century. Are there computers and computer-literate teachers? Are the classrooms on-line? Does computer use seem well integrated into classwork? Are the computers available to all children?

Even with a state-of-the-art computer program, children need an accessible school library. Many school funding cutbacks have resulted in closed libraries, shortened hours, or no trained librarian. Can students check out books?

In most states, scholastic achievement tests are given to some or all students. The results are often published in local papers and considered a sure indicator of the school's fitness. By all means, check the test scores, but don't make them the sole basis of your selection. They're just one piece of information, so they can be misleading. In fact, some principals see to it that the entire student body is drilled to test well. Meanwhile, other schools emphasize other methods to measure learning. A different measuring process is performance-based; one example of this kind of student evaluation is the portfolio (a folder of the child's work each semester). Sometimes student self-assessments and journals are included as part of the portfolio. Such an evaluation system is more labor-intensive for staff but gives a richer, more personalized look at each student's accomplishments, strengths, and weaknesses, emphasizing comments rather than grades.

Many education experts feel that the traditional multiple-choice tests do not give a complete evaluation of a student's talents and abilities. A new theory, proposed by Harvard psychologist Howard Gardner, identifies seven kinds of intelligence. These are linguistic, logical-mathematical, musical, spatial, bodily-kinesthetic, interpersonal, and intrapersonal. Truly accurate testing would evaluate a student in each of these areas.

Many school districts, including New York City's, are now sending home annual reports that compare a child's school with the district in general. These school report cards include information on how many students are enrolled and how many the building was designed to hold, the sex and ethnicity of the students, the number of suspensions, and how students did in standardized tests. While informative reading for parents, however, these reports don't tell the whole story.

Look for parent participation in the school. Is it welcomed? And do parents really get involved, whether in a PTA or other support group? The more a school encourages parents to participate, the more enriching the environment will be for the students. A group of strong, committed parents can make the difference between an adequate school and a superior one. These days, public school funding is bare bones and being cut further every year. When parents get involved, their fundraising efforts can generate computers, field trips, a piano, or sometimes simply enough textbooks. And parents who volunteer in the classroom extend teacher resources.

A good school staff is not threatened by parents coming and going throughout the school day. Ideally, a school welcomes parents at all times and in all areas. The most enlightened schools have parent members on teacher selection committees and/or parent councils, as well as school-based management.

Many experts feel that a school is only as good as its principal. The person at the top sets the tone for everything that happens on campus. A successful principal puts a lot of energy into the work and is out and about, not behind his or her desk most of the day.

A good principal makes an effort to learn the names of students and to say hello to them. She is available to parents and doesn't bounce parent requests for conferences off on other staff members. (She may ask you to make your initial contact with your child's teacher but reassure you that she is available for further discussions.) Search out parents who have children in the school now and whose values you share, and ask their opinions of the administrator. Make sure *this* principal is well liked and plans to be there next year.

A school may get wide recognition for its open, unstructured environment. Sounds good. Many parents like the idea of a "progressive school," where students are expected to take responsibility for meeting deadlines without teacher coaching. Children in this setting may work on their own most of the time, often in groups. This situation may or may not be beneficial for your child. Maybe, for example, your child needs to work individually with a lot of teacher instruction. Sure, some children get all their work done sprawled on a rug, but others are too distracted unless they're in an old-fashioned classroom setting.

School facilities vary greatly. Some schools have huge playgrounds and strong athletic programs. Others may have very little outdoor area and no formal sports teams. Many very prestigious private schools have little more than an alley for a yard.

If your child is a budding musician, you need to find out what kind of music program the school offers. Is there a school orchestra or band, and music lessons? Are there instruments available for rental? If your child is interested in art, inquire about who teaches the art classes. Some schools today make a great effort to bring in innovative local artists who develop programs far beyond the scope of those grim art classes most of us remember.

For children in middle and high school, there are additional questions. What is the absentee rate of students? How does it compare with other schools in the district? Is the student population stable? In other words, do most of the students who start the lowest grade finish the top one? If so, it means fewer students coming and going, who may cause a disruption to all students. The continuity of the student body affects classroom work as well as friendships.

Making Your Child's School Better

Now that you've made your school choice, how do you ensure that it's an enriching experience for your child? Get involved. Parent participation can ensure you get the best school experience possible.

You'll be at a great advantage just getting the firsthand knowledge of the school that comes from being an involved parent. You'll be better able to evaluate your child's remarks about her school life and to ask questions of her. You'll get a sense of what the classrooms feel like, what the principal is really like, and if the restrooms are really scary or dirty.

In every school, there are the dynamo teachers and the mediocre ones, the teachers who are surrounded by students eager to be in their orbits and those who do the absolute minimum. As you get involved in school, you'll start hearing about the inspired teachers—the ones you want for your child.

A diligent search for the best teachers for your child requires taking time off from work. It calls for visiting the potential classrooms the semester before. You will then be able to picture your child in this particular environment, a far more accurate and personalized assessment than relying on hearsay and the opinions of other parents.

Very few schools permit parents to select their children's teachers, however. If they did, everyone would be in Miss Berry's class, and no one would be in Mrs. Barkley's. Parents are told, politely, that decisions are made by computer or "in the best interests of all the children." Or, "all our teachers are excellent."

You know better than that. So how do you get your child placed in the dynamo teachers' classrooms? And without feeling a little twinge of guilt, knowing that getting your child in the exciting classroom means another child will be stuck with a lackluster one? After all, *every* child should have dynamo teachers.

You deal with this moral twinge by reframing the problem. You're looking for the best match—not the best teacher. In all honesty, not every student responds well to the same teachers. Your daughter may need a soft-spoken teacher to encourage her out of her shyness. A peppy teacher may overwhelm her. A teacher who hands out weekly assignments on Monday and doesn't pace the students may not be right for a child who needs a close, steady hand.

After you've visited the possibilities but before "the computer" goes to work on assignments, make an appointment to talk with the principal. You'd like a short, friendly, get-acquainted chat. Sincere, but not fawning. Let her know that you are impressed with the school and plan to be a very hands-on parent. Don't ask for specific teachers. Tell her that you can be counted on for help during the year—and mean it. Even working parents can find ways to contribute (see the next section). And—surprise, surprise—it seems that the children of helpful, visible parents often wind up with the school's star teachers.

Don't make your get-acquainted chat a brag section about your child. Inquire about the school. Make a brief positive statement about your child, something that indicates your child's personality, so that the principal will have something to base her class assignments on. If you feel strongly that one particular teacher would be appropriate for your son, mention it, but don't demand it. "We noticed that Miss Santini works especially well with the quieter children in her classroom. She seems to have a gift for getting them involved in group activities. In preschool, our Maria had a hard time including herself in groups. She needs a little encouragement to join in. We think she would blossom with someone like Miss Santini." The operative phrase here is "someone like."

Also make an effort to meet the school secretary or administrator. The office is at the heart of most schools, and a good relationship with the person in charge there can smooth over problems large and small. She will be keeping track of your child as he progresses through "her" school and may actually get to know your child better than the principal. She, too, may be able to manage a good match for your child.

At my daughter's school, the office manager knew all the children, and the principal was quite removed. There was very little changing her. She'd been a principal for twenty years—her way. The office manager made the school acceptable. She greeted the children in the morning and spent her breaks in the playground. She was the person to cultivate. She watched over sick children until their parents arrived.

At the end of every school year, request another, brief meeting with the principal (or, in a pinch, do it on the phone). This will give you a chance to tell her, candidly but positively, how the school year went from your perspective and to help pave the way for next year's classroom assignment.

To make the most of any teacher/parent conference, let the teacher do most of the talking. Hear what she has to say before you begin. Don't argue. Don't interrupt. Absorb. Take notes.

As she explains problem areas, identify in your own mind the sources of these problems. If you haven't been supervising your child's homework in the manner the school would like, admit it. Tell the teacher that you are responsible in part for your child's tardy or undone homework, if that's the real story.

If you feel the source of the problem is the classroom, this is the time to bring it up. Delicately. Plan your words in advance. Get as much detail from your child as possible. Comments such as "Michael says he can't do anything to please you" aren't enough to generate a substantive discussion.

Bring up the problem in a way that assumes the teacher's goodwill. Don't put her on the defensive. Try "Michael seems very discouraged about school. I think he feels that he is not valued. What kind of things can we do together to work on this?"

Ask the teacher how she thinks everyone involved (teacher, student, and parent) can improve the situation. Work together to set up a timetable for improvement. Agree on a way to communicate (by phone or by notes) about how the situation progresses.

End the conference on a positive note. Take time before the session begins to think of a couple of examples your child has mentioned he *has* enjoyed in class. "Michael has told me several times how much he enjoys the poems you read to the class after lunch. It's inspired him to write some poems of his own." Follow up the conference with a short thank-you note. The teacher will know you're interested in helping your child succeed in school. That alone often works subtle wonders on teachers' attitudes, making them more aware and attentive to the involved parent's child.

Through all of this, however, realize that your idea of a dream school may be locked in the 1950s or 1960s. Forget any memories you harbor of your own school days. That was another era, one of smaller classes and bigger budgets, when almost everyone went to the neighborhood school and there were plenty of stay-at-home moms to augment the official staff. Of course, none of these elements apply to today's reality. Understand that today's teachers carry a heavy load—more kids, more responsibility, and more accountability—all with fewer resources.

Ways Working Parents Can Help Out at School

Whether it's public or private, every school is enriched by parents who volunteer in the classroom, help out on field trips, and work on fundraising projects that provide extras the tight budget can't include. Even the most expensive private institutions expect parents to contribute in ways beyond giving money.

Impossible for a working parent," you shout! *"Not all volunteering is done during school hours,"* we shout back. Some schools, with an active group of stay-at-home moms who volunteer, may not seem to have a place for a working parent to help out. Be persistent. Meet with the key people and point out how much more could be done by tapping the talents of the working parents.

> *When Robey started first grade, it seemed there were these moms who were at the school all the time. They were like the shadow government. They arranged a new-parent lunch that working parents really couldn't participate in. I couldn't. I'd get notices about library committee meetings on Tuesdays at ten in the morning. It really bugged me. Then the organizing meeting for the school's big event of the year, the spring carnival, was announced for a Friday morning. I collected myself and called the chairperson on the phone. I told her that, as a working parent, I felt I was unable to contribute in the way I would like, because everything was scheduled during the workday.*
>
> *She told me that that's when most parents were available. I insisted that that was not true. No one with a regular job could get to that meeting. I'm not a very pushy person, but I was mad. I said, "I would like to see the meetings scheduled so that all the parents could attend—not just a core group." She put up more resistance. She liked her Friday morning meetings. But I kept pushing. I said I wanted to take it up with Ms. Garey, the principal.*
>
> *Finally, she said—very begrudgingly—that maybe the meetings could be held on Wednesday nights. And they have been for three years now, with much bigger turnouts!*

Here are a few things that parents who work regular nine-to-five jobs can do:

Participate in a phone tree (a system for passing along urgent information to all parents in a hurry). Phone calling is usually done at night and/or on weekends.

Sew costumes, design or type programs, or paint scenery for school performances.

Help in the school garden on a Saturday morning.

Work the Sunday pancake breakfast fundraiser.

Help with the parent or school newsletter. This may include interviews for stories, typing, or collating.

Attend parent group meetings. Point out the importance of holding meetings when everyone can come.

Join an event committee for the school carnival or a community fundraising effort.

Volunteer at the carnival and/or book fair.

Take a morning off and chaperone a field trip.

Get your company to be a school sponsor. Donate excess office supplies, old equipment, or new equipment.

Publicize school events by getting PSAs (public service announcements) on the radio or in the local paper.

Approach local businesses to post flyers in their store windows, buy ads in programs, or underwrite refreshments.

However you decide to help your child's school, be reliable and punctual. Better to make a once-a-month commitment you can keep than a weekly one that you have to cancel.

Parent participation is equally as important for children as they move into the upper grades. In recent studies, children in grades six through twelve whose parents were involved in their school (attending PTA meetings and/or back-to-school nights, plays, and sporting events) were less likely to use alcohol or drugs.

eight

Before and After Work

How you get out the door in the morning—late and frazzled or on time and (relatively) unfrazzled—sets up the whole workday. Working parents can, with deliberate effort, begin the day on the right foot. Doing so also helps your child begin his day more relaxed and ready for child care or school.

Organizing Morning Routines

Getting out the front door on time—and later, out the caregiver or center's door—does not come easily to most working parents, if at all. Theoretically, you may have allowed plenty of time for dressing, eating, brushing teeth. But then there's that unexpected something. A child refuses to get dressed—or takes off what you put on him. You have to contend with a lost shoe or favorite toy. A misplaced briefcase. A tantrum. Dawdling. Dawdling can be the worst.

Even though they usually are past the tantrum stage (but not necessarily past the dawdling), school-age children can present parents with early-morning problems: they can't find a field-trip permission slip or they're feeling sick on the day of a big test. And there's an added pressure for school-age kids: they essentially have a time clock to punch:

While parents can get younger children to most child-care programs at a time that suits their schedule, schools demand punctuality.

Here are a few ideas to give you a fighting chance at getting the day off to a decent start.

Mornings begin the night before. That includes meal making. Set out cereal bowls, milk glasses, spoons, and so on. Have the cereal box handy. Defrost orange juice. Check for the right change for buses, trains, and lunch money. Take lunch orders the night before. And make lunches then, too (see the next section for easy lunch suggestions). Make this a rule. All orders in by 8:00 P.M. or you'll use your own discretion. Assign children the task of filling lunch bags with nonperishables.

Pick a special spot near the front door where all family members can put everything they plan to take with them in the morning. Ground zero can be on one end of a table, in a big basket or box, or on the seat of a chair. Preschoolers may like to think of it as a cubby at home. Everything that doesn't need refrigeration should make its way there before bedtime: handbags, backpacks, keys, toys, sports equipment, umbrellas, schoolbooks, snowsuits, jackets, tapes for the car stereo, stuffed animals, notes to teachers, show-and-tell treasures, permission slips, parent-initialed homework. Incorporate the special spot into your weeknight routine. Call out reminders before bedtime that everything needs to be by the door.

Many parents of preschoolers share a little secret. They think they're the only ones in the world who do it. They don't want the neighbors knowing about it. Or the grandparents. And if the other kids' parents were to find out, they might not let their children play with them any more.

What's the secret? Their children don't wear pajamas to bed. No, we're not talking *au naturel* here. Their kids are sleeping in their day clothes: the T-shirts and sweatpants (or underwear) they wear to child care. We know, this is not how Donna Reed would have run her house.

Despite appearances, this sleeping-in-day-clothes habit is not necessarily parent generated. Today's children challenge the logic behind changing into special sleeping clothes that look, to them, suspiciously like their daytime outfits: cotton knits, elastic waistbands, stretchy stuff, T-shirts. So relax.

Dear Beaver Cleaver never wore sweatpants to school. In those days, daytime clothes were a lot different from pajamas. But there's been a pajamatization of children's play clothes, even school clothes. Everything is sweatpants and T-shirts.

If your child wears soft, stretchy clothes, why not get him dressed the night before? We'll guarantee that his friends are doing it. Once a child is toilet-trained, she should be able to go twenty-four hours in an outfit. The time to change is after a bath and before climbing into bed. That way, they go to bed clean. It's easier to make the change after a bath anyway.

When your children are a little older and it's time for them to wear "more formal" clothes out of the house in the morning, at least plan outfits the night before. Here's a good approach: pick two choices and ask "Which one do you want to wear tomorrow?" (A lot of school districts are eliminating this problem by requiring uniforms for students.) And in the best set-a-good-example spirit, get your own clothes ready the day before. Pretend that every day is a first day on the job.

If your kids watch TV in the mornings, set firm rules. Decide on the amount of time and the latest your children can watch—no TV after 7:30, for example, if that's what it takes to get everyone out the door on time. Morning TV should be a treat for getting ready on time or ahead of time, not the main event.

If your child is already in the habit of dilly-dallying over *Sesame Street* or MTV or having all his clothes brought to him in front of TV so he can get dressed there, these new rules will not be welcomed. Such rules are sooooooo much easier to begin at birth—this is the never-miss-what-you-never-had school of thought. But children can learn new morning routines if parents are firm and consistent. But if you flip-flop, give in occasionally, or waffle, you'll end up spending precious time in power skirmishes.

Remember that young children cannot tell time. "Five minutes and we have to leave" means nothing. Your fretting that "it's seven-fifteen already" is Greek to them. "Hurry up" and "soon" are about as much as preschoolers can understand. Use time markers they can understand, such as "after you listen to *Baby Beluga*, you will have to put your jacket on." This sense of time structuring also helps children begin grasping the concept of sequence. Older children may grasp the concept just fine but still resist it early in the morning.

Easy Lunches Kids Will Eat

Children like to feel they have some control over what they put in their mouths. They learn very quickly that eating certain foods in specific amounts seems very important to adults, and it drives grown-ups crazy when children won't eat according to plan. It becomes a game. A contest. And they'll play it no matter whether you're around or not.

Kids trade lunches. They hide lunches. They throw perfectly good food away. All of which is very frustrating to nutrition-conscious parents. So parents need to be a little creative themselves. In this sense, being creative means giving them nutritious foods strong on kid appeal.

When you plan your child's lunch (and other meals), offer a choice. Don't insist on one thing, as in "You're eating a tuna sandwich and that's it, young lady." A better approach would be to ask "Would you like a tuna sandwich or a chicken sandwich? Do you want mayo on both slices of bread or just one? An apple or banana? How would you like your carrots cut up?" Such questions will assure most children that they have somehow shared power with you and that they're in control of their own destinies (lunch box destiny, anyway).

If you suspect your child is trading lunches and not getting the nutritious end of the deal, try cutting sandwiches and fruit in half and suggesting, "It's okay to trade half your sandwich if you eat the other half yourself." Some kids will buy this approach; some won't. It's worth a try.

Some children demand the same lunch every day for months, even years. It has to be peanut butter and jelly—and only certain brands. No substitutions, please! If it's halfway nutritious, go along with it. Remember, a parent can get too caught up in making every meal a paragon of basic food-group virtues. Take the long view and make up the nutrition at the next meal. If your child wants to skip a meal or a certain food, let it go.

Getting your child started out on lunches of chips and sodas encourages bad habits that are difficult to break. There are plenty of healthful alternatives. Boxed juices cost the same as Cokes, and they don't spoil.

Make lunches after dinner. You can make a peanut butter and jelly sandwich and refrigerate it the night before without compromising its appeal. You can even freeze a week's worth. Tuna, chicken salad, or cheese sandwiches can all be made and refrigerated ahead of time. More perishable sandwiches can be partially assembled: portion out two slices of bread in a plastic bag and seal, then fill in the morning. Experiment with breads: find one your child likes that won't get soggy quickly. Put graham crackers and sliced fruit in separate plastic bags.

Begin lunch planning with a brainstorming session at the kitchen table. Come to the meeting prepared with your own suggestions. Try making your own granola. A big batch, made on the weekend, can last all week. If your child hates plain apples, maybe she would eat one if you sliced it and made mini peanut butter sandwiches with it. Spice up a plain old sandwich by shaping it with a cookie cutter. Then she'd have fun eating Mickey's ear or some other fun shape. What ideas do your children themselves have? Throw out a few challenges. What can they think of to slather peanut butter on? What could they fill a pita bread with?

Most kids seem to have taken a secret oath to hate exotic foods. But they don't know exotic until it's pointed out to them. Tell them rice cakes or tortillas are exotic and the mouth shuts. Treat these items like wheat bread, and you're in like Flynn. No food is exotic if it's on the family table regularly and they've been expected to eat it since they started on solids: chayote, cherimoya, jicama, tofu, even oysters.

Another major quirk children have is a highly developed affinity for shapes. They'll eat spaghetti but not fettuccine, or vice versa. Elbow macaroni but not bow ties. They swear the two taste different, and there's not much you can do about it. They'll go for cucumbers cut in spears but not circles. They're two completely different vegetables in their eyes. Even a jaunty, diagonal slant to a carrot slice can ruin the taste of it. So don't assume that a child who doesn't like slices of cheese wouldn't be pleased with spears.

Individual-size cans or cups of heat-and-serve pasta are quick but very expensive; buying the same-shaped noodles in the larger size and apportioning them yourself in plastic containers is much more economical. If your child protests, explain that you can give him *more* dinosaur noodles this way. These days, microwaves are commonplace in child-care centers and schools, but they may create a problem if your child's teacher is overwhelmed by requests to microwave ten cups of SpaghettiOs at the same time. An old-fashioned, unbreakable thermos may be a better away-from-home solution.

Make sure your child can open containers by himself. You don't want him sitting for twenty minutes, waiting for help from a busy teacher. Practice with him at home.

Perk up lunch with fun food. Yogurt in a cup, to be eaten with a boring old spoon, isn't nearly as fun as a yogurt dip, where sliced fruit serves as edible spoons.

A ham and cheese sandwich may routinely come home uneaten. Try rolling the ham, cheese, and bread separately, then instruct your child to take a bite from each. This way, they're not eating a sandwich; they're playing a game. Or roll up the whole sandwich, jellyroll style. This shape will be infinitely more fun to eat.

When your child takes a shine to a "dinner" food, such as macaroni or stew, tell her how lucky she is; there's more of it for tomorrow's lunch! Remember, "there's more" is a more preferable term than "leftover."

Large portions can seem overwhelming to a young child, so cut, slice, and package everything in small portions. Some children need to nibble several times during the day. Package accordingly and this will improve overall consumption.

Keep lunches safe: Keep hot foods hot and cold ones cold with thermoses or cold packs. Explain basic food safety on a level your child can understand. Make sure she puts her lunch box in a safe place, away from sunny windows or heaters. Explain that some foods should be thrown away after lunch, such as tuna salad sandwiches. Since some children eat part of their lunches on the way home from school, they need guidance on what is perishable.

Wash out and sanitize your child's lunch containers every day. If she throws a brown bag in the bottom of a backpack, check every night so you can remove bananas and other squashables before they ooze all over.

Finally, watch which foods your child is enjoying at breakfast and dinner. Is there some way to incorporate these winners into the lunch menu?

Commuting Tips

There are basically two kinds of commuting: the part when your child is with you and the part when you're alone.

When your child is in the car, the length of your commute and your child's temperament are the two big variables. A short hop to a center that's a half mile away takes little planning and patience. Spend this short morning travel time helping your child anticipate the fun things in the day ahead. Talk a little about what's in store for her. Use the home-again ride as debriefing time.

A longer ride with a child requires planning. Some children, especially infants, are lulled by a car ride. Others are content to watch the world go by. Still others want to be entertained. Your priority, of course, is safe driving—not being "on." (See next section for winding-down strategies and Chapter 13 for car safety issues.)

Now let's talk about *your* time alone in the car. Except for carpoolers, commuting is a solitary time. Even in a bus or train, most people keep to themselves.

> *Before I had Lindy, I endured the forty-five-minute train into work. I was acutely aware of all the people around me. I would sit and wait for my stop. Sometimes I would read the paper, but mostly, I just sat. Now, it's really strange. I look forward to the train. Nobody knows me. Nobody is tugging at my sleeve. I love the anonymity. It's like an oasis. What used to make me tense now leaves me relaxed. I watch the people around me with amusement. I make lists of things to do. I find I read more. Sometimes I finish some work papers. Sometimes I read a novel.*

You can continue to view your commuting time as nothing more than a necessary evil of the working life, or you can look at it as a positive, even refreshing part of the day. Yes, you have to negotiate traffic or keep an eye on strange characters across the aisle, but you can also think of it as (trumpet fanfare, please) time alone. Make it productive in the best sense of the word. There are two points of view on what constitutes productivity: getting more or getting less done. Which sounds good to you? Listen to *your* music, books on tape, or your favorite drive-time deejays. Alternatively, dictate into a tape recorder, make notes for a meeting, or work on a sales pitch.

Winding Down, Not Up

That first hour after you pick up your child from child care is the most difficult, demanding, draining hour of the day. At your most exhausted, depleted by a hard day's work, you're face-to-face with a child who's at her whiniest, crabbiest, and most petulant. Clearly, it's not the best timing in the world. Some parents even call it the suicide hour.

For those who choose to live through it, there are approaches to make this hour go more smoothly. First, understand why the same child who has been, according to the caregiver, "a little angel" all day can switch moods the moment she sees you. She may have been quite content to play with a friend or listen to a story. Then she sees you and suddenly, she's fussy, crying, defiant—displaying behavior the caregiver has seen little of all day.

It feels like she's dumping on you. And in a way, she is. She's letting her hair down. She feels safe enough to let herself behave in a less-than-perfect manner. No matter how strong her bond with her caregiver, you are the person she feels truly sure about. She's been showing her public face to her world all day—sharing toys she'd rather not share, waiting her turn when she'd rather not wait, being quiet at story time—and she's built up a lot of emotional tension. She's ready for a little collapsing.

Try to see this pickup time scenario from your child's perspective: You swoop in out of nowhere and expect her to get her things together instantly (move, hurry, hurry) and you're out of there. To her way of thinking, you've left her there *all day* and suddenly you're sweeping in with all these demands. What's your problem? To a child, your behavior seems a little weird, maybe even a lot weird. To get some sense of control, she may dawdle a little—put the book away slowly, walk at a snail's pace, take forever finding her stuffed bunny. Forcing her to move faster only makes the situation worse. Let her have some feeling of control by allowing her to collect things at her own pace. Showing more interest in what she's been doing than in beating a hasty retreat may get you out faster.

Child-care centers are not hurry-up environments most of the day. After all, children are there eight to ten hours, so there is (or should be) time for everything. Parents can burst into the center in a manner that shatters the calm the caregiver has tried all day to establish, producing an inevitable clash.

Likewise, children in after-school programs may not want to leave the moment parents walk in the door. You may arrive in the middle of a basketball game or an exciting checkers match. Your child's request to finish the game isn't unreasonable, except that you've probably got a million things to do. If this becomes an issue, explain that you have to get dinner on the table, walk the dog, or whatever other pressing issue you have on your mind. Suggest that he ask a friend to take his place in the game or, if he balks at that, enlist the caregiver's help in finding a stand-in. At this age, you can also give your child the responsibility of being "nearly" ready at five o'clock, because she knows that's your usual pickup time. You can also tell her that on Wednesdays and Fridays you can manage a little slack, but on the other days, you would appreciate help in getting out quickly. Serious pickup problems may be a contest of wills and need serious discussion, and even the caregiver's assistance in getting out with some speed.

A Radical Thought

Recognize the fact that there's no law that says you absolutely have to pick up your child *straight* from work. If you have just enough time to drive from work to the day-care provider before they close the doors or start docking you a dollar a minute, then no, you can't afford to dilly-dally. But if you usually pick your child up at five-thirty, and the pickup deadline is six or six-thirty, well . . . you could occasionally take a few minutes to yourself to recharge your batteries. Get a cup of cappuccino. Grab a quick soda or juice and read the paper, even if it's in the car. Fifteen minutes of National Public Radio, a Snapple, and the Style section of the paper—all savored in the parking lot of 7-Eleven—can be rejuvenating. Taking a later bus or train may give you time to walk a little slower and do a little browsing or window shopping.

On the Ride Home

Arms full of backpacks, pictures, and wet clothes, you make it into the car or to the bus stop and take a long breath.

Some children chatter the whole ride home. Some refuse to give up one little clue to what they did all day. For the tight-lipped ones, hold off asking about their day until they've settled in a little. Then proceed casually.

Talk about what you see on the way home. Point out familiar landmarks, maybe the birds that always roost on the same end of a telephone wire. This is something the two of you can check on every evening. "There are those birds again." Count the birds together. Admire the flowering trees. See if you recognize the same people at the bus stops. Do you often see the same man walking his dog? Make up a name for the dog. And the man.

Draw your child out with open-ended questions. Not "Did you have a fun day?" but "What costumes did you put on in the dress-up corner?" "What stories did you hear before naptime?" Some children may feel that any question is an invasion, and they might respond better to the less direct approach. Try floating a line such as "I wonder what you dressed up as today." A variation on that theme might be, "I'll bet you and Tyus had a lot of fun in the playground."

Play some soothing music on the tape deck. If you can stand to listen to a little Raffi, do it. Or plunk in a favorite story tape. Spend time thinking about what routines work for your child. There is no all-purpose solution to the end-of-the-day commute.

When James was first going to child care, he had one special stuffed animal, a funny-looking blue dog named Lulu, that we always kept in the car. Lulu liked to live in the car, so we always left her there. James looked forward to saying "hello" to her when I picked him up after work. He cuddled Lulu on the ride home. It was almost like having a real dog in the car. She seemed to relax him.

Sometimes fussiness can be alleviated with a light snack on the way home. Offer your child crackers or granola bars as a quick pick-me-up. Bring a bagel for a young child to gum. Keep boxed juices in the car or a backpack. This little snack can become a transition that's looked forward to at the end of your child's day, calming and diverting his initial fussing. If your child is in family day care, bring an extra bottle or drink and label it "Save for Tammy." Ask the caregiver to keep it cold until you pick her up.

Some older children like to sit quietly, earphones on, listening to music. Others want parents to tell them everything that's going to happen when they get home: what's for dinner; what's on TV; do I have to take a bath?

When Your Child Talks Nonstop on the Ride Home (and at Other Times)

If you've got a chatty child, those after-work hours may coincide with his chattiest time of the day. Some children need to converse at just the time their parents yearn for quiet. Perhaps you can weather this part of the day better if you understand what's behind all the talk.

There are some children who, from the moment they construct their first noun-and-verb sentence, are off and running in the conversation department. They chatter (as opposed to "chat," which is a two-way dialogue); they prattle; they ask a lot of questions; they tell you everything in slow, excruciating detail.

A child who talks on and on is a mixed blessing. On the one hand, you're thrilled at such verbal skill, openness, energy, and sociability. On the other hand, there are times you can feel bombarded by the nonstop barrage of words and wish for silence, especially after a hard day at work.

> *My son was in a nonstop chatter mode from the moment I picked him up at child care to when we walked in the house—an hour-and-a-half drive! I was exhausted from work and became more exhausted by his chattering. In desperation one night, I gave Brendan my watch and instructed him not to talk for a whole minute. He complied and then gave me back the watch, telling me that now I had to talk for a whole minute. Before that remark, I had never realized that I had been so withdrawn on the ride home that my son was doing whatever he could to get some attention.*

Remember what we've said about children building up a lot of energy at the end of the day in anticipation of seeing their parents again? Much has happened, and they can't wait to share it. If a child is doing a lot of nonstop chattering to a nonresponsive parent, the solution may be to find more balance by asking more questions, telling your child about your day, or commenting on what's going on around you. And it's okay to ask for a little quiet ("Let's talk for a while and then let's have some quiet time.") Suggest listening to a few favorite music tapes. And, of course, you can say, *occasionally*, "I don't feel like talking right now."

Before deciding how to handle a supertalker, it's important to understand why your child is talking so much. Some children have a lot of energy, and talking is one way they expend it. They *like* to talk. But for other children, it may be their way of demanding the attention they need and crave but aren't getting.

With some kids, constant talking is a way to become the center of attention. Children need to learn how to be content without being in the spotlight and how to be respectful of other people's feelings. They need to be told, "Now it's your sister's turn to talk." Help them learn that getting along with people depends on a give-and-take, two-way conversation. Otherwise, people will pull away from them and avoid them—and they may never know why.

Children who chatter away usually talk to everyone they meet, including the mailman, the cashier at the market, and anybody who walks through the front door. Some adults may find this kind of behavior very engaging or amusing. Others may be turned off by it, at least some of the time. They may feel trapped and unable to get away without hurting the child's feelings. Parents may need to intervene for everyone's sake by saying things such as "Why don't we let the man work on the plumbing now?"

At Home

Now you know what your dad felt like when he made his way home from work, stumbled in the front door and shouted, "I need a drink," then sank into his chair for an hour. Immobile. Unreachable. Grouchy.

Wouldn't part of you love to get that little bit of peace and quiet without the fallout? Coming from a generation more enlightened than that of your father, however, you can't bring yourself to demand such isolation. You also remember what it felt like to be the child in that scenario.

A better approach is to give your full attention to your child for the first half hour or hour until she has settled down. Even just ten minutes when you first greet each other can make the difference in how smoothly the evening progresses for everyone. Do you really need to listen to all your answering machine messages the moment you walk in the door?

When you look at the day's mail, sit down together. Treat junk mail as family mail or her mail. Young children love getting mail, and fourth-class bulk rate is just as absorbing to them as first class. You may not have much interest in a flyer from the supermarket, but to a child these glossy pictures of food can be very absorbing. Have her check out sale catalogs from department stores.

If you need to do a few preparations in the kitchen to get dinner on the table at a reasonable time, work up some equally important, age-appropriate routines for your child. Maybe she can empty out her own lunch box. Add a dry snack to the dog's bowl. Or say hello to favorite stuffed animals. Find a small, simple task that becomes hers.

Enlist your child's "help" with a few chores such as unloading the dishwasher or straightening up pillows on the sofa. He might get bored quickly, but that's okay. If you tell him to go play in his room while you do chores, he will feel abandoned. Ask for his help and you'll get it for a little while. When he drifts into his room because he's lost interest, that sense of abandonment isn't an issue for him.

School-age children may want to make contact with their room for a while before joining the family. They may have family chores too, such as walking the dog or taking out the garbage.

Preparing Dinner

Encourage children to help get dinner on the table. Preschoolers can have simple tasks; older children larger responsibilities.

Getting dinner ready together is important for many reasons. It's not just about chores and learning responsibility; it's also about being together as a family. And the kitchen is a great place for a busy family to spend time enjoying one another's company. Even infants can enjoy this preparation time, settled in an infant seat-with-a-view, or, if there's room, on a floor blanket. Besides, it's a much easier setup than one that requires your running back and forth to another room to check on the youngest member of the family. Arrange a safe and appealing spot in the kitchen where you can turn and chat, where he can hear your voice, see your smile. This is especially important on workdays. You've been apart for a long time, and he will be going to sleep soon. Make this time count.

Young children don't know that getting dinner ready is considered drudgery by most adults until you explain it to them. So don't. They think playing in the kitchen with all those great toys (you call them pots and pans) is a highlight of the day.

As children begin to move around on their own, they can be encouraged to go into the kitchen with a hearty "Let's make dinner." Pull out a few pots and pans for them to play with. Put a few Cheerios in a cup for them to mush up.

As they grow, children can have regular tasks, such as putting out the napkins. Then, later, they can graduate to setting the table, then clearing it.

A few suggestions:

Sharing a healthy snack before preparing dinner can take the edge off.

For a fast salad, use prepackaged lettuce.

Prepare two nights' worth of entrees at once.

Keep an emergency meal, such as lasagna, in the freezer for an especially frazzling night.

A rice cooker, bread baker, and microwave are invaluable appliances.

Sit down to eat together but allow children to be excused when they get fidgety.

Bring children into the dinner table conversation.

Things to Do on a Warm Summer Night

One of the nicest things about the summer months is that the longer evening hours of daylight give families time to be together outside after dinner. For working parents who don't see daylight in their own homes until the weekends during the winter months, this can be a relaxing, treasured time.

Traditional family schedules might even be rearranged to get outside before the sun sets; maybe a quick snack or a salad when you arrive home, some time outdoors, and then an oh-so-fashionably late dinner after dark.

Take advantage of this time. It's a long time between weekends. Set aside one or two weekday nights for outdoor family activities away from TV reruns. Here are some suggestions:

- Walk/saunter/stroll/hike
- Ride bikes and trikes
- Rollerblade/walk
- Walk to errands such as returning videotapes
- Walk to a nearby ice cream parlor
- Shoot baskets
- Play hopscotch on sidewalk
- Draw with chalk on sidewalk
- Play board games on patio/lawn/balcony
- Play cards or dominos on patio/lawn/balcony
- Garden
- Design art projects for completion on porch/balcony/roof
- Play baseball
- Visit neighbors
- Walk dog
- Go window shopping
- And, of course, eat dinner outside

Things to Do on a Cold Winter Night

Winter nights can be cozy. Staying together in one room on a below-freezing evening both lowers the heating bills and stimulates family togetherness. Make sure your child has enough space in the room to work.

Winter nights also seem to suggest nourishing, traditional foods, especially those you can prepare together. Even with toddlers, you can make hot chocolate or a warm fruit brew together. As children get older, the possibilities for family cooking increase: Jello-O in special shapes, baked bananas, applesauce, popovers, and, of course, popcorn. Have a popcorn tasting. Try different flavored corns or compare microwaved and stove popped. Blindfold each other and see who can tell the difference.

Other ideas:

Play board games, such as Chutes and Ladders, Scrabble, chess, and checkers.

Play card games, such as Concentration, War, Go Fish, Casino, and Hearts.

Make videos or audiotapes to send to friends and relatives for upcoming birthdays.

Hold family meetings (see Chapter 12).

Talk about the change in seasons. Check the newspaper for the sunset and sunrise times.

Huddle together under an old comforter and look at/read favorite books.

Have a teddy bear or doll party. Of course, this is an anywhere/anytime activity, but when your child holds a tea party at the kitchen table while you're cooking or in the living room while you're reading, you have the not-to-be-missed opportunity of overhearing the conversation. Many a bear will tell stories and reveal secrets you might not hear directly from your child.

Since Seasonal Affective Disorder (SAD) is getting more and more recognition as a cause of depression during the winter, plan family gatherings in rooms with an abundance of light. Lights (especially twinkly, holiday ones), bright curtains, plenty of lamps, and plants make rooms cheery and are uplifting for young and old.

Helping with Homework When You'd Rather Put Your Feet Up

As a working parent, the last thing you need is to work a double shift, moonlighting as the "homework police" as soon as you get home from your day job. But unless you are blessed with a motivated self-starter, you will need to be part of your child's homework routine on a regular basis.

With some children, your help may be minimal and occasional. They may be able to handle routine assignments pretty much on their own but need assistance with special projects or reports. Other children need help every night for most of their school years.

A decided advantage of after-school programs is that they oversee completion of all or some of your child's homework assignments. Even if your child arrives home with all his homework completed, however, reviewing it with him will give you a clear idea of what he is studying and how well he grasps it.

Children who are home alone in the afternoon and are expected to do some of their homework then will likely need to go over it with parents.

Most of us are carrying the memories of our own homework days: trying to finish geometry before *Laugh In* started, for example. Now there's a second-grader in your living room who needs help before the next day's spelling test and a fifth-grader who, having a hard time understanding the math homework, is showing signs of extreme anxiety.

Your first step should be to check for any permission slips, assignment sheets, or letters to read and/or sign. Younger children are often simply forgetful about homework and notes, while older ones withhold information with the skill of a professional spy.

Decide together on a special time to go over schoolwork. It might be right after you get home or after dinner. Children need some time to unwind after school, but they shouldn't put off homework until late in the evening. The best time to tackle it is usually after a snack and a chance to play or relax a bit.

Provide a conducive place to work that's comfortable, well lit, quiet, free from distractions, and spacious enough to allow work to be spread out on a desk or tabletop. Some children work better in their rooms, while others are more productive when surrounded by low-key family activities. In some families, children sit at the dining table and work while parents do chores nearby. This approach makes homework part of family life, rather than separate from it.

Most teachers consider homework an essential part of the school routine—even in kindergarten. It is meant to gauge how much a child is learning in class, promote good work habits and reliability, and encourage independent work. For many students, their report-card grades reflect how diligently they did their homework.

Helping with homework does not mean completing it for your child. Granted, doing it yourself may be faster, easier, and tempting after a hard day at work. Parents have the responsibility to see that homework is completed (legibly), but they are not responsible for doing it. That is the child's job. The parent is merely the coach.

It is important for teachers to see what mistakes are made, especially the more common ones. If you help your child through a particularly difficult addition problem or edit his term paper to Pulitzer level, the teacher may have a hard time figuring out that your child really hasn't grasped basic addition or grammar and needs more help. Seeing that a child has made a serious attempt to do the work but hasn't been able to master it is more valuable than thinking he has completed it well by himself, when in fact, he has received help. Teachers want sincere and thoughtful attempts, turned in on time.

Of course, this doesn't mean you can't set standards of spelling, neatness, and completeness. If the assignment is to write a two-page book report and your child only wrote a short paragraph, for example, you should by all means make it clear that she should complete the assignment as stated by the teacher.

Here's how to help without doing the work:

Read the assignment aloud, then ask what your child thinks the teacher is asking for.

Watch your child go through the first few questions or problems to see what she can do on her own. Then if she needs guidance or assistance, offer direction, but not answers.

Help locate instructions, source books, directions, definitions, etc. Explain how to organize work, review for a test, and do research. Point out glossaries and indexes and how to use them.

Find out about long-term assignments, so you can help pace the work. Book reports should be tackled the same way. Dividing a two-hundred-page biography of Harriet Tubman into ten nightly sessions beats trying to absorb it all in one night. For many children, this kind of pacing doesn't come naturally.

Make sure your child has the right supplies: plenty of pencils or pens, paper, notebooks, dividers, poster boards, etc. These days, the right supplies often include a computer equipped with word-processing software and a decent printer.

Children work at different paces. Joannie may zip through an assignment in fifteen focused minutes while Johnnie takes an hour, because he gets sidetracked several times. Try to understand your child's individual learning and working style. If the work is getting done satisfactorily, acknowledge that achievement. If an assignment is difficult, add a note of your own so the teacher will know that a serious attempt was made to do the work. "Jenny really tried. We spent a lot of time on this." If the amount of homework and the level of difficulty are frequently overburdening, talk with the teacher.

Juggling Time, Space, and Sanity

TRYING to cram thirty-six hours' worth of commitments into twenty-four-hour days forces working parents into often doing two things at once. You no longer have the luxury to tackle life sequentially. Being a working parent calls for making clear plans for everything, from getting dinner on the table to making sure there's food in the house when you're two thousand miles away. You're constantly juggling several balls at once, and single parents even have an extra ball to juggle.

Grocery Shopping with the Kids

Never has the old maxim "He travels fastest who travels alone" been truer than in a supermarket. Shopping alone, a parent can fill a basket with necessary—and only necessary—items, getting out the door lickety-split. With a child, it takes up to twice as long. The trip that normally takes you thirty minutes takes forty-five minutes when you bring a little one along. But, of course, the extra time is only part of the story. There's also all the drama of keeping your eye on your young child while trying to move efficiently through the aisles. The degree of difficulty and stress increases, sometimes exponentially.

But sometimes you can't avoid bringing a toddler along. You may not have a place to stop for groceries on the route home from work or time to shop before the child-care center closes. Or you simply want to see your child after a long day, and while no one in her right mind would call grocery shopping "quality time," it *is* time together after nine or ten hours apart.

So there you are, midaisle, a two-year-old in the shopping cart jumpseat or a six-month-old in one of those carts with a padded baby seat attached (finally supermarkets are wising up). All you're asking is that your marketing go as smoothly as humanly possible.

A smooth—or at least smoother—trip begins before you set foot in the store. A nursed, bottled, or fed child will be a much better companion. And, likewise, a fed parent is a much better companion. In other words, no one should go to the supermarket hungry. It makes people edgy and impulsive and lines the market owners' pockets.

Bring toys along. Keep them in your bag or stuff them in your pockets until you sense a need for diversion. For the booster-seat-bound, bring toys that can be looped onto the cart handle instead of ones that can be dive-bombed off the side of the cart.

Now that you're a working parent, every little dash to the market for one or two items is a chunk of time that could be better spent. Even if you are not, by nature, much of a list maker, keeping track of what you're out of and low on can cut down on the number of trips each week.

Older children can help on market trips by always being responsible for getting certain things, such as lunch items or cereal. They can be kept quite occupied by matching coupons to products on the shelf.

As a working parent, you might find advantages to shopping at odd hours. Are you up with a perky infant at six o'clock on weekend mornings? You may not be ready to tackle anything that requires actual thinking, but an early morning trip to the grocery store with no crowds, the shelves recently restocked by overnight crews, easy parking, and a child who is a fine fettle may be just the ticket. This is as good as it gets.

Alternatively, shop by yourself after your child goes to sleep.

I'm a morning person, so Erin's early-morning wake-ups were never really a problem for me. They were for my husband, Ernie.

So when Erin was a baby, I found a way to kill two, more like three, birds with one stone. I'd take Erin with me and do the grocery shopping really early on weekend mornings. We'd get there before eight o'clock and the shelves would be well stocked and the lines were short, if there were any. Erin was very playful and content to watch the world around her. And Ernie got to sleep in.

Or . . . maybe someone else could do the grocery shopping. Some of it, anyway. Even in these enlightened times, it's usually the same person in a relationship/marriage who assumes marketing chores. Well before a couple has children, it becomes an accepted assignment. Maybe that person does most of the cooking, so knows what's needed. And maybe that person doesn't trust anyone else to do a good job. But maybe now it's time to share the task. (See Chapter 12 for further discussion on sharing chores, including marketing.)

Granted, grocery shopping is a skill. To get everything you need (and nothing you don't need) takes practice. But it's not like ballet. You don't have to start at age ten. Adults can learn to be proficient grocery shoppers. Just cut your partner a little slack and give him a detailed list. The first few trips may not be perfect: he didn't get the ketchup, bought some gourmet soup when you needed plain chicken broth, and confused baking soda with baking powder. You may need to spend a little time prepping the new shopper. Draw a map leading to the hard-to-find items that the grocer hides in strange places. But it's worth the effort. Think of all those grocery shopping trips you might be able to avoid in the future.

Restaurants with Kids

One of the ways working parents save time is to eat out. Even a fast-food meal eliminates grocery shopping, cooking, and cleanup. But even a fast-food meal costs more than a meal prepared at home. You want it to be worth the cost. You want it to be relaxing.

Let's face it: A restaurant meal with children is always a chancy thing. Sometimes it works out beautifully, and sometimes it seems like money down the drain. The restaurant meal from hell includes crying that won't stop, followed by your walking back and forth on the sidewalk with an inconsolable child in your arms while your food gets cold and your spouse sits inside alone. And you get to pay hard-earned money for this nightmare.

Making restaurant meals work (meaning everyone who came in together, eats together—at the same time—with a minimum of crying and rambunctiousness and no icy stares from other customers) is a matter of both temperament and technique.

Some babies are to the restaurant born. They seem content to gaze around the room, amuse themselves quietly, and eat with a reasonable amount of dignity. Others—perhaps even siblings of the above-mentioned parent's delight—find restaurants pure torture. They feel they're being forced to remain in one place when they'd rather be moving around. Forced to eat food they don't like. Forced to sit still forever.

If you're dealing with a child who finds restaurants difficult to bear, begin by selecting places that truly welcome children. This is not the time to push back the frontiers of child acceptance. You can't work on two fronts at once—soothing a fretful child and enjoying your meal at a restaurant that sees itself as a haven for adults. Stick to youngster-friendly restaurants: the kind with kids' menus, high chairs, booster seats, booths, other children, fairly quick service, and a generally relaxed environment.

Room noise is also a good sign. You don't want to go someplace where you can hear a spoon drop (or, for that matter, "Mommy, I have to go pee pee") from across the room.

The concept of "A" tables is one thing for celebrity bistros and quite another for families. The "A" table for a family with a baby is one that is off to the side, usually a booth. You want the quietest part of the room if you're trying to lull a baby to sleep or nurse unobtrusively. And for families with preschool and school-age children, "A" tables are ones with plenty of diversions nearby to keep youngsters entertained, such as a fish tank, a picture window looking over the ocean, or even the parking lot, which provides other people to look at.

If you have kids over the age of one and a half or two years, discuss your plans with them before you set out for the restaurant. Let there be no surprises. Better they know in advance that "they probably won't have grilled cheese sandwiches at the Chinese restaurant. But they will have rice." Let them adjust to the no-grilled-cheese idea before they sit down to eat. After all, most adults go out to eat with some notion of what kind of food they're going to have—"No, I don't feel like Italian food tonight. I've got my heart set on a juicy steak." Children deserve the same courtesy.

This is also the time to discuss your expectations of what constitutes a decent meal. Head off visions of french fries, a Coke, and ice cream before you open the menus.

As always, parents need to set limits for restaurant behavior. These rules should also be discussed before leaving home. Talk about the physical parameters: Will your child be required to sit at the table the entire time? Can she walk out to the foyer by herself if she gets antsy? Make clear there is to be no running, no loud noises. And, no matter how much she hates the food, there won't be any "yucks." Talk about acceptable ways to decline food. Agree on the limits together. And remember, good restaurant behavior *can* be learned.

How much latitude you allow your child in restaurants depends to a great extent on the environment and respect for other customers. Each restaurant and meal might be a little different. A noisy fast-food spot, with so many distractions that children's voices are only part of a general dull roar might permit more relaxed guidelines than when you dine in a quiet place, where your child is the only youngster. Sometimes it's okay for children to slip under the booth and pretend they're in a fort—and to "flirt" with the older couple in the next booth. Sometimes other customers love the attention of a child (for a while anyway); sometimes they don't.

Parents are role models for how to behave in restaurants. From keeping your napkin on your lap to how you interact with the server, your child is observing it all. A parent who treats waiters and waitresses with courtesy is showing a child how to do it properly. Once you agree that you are ready to order, that means no dawdling, no changing your mind (well, maybe occasionally), and "pleases" and "thank yous" all around. Older children can order their own food or ask for refills on the water.

A successful restaurant meal with children, even preschoolers, is usually one where children are included in most of the conversation. Imagine if you had to sit for an hour while people talked around you. Bor-ing.

Several years before I had my baby, my husband and I were having dinner at a Japanese restaurant in the neighborhood. A few tables away, I noticed a woman who was a very high-profile news reporter in the city. She was dining with her husband and their child, a girl about six years old. The parents talked the entire time, and the only time they acknowledged their daughter was when they ordered her to finish her food. She sat, lost and alone, for over an hour. My heart went out to her. That was a lesson in how not to take a child to a restaurant that I never forgot.

If your children are typically at their most fretful around dinner time, it's like swimming upstream to attempt eating dinners out (except fast food). Try breakfasts or brunches instead. Or the occasional early dinner.

One way to make meals out more workable is to put together a "Restaurant Box." Keep it in the trunk of your car or hall closet, and use it at no other time. Fill this box (or bag) with surefire tricks to make restaurant meals enjoyable. Depending on the ages of your children, include a deck of cards, pencils, and a pen (for a game of hangman while you wait for your food to arrive), small coloring books, maze and dot-to-dot books, miniature games, even a few tiny cars or animals. Travel toys (Etch-A-Sketch, a miniaturized version of Battleship, etc.) are perfect. The key to making this strategy work is to put the items back in the box after you leave the restaurant and leave them there until the next outing. That way, your children won't get sick of them or lose them. Bringing an old favorite toy or game from home (except for perhaps an emotionally charged stuffed animal) doesn't hold the same appeal.

Many parents keep a few emergency food provisions with them for times when nothing on the menu seems palatable. Store a few nonperishable favorites in a bag, or pack a small bag of food before leaving home. Then your child can mix his regular food with choices from the menu.

Children, especially those in this fast-food generation, have a hard time waiting for food to be prepared and delivered to the table. The ten or fifteen minutes it takes in real restaurants can be torture. To fill the time—and the stomach—bring along a few hors d'oeuvres from home: a little bag of carrot sticks, Cheerios, or raisins. Eaten unobtrusively, they can take the edge off the wait. Another suggestion is to bring along a small jar of peanut butter (it keeps without refrigeration) and make a little sandwich with the bread or rolls the restaurant puts on the table. Filling, nutritious, and, in younger eyes, fun! What more could you ask for?

If your toddler hasn't mastered adult utensils yet but is a whiz with his kid-size ones, bring them along. And to minimize spillables, request that drinks be served in disposable cups with lids. Ask for extra napkins before you need them. This goes for the check, too.

After leaving a restaurant, children appreciate being complimented for a job well done. Comments such as "I thought you handled yourself very well in there" or "I was pleased that you didn't make a fuss over the pickles they put on your burger" go a long way toward ensuring a repeat performance of good behavior.

Sometimes going out to a restaurant seems appealing simply because you don't want to fix dinner. If you've had a rough day but the kids are fidgety, it could well be a recipe for disaster. In theory, restaurant food is a good idea, but perhaps you're better off ordering in or taking out. This is especially true if your children are at a particularly fussy age. Make it easy and get take-out food (with the kids in pajamas at the drive-thru window) until this stage passes.

Juggling Children's Appointments During Working Hours

Children seem to have a lot more appointments than adults. All those DPT shots. Orthodontia. Teacher conferences. Some are routine; some are semi-emergency. Most come at an inconvenient time.

One way to cut down on the amount of time you're away from work for these appointments is to select doctors and dentists who are open early or late—and who are close to home or your child's school or child care. You might be able to get to work on time with a pediatrician who takes 7:30 A.M. appointments, but never with one who starts the day at 9:00 A.M. That convenience alone may be reason enough to select the early-hours doc. Some medical professionals also have one day a week when they take late appointments. That could help, too.

Health maintenance organizations (HMOs) usually have after-hours pediatric walk-in clinics. You may not get to see your regular pediatrician, but you do get to see one of the staff doctors who can diagnose an ear infection and write a prescription. Some HMOs are going further by offering scheduled pediatric appointments in the early evenings and on weekends. This option is definitely worth checking out.

If you have to make appointments during work hours, which is inevitable even with the best health programs, think ahead to what time would work out best: getting to work a little late, leaving early, or taking a long, late lunch?

For some medical appointments, such as simple checkups and regular shots, a nurse-practitioner can be as desirable as a pediatrician. Going to a nurse-practitioner gives you more time flexibility, since you then have two professionals with whom you can make appointments. Make sure, too, that you get to know the office receptionist. She may call you when there's a cancellation or work you in sometime between appointments, whereas she might not have made the effort if you were a faceless stranger. Ask her what the best times are to avoid sitting a long time in the waiting or examining room. Also find out what walk-in services are available.

Always allow plenty of time for an appointment rather than getting your hopes up that you'll be in and out in half an hour; that way, you might occasionally be pleasantly surprised.

Bringing Work Home . . . and Getting It Done

To get work done at home, begin by paying attention to your child. You won't have a chance until you've met her needs and given her plenty of time and attention. The secret is to get your child settled into an activity *first*. This activity could be sleeping or playing with a puzzle or building set. Some mothers can read a report while nursing.

Apply the "we both have work to do" approach. Don't let your child fend for herself. Suggest some possibilities to occupy her. Sit at the table with drawing or writing supplies for your child, and suggest that she draw while you work.

You know your child and what is likely to pique his interest. Should you stop at the video store on the way home and rent a special tape? If you have a family policy of not renting movies on weeknights, bringing home a video will seem very special. Your child will know you mean business.

If you are really serious about getting work done at home, read the "When You Work at Home" section in Chapter 5. The same issues apply whether you are a full-time worker at home or an office worker who has paperwork or reading to do at night.

When there's important work that absolutely has to be done, such as preparing for a staff meeting the next morning or turning in a final report, consider hiring a caregiver for the evening. You would if you had tickets to the opera, wouldn't you? If this is just as important, spring for the expense.

Maybe your child can spend an hour or two at a friend's home. Make a formal request with the parents and offer them a speedy reciprocation. Keep phone numbers at work, so you can be ready for emergencies as they arise. If you ask another parent to take your child home from child care, you'll need advance planning, since most places will not release children to anyone who hasn't been designated on the information form (sometimes a fax will do). When you ask a parent to take your child home, call the caregiver and tell them of the change of plans. Then ask to speak to your child and tell him directly who will be taking him home.

If you bring work home regularly (but not often!), take the time to help your child develop the skills she'll need to wait and survive. Be honest. Prior to the night you need to work at the dining room table, explain about your work and that you need to practice. Make it a collaborative effort. "I'm going to work at the dining table, while you work on your puzzles on the coffee table." Explain that the more you are able to concentrate, the quicker you'll be able to get your work done and back to being Mommy again. Practice being apart/together by writing bills or personal letters at the table. Offer encouraging words when your child allows you to work without interruption. "I do my thing and you do your thing."

Bribing your child with sweets or toys to "be good" while you work should be considered carefully with an eye toward the long term. One bribe and you've set a precedent. Children need to learn that sometimes emergencies happen. You might offer to spend some extra-special time with them the next night, perhaps reading a favorite book twice. While it might fall into the broad bribe category, such a promise is a far cry from offering candy or ice cream.

Once your child understands to some degree the concept of time, give her a choice on how she'd like to organize your time. Let's say you've got two hours' worth of work. Tell your child that you could do it all at once, so you'd be done sooner. Or, after every half hour or so, you could take a fifteen-minute break and play together.

Even with workable strategies, you can't work at home every night, unless you do it after your child's bedtime. This is one of the reasons it's important to establish a bedtime routine and schedule.

Business Travel

The average person who travels on company business takes between four and five trips a month and spends five nights away from home. A lot of these travelers are parents who must wrestle with both the logistics and guilt of being away from home.

On rare occasions, employers may pay for the expenses of bringing a young child along. Of course, this treatment is definitely the exception, reserved for star employees who are lactating! While most working parents leave their children at home, 14 percent of the 276 million business trips in one recent year included children. For the other 86 percent, there are ways to minimize the stress and lonesomeness that everyone involved feels.

First, time your trip carefully. The killer trips are the ones when you miss a birthday or other special event, such as a school play. Keep track of school events on the kitchen calendar and/or in your daybook and try to work around these can't-be-missed dates.

There will be, of course, business trips over which you have no control, ones you must go on no matter what you'll be missing at home. Fifty sales reps are not going to schedule around a kindergarten play. In these cases, ask your spouse or a friend to make a videotape of the special event, so that you and your child can watch it together when you return. No, it's not like the real thing. But it's next-best.

There may also be times when you have to leave a sick child. When you're faced with such a situation, make doubly sure you can be reached at all times. It can be soothing for both you and your child just to hear a loving voice over the phone. And there may be a time when you have to do what was previously unthinkable: cancel a trip because your child is very sick.

Just as I was about to leave on a three-day business trip to Memphis, my little boy started showing symptoms of strep throat. I knew I wouldn't be able to give 100 percent to the trip, worrying about him. But I also knew that my supervisor would hit the ceiling if I canceled. There was really no good solution. I went to Memphis, but I really resented having to make such a decision. My husband used a few sick days to take care of things, and that put a strain on our relationship.

Whether you go away or stay home with a sick child is usually a matter of opting for the lesser of evils. Each scenario is different. The availability of loving care while you're gone and the consequences of not going must be weighed each time. Always ask yourself if there is a compromise. Could you, for instance, shorten the trip?

When you leave for a trip that lasts more than a day, you might think that it would be better for your child to be with a doting friend or relative, rather than stick to child-care routines. Mull it over carefully. Your leaving may be all the change in routine a child can handle at one time. Going to a familiar child-care situation may be important for a child to feel the world hasn't gone topsy-turvy.

When I was about four, my mother had to go away on two important business trips. She had to get two weeks of training for her new job. They were scheduled a month apart. It seems my parents never seriously considered my father taking care of me during those weeks. They sent me to my grandparents for one week and to an aunt's house the other. I still have memories of those events. I knew my grandparents very well, and they doted on me. I loved being with them. We had a grand old time. But I didn't really know my aunt. She had four children, and my parents thought they were doing me a favor putting me with a lively family rather than two old people. But I felt lost and abandoned and miserable. It was too much. Maybe another child would have loved the excitement, but I was used to the only-child life.

There are differing opinions on what time of day is best for a parent to leave on a trip. Some experts suggest taking your child to school or child care just like a regular day and leaving from there. Some trips can be completed in one day only if you catch a 6:00 A.M. plane or train. The fewer nights away from home, the better, even if it means a change in the morning routine. Evenings are the most difficult time of the day for children; as they wind down from the day, crankiness, illness, and sleep problems may emerge.

Explain your travel plans as much as possible. Very young children may need to hear that you'll be back just before bedtime or "after two bedtimes."

Tell your child about what you'll be doing and where you'll be going. Use a globe, a map, or brochures—whatever they can absorb.

Even though you're not there, you can leave your child reminders of your love, such as Post-it notes in a drawer or lunch box. A silly drawing on their pillow. Send postcards if you're away more than two days even though they may arrive after you're home. And make full use of faxes, which are great for checking homework. Buy and/or cook some favorite meals for the family to enjoy while you're gone. Tape a story so they can hear your voice.

And of course there's that old standby: phone home. Ask your child what time of day he'd like to talk to you. Maybe he'd like a little chat before he sets off for the day or to tell you about his adventures when he gets home. Whenever you decide to call, keep your promise. And remember time zone differences; will you be able to make a call when your child expects it?

You may decide to assuage your guilt by bringing home lavish gifts. Think twice. A child who begins to associate your trips with fancy presents will ask, "What did you bring me?" before she says, "I missed you." Token gifts or souvenirs like hotel soaps or postcards are okay. But save the jumbo Duplo or Lego sets for birthdays.

Coming home after a business trip is wonderful, but you may not get an effusive reception when you return. You may, in fact, get the cold shoulder instead.

I had to be away from Lamar for five days when he was a year old. He stayed with his grandmother, whom he adores. I called every night and talked to him on the phone. My mother said he was fine and playful and didn't seem upset. The last day I was away, I thought about him all the time—the whole drive from the airport. I rushed through the front door. Lamar and my mother were playing a game on the rug. He looked up and then went back to the game. He acted like I wasn't there. I was devastated. When I tried to pick him up, he pushed me away.

Such behavior is actually good news, a sign that things went well. Yes, you want your child to miss you on one level, but the fact that he ignores you when you return is a strong indication of the good care he received while you were gone.

> *I noticed with my kids that I either paid for the trip before or after. When they were real cranky before I left, they were happy to see me when I got back. When they didn't seem to care that I was going away, they were real whiny when I walked back in the door. Always one or the other. But luckily, never both.*

Business travel involves the entire family: traveler, children, and the spouse left at home. Everyone's life is disrupted. When a parent goes away on business, the parent left at home to cope with everyday life has more than usual to deal with. The spouse at home is left fully responsible for child-care arrangements, grocery shopping, meals, bedtimes, baths, and all the rest. Not only is it a lot of physical work, it's also emotionally draining to go it alone. That person becomes an instant single parent without any preparation.

Routines change when one parent is away. Remember when you were a child? On those nights Dad didn't come home for dinner, you got to relax a few rules. You could eat in front of the TV, have McDonald's, generally break Dad's rules. That scenario transcends generations, because the parent at home always wants to make things easier. There is a sense that the stay-at-home parent is in collusion with the children against the stern disciplinarian figure who is away, even if that person isn't really much in the discipline department. One parent's absence provides a chance for the kids to stay up later than usual. Skip a bath or two. Eat fast-food meals. Parents sometimes allow their young children to sleep in their beds with them while their spouse is away.

Why is this cat's-away-the-mice-will-play attitude so pervasive? The stay-at-home parent may understand intellectually that the trip is important, but still . . . it feels like he's been left home alone with a big responsibility, so breaking a few rules seems to balance things out.

The "regulations" that get cast aside during this period may be Dad's rules or Mom's rules. They may in actuality be rules—or ways of doing things—that both parents had agreed on together. But a business trip changes all that.

Sometimes the business traveler returns home to both an angry spouse and angry children. Having to handle the routine alone for a few days can be extremely difficult. And maybe something happened, like a child had an earache and didn't sleep all night. The caregiver didn't show up. Or he was given a rush assignment or extra work, on top of being the only available parent.

In these cases, it's best to talk things out. Acknowledge the situations and difficulties both of you had and express appreciation verbally and in other little ways. The "stay at home in the thick of things" parent may need to get out for a while or sleep late on the weekend. If you're the business traveler, give the gift of time.

Business trips are especially draining on single parents. It may not be possible for a single parent to keep her child in the routine child-care situation. If you are a single parent, see if your child can stay with relatives while you're out of town.

Conventions

At one time, no one would consider taking children along to a convention. Part of the purpose, whether verbalized or not, was to get away from family. Work and revelry, hand in glove. While some conventions still encourage a strong high-jinks component, more and more are becoming family-friendly. Sort of like what's happening to Las Vegas— which now offers adult fun for those who want it, family fun for others. And *family-friendly* means, to a great extent, providing good child care and/or activities while parents are occupied.

Should you consider taking your child along to a convention? First, find out about child care. There must be some reliable services available, whether you have to make your own arrangements or the convention planner can take care of it. Of course, you must be fairly confident about these arrangements, or you won't be able to concentrate on the work that brought you there in the first place.

Second, take a long, hard look at the schedule. When will you be able to spend time with your child? Are there long lunches where you wouldn't be missed? Does the afternoon session usually end early, with most people heading for the bar to continue informally? What would it mean to your work (career, reputation, etc.) if you didn't party with the others? Are other parents bringing their kids? Are you expected to put in ten- to twelve-hour days? Or could you turn the convention into a minivacation by staying the weekend and seeing the sights? Might there be a chance, for instance, to show your children New York or Miami? (Keep in mind that the same issues may arise in this situation as when parents take young children to the office: your coworkers and bosses will be witness to the parenting side of your life.)

Third, what will the weather be like? Chicago in January? What does that mean if you take your children? Taking a baby in and out of taxis or taking a twelve-year-old to the Art Institute? Consider how your child will be exposed to extremes of hot or cold—or a rainy season—as well as what the location has to offer someone your child's age.

Fourth, take another long, hard look at your child's age and temperament. There are no hard-and-fast rules about which children should and shouldn't go, but imagine how your child will adapt to temporary child care, strange rooms, unfamiliar schedules. And what about missing school?

The most basic convention child care consists of a babysitter who comes to your hotel room. For infants, this setup may be the best, no matter what else is available, because it offers a minimum of noise and distraction. You will also probably feel the most at ease with this kind of baby care. Prices for this kind of care vary greatly depending on geography; it may be significantly more or less than the going rate in your hometown. Such arrangements must be made in advance of your trip, not after you arrive. Many major hotels provide names and numbers of babysitting agencies that work with their guests regularly. This regular business association can be reassuring to convention-going parents; the assumption, of course, is that the agencies have provided reliable sitters in the past in order to be recommended by the hotel. In hotels that don't have formal agency lists, the concierge may be able to provide names of sitters. Again, any problems would probably have gotten back to the concierge. Using the Yellow Pages can be more risky. It may be fine to locate agencies in your hometown, when you have time to check references, but in a convention city, you must rely totally on the agency's screening process, which is always chancy.

For toddlers and older children, the best option is group care, which is available at some—but definitely not all—conventions. Many convention planners use companies that specialize in temporary on-site child care (such as KiddieCorp and American Childcare). These companies provide their own staffs, trained in short-term arrangements.

There are two locations at which group child care can be offered: in hotels and at the convention center. In cold weather, hotel child care may be preferable. Children don't have to face the elements and can stay warm and toasty. Hotel care can be offered in suites or meeting rooms. Meeting rooms have an advantage over suites, since there is usually more flexibility in size and furniture arrangements. On the other hand, suites have their own bathrooms; in a meeting room, the closest rest room may be far down the hall.

If none of these options appeals to you, you might consider taking your caregiver with you. This is probably only possible if you have nanny, au pair, or relative care, but it might also work with a regular nighttime babysitter or a college student who is free to travel during vacations.

If you are considering taking your child to a convention, there may be other employees who are pondering the same logistics. Put out feelers. Find these parents. Maybe you can share the cost of care, or approach your employer for some help.

Conventions that do not provide child care can sometimes be prodded into it. It takes a concerted effort by attendees who demand these services. As expected, organizations that have a high percentage of women members are often the most enlightened. At the American Association of Law Schools conventions, for example, where a high percentage of members are women, child care is considered an essential.

A booksellers' association provided child care for several years during its convention, but it was contemplating doing away with it until members spoke up and demanded it continue to be offered. A portion of the convention-center space is set aside for child care, and one year, Mr. Rogers stopped by to visit the kids there!

Some convention planners are reluctant to provide child care, because they worry about liability if children hurt themselves or get sick. However, using a child-care company shifts the responsibility for risk onto the provider company. These companies may also have on-site personnel trained for medical emergencies. Hiring such a company relieves organizations or planners of the hassles of setting up child care themselves.

Companies that provide convention child care should be evaluated in much the same way as regular child care. Necessary components include:

- An enthusiastic, qualified staff (adults!)
- Nutritious snacks and drinks
- A planned but varied schedule
- Enough space for the number of children
- Age-appropriate care (preschoolers and preteens have different needs)
- Liability insurance
- Strict check-in/check-out procedures
- Emergency procedures

One innovative security measure offered by some convention child-care programs is to take Polaroid snapshots of the children, parents, and all people authorized to pick them up.

Weekend Time: Too Much to Do, Too Little Time to Do It

Weekend time: there's never enough of it. Blink once, and it's Sunday morning. Blink again, and it's Monday—back to work.

In most families, weekends are crammed with chores and errands. Doing laundry, housekeeping, and yardwork; buying a birthday present for Jeremy's friend's birthday party; dropping Jeremy off at the party; picking him up at exactly 3:30 P.M. (a time that cuts off the entire afternoon); getting Heather to soccer practice; making a quick trip to the dry cleaners; then heading to the bleachers to cheer Heather on and gulp down some team punch. And then, of course, you notice that Jeremy's shoes are torn and he'll need new ones before school on Monday.

Sound familiar? And that's just Saturday.

What defines a good family weekend? Probably getting all the essentials done, having a fun and relaxing family outing, plus time for yourself. All three in one weekend: is that possible anymore? Yes. Here are a few suggestions for a triple-treat weekend.

When your child is very young, temperament is the great determinant of how weekends can be successfully scheduled. Your child may need to have weekends mirror the weekdays, following the same flow of activity, feeding, and napping. Too much variation can make her very fussy, and she needs to stick to her child-care schedule, so you need to work your plans around her. Do errands and go on outings when she's accustomed to being active. This means feeding her when the caregiver does and putting her down for naps close to the time the caregiver does. This kind of planning can result in your child displaying a happy disposition during your busy day. This stage won't last forever. As your child gets older, you will gradually be able to follow a more flexible weekend schedule. But for now, know her limits.

Then there are the children for whom a schedule doesn't seem to matter. They play whenever there's some action, eat when food is offered, and collapse in a deep sleep whenever they're tired. Parents of these adaptable children have much more latitude.

When your children are older, hold a family discussion or meeting (see Chapter 12) before the weekend starts—perhaps on Wednesday or Thursday evening. Ask everyone for their ideas on what they want to do and what needs to be done that weekend. The list may include going to the mall, buying a new tire for the bike, doing laundry, getting Rollerblades repaired. But don't stop there. Add the fun stuff to the list, too, such as renting *Winnie the Pooh* (again), going to a park, or browsing in a bookstore. If you follow this strategy, everyone knows what's on everyone else's minds, and a master plan can be put in place.

Getting Chores Done So the Good Times Can Roll

Including children in the chores is good for many reasons. They develop a sense of responsibility, make the work go faster, and learn new skills. Doing chores together also provides a chance to chat. Begin early with the concept of family chores ("Once we get our chores done, we can go skating"). Little ones can help fold laundry. Not a bad assignment, especially when it's all toasty warm from the dryer and you can dance to your favorite music while you fold. Saving some of your favorite tapes or CDs just for chore time can shift the sense of pure drudgery to partial drudgery tempered by some high-energy tunes.

Very young children are probably the most enthusiastic helpers—in their own way. With their toy mops, brooms, and dustpans, they're happy working beside you. Isn't that better than calling to you every five minutes from another room to come and see what they're doing.

Be flexible in your approach to chores. Take car washing, for example. On a warm day, washing the car with kids can be a fun way to be together. But remember that this method is time-consuming; it can take a good part of the day. If you have a lot to do, it's better to head for the car wash and be done with it in fifteen minutes. Be open to both possibilities.

To save yourself some time on the weekend, try doing one of your major chores during the week. If you always do the grocery shopping on Saturday mornings, try sneaking out to the store on Thursday after the kids are in bed (assuming, of course, someone's watching them). Or do the laundry a load at a time after dinner during the week (assuming you have a washer). Try a new schedule. You'll find a wonderful sense of freedom on the weekend. Found time . . . for fun.

Combine errands with exercise. Ride your bikes, push the stroller, or walk briskly to the video store (even toddlers can ride in child seats). Turn a quick trip for a carton of milk into a pleasant walk.

Make the most of a time-consuming chore. If you do your wash at a self-service laundry, scout out one that's close to a park or a block away from a pet shop. The old standby, even if it's close to home, isn't always the best choice.

Set a pace you can live with. Cut down on weekend commitments. Don't overschedule. Say no occasionally. No, you tell your son, you can't drop him at Brian's house at noon. You can do it at two o'clock when you take Stacey to gymnastics. Alert your children before baseball or soccer season that they might miss a practice or two because of scheduling conflicts. Scout out team-member parents for carpooling prospects.

Free and Low-Cost Weekend Outings

These days, a family outing to the movies costs as much as a splurge at an amusement park not too long ago. So where do you go?

Upcoming activities. Check the weekend sections of local newspapers for listings. These are often community events that need no prior planning or advance-purchase tickets, including school and church carnivals, stamp shows, baseball card shows, cat and dog shows, swap meets, and farmers' markets. Many colleges, from universities to junior colleges, offer children's programs on weekends.

Docent- and ranger-led walks. Many parks offer special family hikes that take into account children's pace and endurance. Some are even on stroller-accessible trails. These walks are often free but require advance reservations.

Reading. Take advantage of library or bookstore-led story hours. Once your child has settled in and is listening to the stories, you can slip over to the magazine rack or browse the new fiction section. You may also arrive early for the story hour and spend a few minutes together picking out magazines for you to read while your child sits near the reader. (See the next section for further discussion.)

Museums. Attend organized museum activities, such as sketching in the galleries, making papier-mâché masks on courtyard tables, and learning Aztec dances on the lawn. Get on museum mailing lists, so you'll be alerted to upcoming events. These activities can range from free to expensive. (See next section.)

Do things together. Don't just sit and watch your child skate during a Saturday morning trip to the local rink. Rent a pair of skates and get out there, too. Find art classes that encourage parent and child participation, not kids-only classes. Enroll in "mommy-and-me" and "daddy-and-me" classes on the weekends. Many of these classes are geared to very young children.

To make the most of all these outings, call ahead and find out what to expect. Is there a place to eat? Do they sell food? What kind? Can you bring your own? Are there places to picnic nearby? Is the event stroller-accessible? What is the parking situation? Is parking free? How far is the walk from the train or bus stop? Are there water fountains? Bathrooms?

The new multiplex movie theaters make it possible for parents with older children to enjoy different movies at the same time. If you think that once is enough for the latest animated film but it's just the beginning for your ten-year-old and her buddy, seeing separate movies can be the solution. Check the schedule to find two movies that start about the same time. When you arrive at the theaters, find an usher and tell him that you'll be in theater #4 while your daughter will be in #2, so when her show lets out ten minutes before yours, you'd like him to let her into #4. Make a plan with your child that you'll be on the left aisle and that she should just walk slowly down the aisle until she hears you call her name. A little bit selfish? Maybe. But many kids like the grown-up feeling of going to a movie with a friend, and this can offer a safe approach to doing it.

Many families invite their children's friends on weekend outings. Consider taking this a step further and suggesting a flexible arrangement with another family: you'll take their son on the first Saturday of the month if they'll take yours on the third Saturday.

Make Sundays special. Not too long ago, when nothing was open on Sunday, families would spend the day relaxing. Take an afternoon drive. Rest and gossip over a long supper. Back then, you couldn't hit Target, Kmart, and Sears on Sunday afternoon. With these great advances(?), a relaxing family Sunday is harder to come by. Maybe you can't recapture those Sundays when Mom cooked a big supper and relatives came over to share the conviviality. But with a little determination, you can set aside part of Sunday as family time. Make Sunday brunch or dinner a time when everyone gets together at the table. Plan special menus that becomes traditional. Sourdough pancakes from scratch with real maple syrup and fresh orange juice. Or turkey and real mashed potatoes. You may not be able to hold a special family brunch every Sunday, but if you miss a week, everyone will just look forward to the next one even more.

Library and Museum Trips for Working Parents

With all the bookstore shelves lined with gorgeous and tempting children's books, is there any good reason for a busy working parent to make a trip to the good old town library? Yes. Make that a resounding YES. Bookstores can't completely take the place of libraries. Even if parents could afford a stack of new books every month, there's still a need for visits to the children's library to promote a well-rounded reading list. Even after a hard day at work. Even on a busy weekend.

Libraries and bookstores have overlapping but not identical stock. Bookstore chains tend to be strong in three areas: the classics in children's literature, serials, and hot-off-the-press, lavishly illustrated books. Many libraries choose not to spend their money on the serial books, which can be bought inexpensively in bookstores. They do have the classics and some of the new books, *plus* shelves of books that can't be found in bookstores, including out-of-print books, books that may not be as visually commanding on the shelf but contain well-written stories, and books on everything from butterflies to soccer.

Most families can't buy every intriguing book in the store. Libraries allow readers to check out books and browse through them carefully before buying. It takes time to evaluate a story. For young children who revel in hearing stories again and again, a trip to the library can help you avoid the common scenario of buying a pretty twenty-dollar book that your child finds uninteresting after the third page.

When a child expresses an interest in dinosaurs, the library offers a stack of books on the subject—for free. Children also learn to take responsibility for the care of a book that's on loan and to return it on time.

Another asset of libraries is the expertise of the librarians. Children's librarians are better informed on children's literature than most store clerks, and they take special pleasure in guiding young readers to good literature. And while they acknowledge the value of encouraging a child's passion for serial books such as *The Babysitters' Club*, they also know what delights are to be found for readers who go beyond the formula books. When a child says that she loves a certain series, the librarian can then guide her to similar books that might also be appealing.

Introduce yourself and your child to the children's librarian. Tell her what kinds of stories your child likes to read and has read. Ask for suggestions. Explain to your child that librarians take the time to read most new books and therefore can be a great help in finding appropriate matches.

Because of budget cuts, libraries are being forced to reduce their operating hours, which can prove a problem for working parents, since night hours and Sundays are usually the first to go. However, most libraries are still open Saturdays.

When you visit the library, allow your child enough time to browse so the visit will feel more like an outing than an errand. Keep in mind that children can be so impressed by the number of books they are allowed to check out that grabbing the nearest ten is more of a priority than finding ones that will really hold their interest. Children get more out of their trips if their parents spend time with them in the children's section, so look through some potential books for your child before you head for the adult section.

Many libraries are now on computer catalog systems. For parents accustomed to the old card system, learning the computer system can be a great opportunity to share an educational experience with their kids.

Once children have learned their way around the neighborhood library, older children may be able to spend time there on their own, doing homework, research, or reading for pleasure. However, librarians cannot be expected to keep an eye on children, and unsupervised children should clearly understand the library's policy for quiet, nondisruptive behavior.

Librarians are united in their belief that a parent's attitude toward reading and books is the most important element in developing a love of reading in children. Homes filled with books, and parents who relish time with good ones, create a book-friendly atmosphere. Telling children that reading is important pales in comparison to actually showing them your enthusiasm for books.

Many librarians feel that parents often stop reading to their children too soon. When the child has mastered the rudiments of reading, parents assume their reading-out-loud days are over, and they send children off to read by themselves. Experts believe that reading to children is something parents should continue to do as long as their children let them. Let the kids do the weaning. Even those who can read by themselves will enjoy hearing books they aren't yet ready to tackle themselves. And when parents read out loud, it gives them a chance to share the ideas in the book and talk about them. At the same time, children also enjoy reading out loud *to* their parents.

While you can easily wind up reading the same book night after night, strive for a balance between your child's need for repetition and your need for variety. Compromise. Say, "You pick one, and then I pick one." Children will get much more out of read-aloud sessions when parents enjoy what they are reading.

My son Alex and I would take turns picking the book for the night. We both had our favorites. I liked reading about Mike Mulligan and his steam shovel, which was a book from my own childhood. It still has an almost hypnotic effect on me. I am as guilty as Alex of picking the same book over and over.

Art Museums, Too

You may have made time for family visits to the local children's museum, maybe a doll collection, and even the museum of natural history, marine animals, or dinosaurs. Does an art museum seem too much for a jam-packed weekend?

Life is more than stegosauri and porcelain-faced dolls. Art is one of the great pleasures of life, and some of the best experiences with art can only be had in museums. Coffee table books and Matisse posters aren't enough. But we know you already suspected that.

Appreciating art and being at home in art museums and galleries is one of those things that's easier if it's cultivated early in life. Much like reading, attitudes toward art are often learned from parents. Just as children of parents who openly relish a stolen hour with a good book are more likely to find joy in reading than the children of parents who find it a chore, when parents anticipate and savor museum trips, children will have a much more open mind. A parent who expresses exhilaration at seeing a Monet painting or an intricate stone carving from ancient Mexico demonstrates to a child what joy art can offer. The child may not be interested in Monet or Aztec art, but the concept is planted and therefore ready to be taken out and explored when she starts to develop her own unique interests.

Children are never too young for a museum trip. They may be too cranky or tired on a particular day, but never too young. Babies in backpacks have the great advantage of sharing their parents'-eye view. Meanwhile, toddlers in strollers can doze off when they've ODd on Picasso.

For working parents, museum visits are usually limited to weekends, when museums are most crowded. Time your trip around your child's best time. One child may be cheeriest and most open to new things at ten in the morning, while another is the most sanguine after a nap. As always, don't go when your child is hungry or tired.

The most important advice for taking children to museums is to not try to see everything in the museum in one trip. See one exhibit, or a wing, or a floor—not the whole kit and caboodle. There may be fascinating costumes in the next gallery, but save them for another day if you sense your child has reached his limit. How wonderful it is to promise your child a return visit! Leave him begging for more.

Basic museum etiquette applies here, so there should be no shouting, no running, no touching, no cartwheels. But talking is allowed. In fact, talking in a well-modulated voice is essential to a stimulating visit. The best time to talk about a painting or sculpture is when it is right in front of you. Discuss why you like it. Why you don't. Such conversations teach children to learn to be critics, in the best sense of the term. They will develop strong likes and dislikes (after all, disliking a work of art can be as important as liking it), and they should feel free to express their reactions. Are they drawn to paintings with animals in them? Or ones with bright colors? Point those out to them. Help them make connections and distinctions.

Don't, however, overload children with facts. If they're not ready to learn or don't care about where the Incas lived or the history of photography, roll with it. The historical and cultural contexts of art don't mean much to children who haven't gotten down to history and geography basics in school yet. Children are more interested in how something was made than where or when. Point out facts that children can understand. That the red dye came from beetles, for example, or that it took ten artists a year to carve a wall. Just the juicy stuff.

> When I went to see a photography exhibit at the county art museum, there was a mother carrying her daughter, who was about three, in her arms so that she could see the pictures at eye-level. I thought that was great. Then they got to a photograph of Ella Fitzgerald, and the mom said: "See that woman? Her name is Ella and she's a very famous singer. She does a kind of singing called scat. She sings like this: scooby doo, wah wah, da, da, da." I was so impressed.

A few generalities: Children like bright colors, animals, weirdness, miniatures, shiny metals, cartoonish drawings, sculpture, and murals. Museum docents we've talked to have a few surprises to add to the list. They say children are also drawn to abstract art, mosaics, and art from India. Save the somber eighteenth-century portraiture for an adults-only outing.

The staffs at art museums want children to visit, and they offer all sorts of things to entice them there, including workshops, special tours, festivals, classes, music, and storytelling events. Many of these programs are free and offered on the weekends. What could be better?

Museum workers can do things parents can't. They make (and break) the rules. They can read aloud a story about an Inca girl right there in the middle of an exhibit of Peruvian art. They can set up tables with paints and brushes on the patio, just steps away from the originals.

Parents who go along on gallery tours designed for their young children can observe how teachers and docents keep children interested. They are trained to present art in child-friendly ways and are expert in engaging children in dialogue that focuses on what they are viewing. They ask questions like, "Can you find the lion in the painting?" or "What do you think the artist felt about the person he was painting?" Or even a simple, "What do you see?"

Great Birthday Parties Without Maxing Out Your Visa

Working parents have less time than their nonworking counterparts to plan their children's birthday parties, but try telling that to a five-year-old with his heart set on inviting the entire kindergarten class for a dinosaur hunt. It may be only one day out of 365, but it can take on Brobdingnagian proportions. Working or not, parents must still deal with their children's primal need for a big day, not to mention the increasingly heavy pressure society is putting on parents to make children's parties lavish and unique.

In some neighborhoods, children's birthday parties have turned into competitive sport—reaching the extravaganza-like proportions once reserved for society weddings. The cake-and-punch days are long gone. Now it seems that real live clowns and ponies are *de rigueur.* Helium balloons are a must. Despite your forty-plus-hour workweek, you've got to come up with something memorable. A theme. It seems like nobody has a party without a theme anymore.

Before you take out a loan and max out your Visa to pay for your child's next birthday party, sit down and think through this whole birthday party craziness.

What are birthday parties about, anyway? Plain and simple, they're meant to celebrate the specialness of someone. And specialness doesn't and shouldn't have anything to do with how much money the party costs.

In the end, what makes a birthday party great? The fact that the birthday child had a wonderful, wonderful time, everybody laughed, and there were fun things to do—the birthday child opened presents and had a cake with *her* name on it. That's what makes a great party.

Different Parties at Different Ages

Parties on first birthdays are really for parents, family, and parents' friends. These can be very warm, emotional celebrations. Perhaps the significance of first birthdays is tied to some very old feelings that stem from a time when child mortality was so high in the first twelve months that reaching the one-year mark was a great reason to rejoice.

First birthdays are special because family and friends take the time to look at the birthday child and comment on this child as a real person. Documentation is important; a camera is as essential as the cake. While the birthday camera of choice these days seems to be the video (either bought or rented), don't forget the power and simplicity of the snapshot. It's still the snapshots that go in albums and on mantels.

The high point of first birthday parties, after the cake cutting, is the group snapshot. That picture will take on special meaning over the years.

Every year we take a group snapshot at our son's birthday party. One year everyone posed with corncob pipes and flexed arms for our Popeye party. Another year everyone wore Groucho glasses and eyebrows. We've got ten years' worth now, and they are probably the one thing I'd grab if we had a fire. We see how everyone has aged, children and adults! Grandparents and great uncles who've since died. It's like a short history of our family.

Preschool Parties

The focus changes for preschoolers' parties. This is *their* day. *Their* party. It's a time of socialization: to learn the party rituals of life; to learn how to be the center of attention, and how to be a guest. One lesson *not* to be learned is how to one-up other children with party excesses.

Preschoolers don't need to know too far in advance about their parties. You may be *thinking* about it for weeks in advance, but *talking* about a birthday party that's a month away is very difficult for a young child. To her, a month and eternity could be the same amount of time. A week's notice is much more in keeping with a young child's sense of time.

With regard to number of guests, one rule of thumb we've heard is to invite one guest for every year. Three guests for a three-year-old, and so on. Another possibility is to plan a small celebration at the child-care center or family day-care home. A cake-and-hats party at the child-care facility is really enough for very young children. It eliminates bruised feelings (both of other children and their parents) and it's inexpensive. Plan a small, warm family celebration at home in addition.

Children this age like to repeat favorite activities from their everyday life at parties. Find out from your child's day-care provider what games and songs she likes, and include them in the home party. Washing dolls in bubble bath and making wild Play-Doh monsters are simple fun, but also perfect party activities for this age.

School-Age Parties

School-age children have the opposite idea of preschool children about what makes successful parties: namely, at the best ones, they *don't* do the same things they do all week. And as children approach the preteen years, they develop a need for sophistication. Or what they think passes for it. So it takes a lot to get them excited.

Ask a child why he didn't like his friend's party, and he'll complain about the food (not enough of it) and that there was nothing fun to do. Ask a child, especially an older one, what makes a party great and he's likely to say something like, "We got to stay up late." Feeling grown-up is what it's all about.

Party Logistics

All children, both birthday child and guests, bring an enormous amount of energy to parties. They have high expectations of having fun. Successful parties let the partygoers express their exuberance, rather than forcing them to sit still like perfect little ladies and gentlemen. Parties that require children to sit through long performances, for example, don't give kids the outlet they need. *They're there to boogie.* Plan plenty of physical activities that are noncompetitive. Depending on the ages of the partygoers, that might be races (the everybody-wins kind), jump rope, or hide-and-seek. Celebrating a birthday during cold winter months, or whenever bad weather hits, calls for ingenuity, because kids still need to get the energy out.

Since birthday parties are important social events in young lives, the guest of honor should be involved from the beginning. Since parents need to begin planning before very young children are told of the upcoming event, this may call for some low-key probing on what kind of party they want. Try sounding out your child with questions like, "Your birthday party will be here in a little while. What kinds of things would you like?" But don't go overboard. Bringing a young child along to a party-goods store is asking for trouble. You'll never get out of there, because there are just too many choices. If you shop alone, *you* make the final decisions. If you feel that the party goods are costing too much, you can scale back and announce that the store was all out of Barney cups so you'll have to use the plain (and cheaper) purple ones.

Many older children love to plan their own parties, design and make invitations, pick out or make decorations, and plan the games. Let them get involved in creative ways.

To avoid hurt feelings, never have your child give out invitations at school. It can be an uncomfortable scene—a power trip for some children, a source of guilt for others. Even if you do invite the whole class, some invitations may get stuck in the bottom of backpacks for weeks. Get rosters from the school, if possible, and mail the invitations.

The best theme parties are tied to what a child is interested in at the time: dinosaurs, dolls, baseball. But having a theme doesn't necessarily mean you have to spend a lot of money on themed party goods. They're fine and fun if you can afford them, but there are other ways to have a great party.

The emphasis on birthday gifts is disturbing to some parents. Their children seem too caught up in what they'll get from their guests. It doesn't seem right that gifts should be a requirement to get through the door. And they shouldn't be. But the gift-opening ritual is important in children's lives. While guests learn to yield attention graciously to the birthday child, the birthday child learns to handle being the center of attention, as well as the social niceties that come with getting either a present you hate or a duplicate gift. Both of these eventualities are predictable and should be discussed beforehand. Ask your child how he thinks these situations should best be handled so the gift-giver's feelings won't be hurt.

One of the best gifts a parent can give a birthday child is to quietly manage the day so she has a wonderful time.

Here are our suggestions for making parties fun:

Have a decorate-it-yourself birthday cake or cupcakes. These are great child pleasers. Put out the cake or cupcakes with tubes and bowls of store-bought decorations, such as sprinkles and tubes of decorator icing. Kids love to create their own works of art.

Take Polaroids. Instant pictures are great fun at *all* ages.

Take group photos. Try one shot with Groucho glasses, another for real. Let the children put two fingers (devil horns/bunny ears) behind each others' heads.

Give out party favors to the guests during the gift-opening ceremony.

Have the birthday child make up party favors, perhaps personalizing store-bought items with names.

Have the guests make their own party favors, such as Shrinky Dinks or yarn bracelets.

Consider a breakfast party for a preschooler. It prevents having to plan around guests' different naptimes.

Serve both ice cream and cake in cones.

Goody bags (loot bags) are *de rigueur* in some crowds. There's no way to avoid them. They can be simple or elaborate, packed with fifty-cents' worth of trinkets or expensive favors. Whatever they are, they must be identical in color, design, and contents. You may think it's a nice idea to have four red bags and four green. You may think it's a nice idea to put fingerpullers in half the bags and fake dollar bills in the other half. But you're asking for trouble. And if your guests are under age three, make sure the contents are childproof. And always make up a couple of extra bags in case an extra child shows up, or a bag gets broken. Good sources of goody bag treats are prize catalogs, 99-cent-type stores, and party supply shops.

Birthday parties are a lot of work. If you're concerned, hire a helper from your child's school, especially if you are short of help from other parents. Don't invite teachers or caregivers from school and then put them to work. Make your intentions and compensation clear and wait for other parents to volunteer before you put them on heavy work detail.

ten

As Time Goes By

THE issues in this chapter—sleeping through the night, toilet training, friendships, and how to encourage creativity—are concerns and challenges for all parents, but they are of particular urgency to working parents.

Making That Nine O'Clock Meeting on Three Hours of Sleep

Yes, there are babies who sleep through the night when they are a month old. Not your baby. Other people's babies. Your baby cries till she's red in the face for half an hour before bedtime, wakes up two, sometimes three, times every night. She has an uncanny knack for timing the first wake-up about an hour after you fall asleep, breaking your deep sleep with an unrelenting, sanity-shattering cry. This routine of waking from the dead, wishing you were dead, spending half an hour calming her down, then lulling her back to sleep is wrecking your life and all its components: your disposition, your marriage, and your job.

And she's such a sweet child during the day.

Or maybe your four-year-old can't go to sleep without your presence in the room. If you try to tiptoe out before he is in a deep sleep (and breathing patterns, you've discovered, seem to be no indication), he turns over and insists that you sit there until he's really asleep. This time-consuming bedtime ritual, from getting ready for bed to the moment you really do manage to tiptoe out the bedroom door unnoticed, can take an hour or two—a big chunk of a working parent's life.

It may be cold comfort, but sleep problems in children from birth to age twelve are common and normal. Moreover, they occur in children of all ages when there are disruptions in their lives, including starting or changing child care or school, moving to a new home, the birth of a sibling, or the arrival of house guests.

It's been estimated that 25 percent of children between ages one and four have temper tantrums at bedtime, so you are definitely not alone. And if you think you are the only parent to let your child sleep in your bed when you know he should be in his crib or bed, well, you've got plenty of company there, too.

There are parents, as well as experts in the field, who will say that the way to solve sleep problems is to let an infant share the parent's bed. After all, they usually say, this is common practice in many cultures around the world. True. But we think this response should be viewed in a larger context. In some cultures, parents sleep with their children because of space constraints and because cultural patterns require a more interdependent relationship between children and their parents. Conversely, the American ideal is to encourage independent and self-reliant children as early as possible. One of the ways we try to develop self-reliance in our children is to create their own sleeping spaces. Learning to sleep separately from parents is part of our larger view of raising children to be independent people; many experts consider this both a mental health and safety issue.

Parents can learn techniques to minimize bedtime difficulties and encourage infants and toddlers to sleep through the night. The trick is to start early and not falter when the going gets rough. And it does get rough. There is no surefire fix-it for sleep problems, no patent medicine that guarantees to have your child sleeping through the night in just three days.

First, parents must remember that sleeping patterns, like temperaments, vary widely from child to child, from the number of hours of sleep he needs to how easily he falls asleep. The best measure of how much sleep a child requires is how he acts during the day. If he's happy and alert, he's getting enough.

Some babies begin sleeping through the night between six and twelve weeks of age. But many have indefinite sleep patterns, in which they continue to awaken, for several months beyond (and many others continue such patterns even longer).

All children, even the best sleepers, have four or five partial awakenings during the night, every night. Adults do, too. Babies, like older children and adults, can learn to deal with these awakenings on their own.

While child development experts vary in their approaches to solving sleep problems, most are in agreement on some basic issues: namely, children can learn to put themselves to sleep, and children need bedtime rituals that help them make the transition to sleep. The experts call such rituals "self-soothing." Some infants are natural self-soothers, and others can learn how to become that way. Parents can help.

It is very important to place a baby in the crib when she is drowsy but still awake. Without it, the preventive measures that follow will fail. By about four months, they can be put in their cribs awake with a transitional object, such as a favorite blanket or stuffed animal, but not with a bottle unless it's filled with plain water. (Anything else—milk, apple juice, sugar water, and so on—can lead to "bottle mouth," a condition that causes severe problems with baby teeth.)

At this age, many babies are accustomed to middle-of-the-night feedings. If your pediatrician feels your baby is at a healthy weight, some experts suggest making an effort to discontinue this feeding, because it is the sucking rather than the milk that is the real comfort in the middle of the night. A pacifier may work just as well.

At six months, babies often develop strong separation anxieties. They fall asleep in their parents' arms or with familiar faces just beyond the crib, only to wake up alone; this is a very scarey feeling for a child of that age, as he does not yet understand where you are when he can't see you. It is important to allay that fear, rather than to exacerbate it by letting him cry. What if your six-month-old is waking up several times a night, crying until you comfort him, and refusing to go back to sleep unless you stay in the room? By now, he's learned how to keep you there. How do you change his routine?

One approach is to spend two or three nights sleeping in a makeshift bed by the side of the crib. Don't offer your baby anything to drink. When he awakens, check to make sure the reason for crying is not a wet diaper or some other physical disturbance. Tell him in a soothing voice, "I'm here right next to you." Say this even if he is preverbal. Assure him you will stay there. *Then stay.* When he realizes that nothing bad is happening (which he feels is due to the fact that you are right there), he will drift back to sleep. This method of soothing takes a few nights to work, but the separation anxiety that overwhelms children in the middle of the night seems to disappear after several reassuring all-nighters.

Of course, the same approach doesn't work for every family. There are other strategies, including the Ferber method. Developed by Dr. Richard Ferber, a pediatrician at Children's Hospital in Boston and an expert in sleep problems, it is a program that changes a child's expectations over several nights. If your toddler wakes up and starts crying, go in and comfort him briefly. Then leave. If he continues to cry, you may go back in for another quick comfort, but wait increasingly longer between each visit. Three minutes, five minutes, ten minutes. You are *not* there to lull him back to sleep: you are only there to reassure him that everything is okay. It is important not to go in with a predictable pattern that is recognizable to your child. He can train himself to wait in anticipation of your estimated time of arrival. If you try this method, you should brace yourself for extended crying sessions. It will take several nights for your child to make the shift from your lulling him to sleep to his lulling himself to sleep.

Families who live with neighbors in close proximity have an added layer of stress and anxiety. They usually find it excruciating to let a child cry for a long time, piercing the night with his wail and waking everyone within a hundred yards. Before you begin your new plan, tell your neighbors about it. Ask their indulgence while you attempt to help your child sleep through the night. They need to know that the cries are not coming from neglect, but rather from concern and an eye to the long term. Also be sure the whole family, including older brothers and sisters, are aware of the plan and understand that this won't be easy. You'll need the whole family's full support.

Children of all ages need bedtime rituals. Many adults have theirs, whether it's the Letterman monologue, a hot bath, or fifteen minutes with a good book. At about one year of age, babies need a predictable bedtime ritual, too, whether it's a bedtime story or a special "nighty-night." This ritual should be finished before your child falls asleep.

Babies need to learn that nighttime is different from naptime. Naptime is a little break, a time to rest our bodies with some plans of what we will be doing afterward. Nighttime is when we do our serious sleeping, and that requires special preparations. To help make this distinction, parents can develop specific routines that signal bedtime but not naptime. This can begin with a different tone of voice, bathroom chores, or a special way of going into the bedroom together. For some babies, this ritual may include a fast feeding, because they sleep well on a full stomach. For other babies, a feeding causes them to wake up and increases their activity level. These babies need to be fed early in the evening. You'll have to experiment to see what your child responds to. Most pediatricians advise that babies learn to sleep with normal voice levels and noise around them, so that they can become accustomed to the typical sounds of family life early on.

Of course, sleep problems aren't just for babies and preschoolers. A recent study of third to fifth graders indicated that 43 percent of them suffer night disturbances. At that age, such disturbances are different from infants' problems. Some youngsters are "poor sleepers," which usually means they take more than thirty minutes to fall asleep and have at least one complete awakening during the night that may require at least thirty more minutes for the child to get back to sleep. The study found that these children were less active in sports and slept in noisier or more lighted rooms than "good sleepers."

At times, these sleep problems are caused by a disturbance in the child's life, such as worry over an upcoming test, fights with friends, or disharmony at home. Parents need to explore the underlying causes for sleep problems and offer assurances that will offset the anxiety. After this, if sleep problems persist beyond two or three weeks, parents may want to consult their pediatrician or a mental health professional.

A child's sleep difficulties reverberate through the family. Everyone is affected. They can turn perfectly fine parents into zombies. They can fray marriages. Interminably long bedtime rituals and nightly wake-ups inevitably lead to discussions of "whose turn it is to go in." One parent may feel that he's gone in to take care of more wake-ups than his partner or pleads that he has a tougher schedule at work the next morning. "You go," is his plea.

Parents need to work together to solve their child's sleep problems. Equal resolve is required to determine the correct strategy and decide who will handle each night's wake-ups.

Single parents are especially vulnerable to the stress caused by a child's sleep problems. They make all decisions alone, including how long to wait before going in to comfort the child, and how long to stay there. They have no one to share the burden of these nightly awakenings. Many single parents deal with middle-of-the-night wake-ups for months with no relief. If you're one of these parents, recognize when you need help. Begin by taking naps when your child naps on those days you are home together. Forget about using the time to get housework done. Sleep is more important. And what greater luxury is there than a nap? Ask relatives or friends if they would sleep over at your home for a night or two occasionally so you can get some uninterrupted sleep.

Are Pull-Ups a Downer?

For working parents, there are advantages to having a child out of diapers and into underpants. Many child-care centers do not accept children until they are toilet-trained, and your list of possible facilities can be whittled in half by that criterion alone. Day-care providers and those centers that accept children in diapers often require that you produce an ongoing supply of diapers for your child.

Let's face it, a child who's graduated to underpants makes life easier (not to mention cheaper). There used to be three stages to toilet training: diapers, training pants, and underpants. A fourth has been added in the last few years. Disposable-diaper manufacturers have craftily created this new stage, between diapers and training pants, and labeled them pull-ups. In your eagerness to simplify life, at home and in day care, you may embrace pull-ups as a great invention. But are they really? Are they the first step in toilet training? Are they developmentally sensitive? Consider what pull-ups mean in a child's life before you throw a pack in your shopping cart.

Pull-ups are very consumer-friendly. But do they shorten or prolong the toilet-training stage? Manufacturers tout pull-ups as making young children feel great about themselves, in particular very independent and grown up. They absorb like diapers but they look like underpants. True enough. In fact, they are so good at absorbing wetness that children are quite comfortable in very wet pull-ups. Is that such a good thing—to be wet and not feel it? After all, the aim of toilet training is *to wear underpants and keep them dry.*

To learn to control body functions, a child needs to know when to use the toilet. One of the signals is feeling wet—uncomfortably wet. Pull-ups offer little help in this area; they are instead designed to mask wetness and therefore do little in the way of training. Real training pants are soppy and uncomfortable when wet. They absorb enough moisture to prevent the most egregious leaks, but they get sopping wet and most children want out of them fast.

Pulling pull-ups up and down like real pants is *supposed* to give them autonomy. But real autonomy only comes when children learn to handle their own bodily functions, a process which pull-ups don't facilitate. What happens when a child grows out of the largest size pull-ups and hasn't learned when to use the toilet? What's the message there—is she big or little? Children in pull-ups may in fact get the message that their parents are no more ready for toilet training than they are themselves.

Timing is an essential element in successful toilet training. It can be achieved only when a child is ready, not because some authority figure (parent or caregiver) decides on an arbitrary time to get it accomplished. If they're using pull-ups, parents may not pick up on some of the important but subtle signals of readiness children give when the time is right.

True, pull-ups may come in handy occasionally, in instances when an accident would be extremely disruptive and returning to a regular diaper for one time would be demoralizing to a child. But they're not for everyday. They are a convenience, not a training solution.

Home Alone: Latchkey and Beyond

In most states, there is no cut-and-dried rule for when you can leave your children home alone. Not only do laws vary from state to state, they also tend not to specify what constitutes neglect. Legally, you are responsible for keeping your children safe. If anything were to happen to your child when you left him alone, you could be charged with felony endangerment. The law expects parents to make the right call.

One state that has more specific guidelines on this issue is Illinois. A law was written there in reaction to the furor ignited when a suburban Chicago couple left their two children, ages four and nine, home alone for nine days. The Illinois law requires that children under fourteen be adequately supervised; still, this law does not rule out being left alone. Authorities are especially concerned about children left alone for more than twenty-four hours (which, in our minds, seems unconscionable), the severity of the weather, and situations in which older siblings are responsible for younger ones.

It's a complicated judgment. When are children mature enough to stay alone? How long can you leave them alone? Is your child ready to be a latchkey kid? How do you prepare her for independence and give a sense of responsibility and resourcefulness? After all, sometime before your children graduate from high school, you should be able to run to the local 7-Eleven for fifteen minutes.

As usual, there is no magic formula for making this decision—not 20 minutes at this age, an hour at that age. It depends not just on a child's age but also personality, maturity, experience, and available backup plans. One twelve-year-old might be very responsible and live within shouting distance of friendly neighbors. Another might live in a neighborhood where her parents don't know anyone and the whole family may be prone to panic attacks about burglars and kidnappers breaking in the back door.

Deciding to leave a child home alone, even for fifteen minutes, must be something both parent and child feel is the right thing to do. If either is uneasy, then it's not time yet. Maybe it's a matter of waiting another few months or a year or two. Whenever you decide to try it, this situation calls for some thoughtful preparation.

If your goal is to prepare your child to be home alone after school, approach it in small increments. One weekend, leave for an hour, then two. Go slowly, just like when you made that first adjustment to child care. This is simply the same process in reverse.

Your trial runs should begin with short, daytime trials. Children are often ready, even eager, to stay home alone during daylight hours. At night, there are more fears, more creaks, more strange sounds. All those horror movies, those Freddy films they were so sure they could handle, come back to haunt them.

When you and your child decide he might be ready to try a short spell home alone, sit down together and go over specific plans. This will give you both confidence in handling this new scenario.

Have an emergency plan. Without scaring your child, develop a plan for a few eventualities. What are the most likely emergencies in your area? A power outage? A blizzard? An earthquake? Plan ahead with your child what he should do in these situations. Keep a rechargeable flashlight in an accessible spot. Tell your child that if he thinks of other possible emergency situations, he should tell you so you can brainstorm solutions together.

Keep a list of easy-to-read emergency numbers in an easy-to-reach place. Talk to your child about when it is appropriate to call 911 and when it isn't. Show your child where simple first-aid supplies such as Band-Aids are kept. Store them away from drugs, prescriptions, and other things that are best handled by adults.

Can you be reached at another number? Make sure he has that number. If you can't be reached, is there a family friend or relative whom your child can call to seek advice or just to hear a friendly voice? Call them before you leave to alert them. Leave their numbers near the phone with the emergency numbers. A fairly inexpensive way for your child to reach you wherever you are is to buy a beeper. A cellular phone is a more expensive option, but it does eliminate that step of searching around for a working pay phone.

Make sure your child is occupied while you're gone with a book, a jigsaw puzzle, a TV show. Leave a nutritional snack ready on the kitchen counter or in the refrigerator.

Latchkey children, who come home from school to an empty house and stay there without supervision until a parent gets home, need some sense of routine to their late afternoons: a check-in call, snack, relaxation or playtime, homework, relaxation again. In some areas, students can call homework lines by phone or modem if they need help.

Don't underestimate the time you'll be gone. If you're gone a minute longer than you planned, your child may start to shift into high-gear anxiety. If a typical trip to the supermarket takes thirty minutes, estimate forty-five minutes so you won't be late. If you call home right before you leave work, prepare your child for delays due to traffic, missed trains, or the weather.

Do you want your child to answer the phone or the door when he's alone? Depending on your circumstances, answering the door may or may not be a problem. In many neighborhoods the most frequent knockers are solicitors, and you probably won't want them knowing your child is alone. It might be better for your child to ignore the knock. If it's a friend or neighbor, the friend or neighbor can shout to make herself known, and then your child can let her in. Set up plans that work for you.

Work out a phone plan. When a child answers the phone, he probably doesn't want the caller to know he's alone anymore than you do. It may be hard for him to think on his feet, so rehearse a standard answer, such as "My mom's in the shower" or "My dad's in the bathroom." Have him offer to take a message for you.

If you have an answering machine, it might work well to instruct your child not to answer the phone when it rings but to screen the messages as they're being left. If it's you, checking in, he can pick up the phone at that point and talk. Anyone else can leave a message on the tape.

Think also about your outgoing recording. If it refers to your absence ("We're not home now . . ."), it might make your child uncomfortable. While adults don't necessarily take such references literally, children might. A message such as "We can't come to the phone right now" might sound more reassuring to young ears.

Ask your immediate neighbors if it's all right for your child to come to them if there's a problem and you're not home. You might also want to leave them some emergency numbers to keep on hand. Check with them every time you leave your child alone. This helps to reaffirm the plan, as well as allowing you to see if they will be home.

Once you've discussed this plan of action with your neighbors, discuss it again with your child present. Children are often hesitant to cause a scene or ask for help, even in a dangerous situation. They can be shy and self-conscious, even when they're scared. Telling some children that they should go next door if they have a problem may not be enough. Take the time to walk over with your son so he can hear your neighbor say she wants him to come to her if he has any concerns.

Follow the same process with phone numbers. After you set up a plan with friends or relatives, have them speak directly with your child, either in person or on the phone, to reinforce their availability. Try a few practice calls before your first "home alone" trial.

Set firm "home alone" rules. Can your child go outside? What appliances can he use? Can he turn on the stove? The microwave? Take a shower? Take the dog for a walk? If a friend comes over to play, can he let him in? If he can, what are the rules then?

After you and your child practice with a few short home-alone experiences, you'll get a sense of what both of you are comfortable with. Be sensitive to any indications that she is being brave just to please you. She may not be ready. You may not be ready. Wait a while and try again. Believe it or not, the day will come when she'll love it when you go out for a while.

Many parents find that leaving one child home alone is much, much easier than leaving two children. Or three. The consequences are frightening as the number of children increases. The opportunity for teasing, taunting, hitting, and worse, without parents nearby to intervene or play witness, can make parents very uneasy about the whole situation.

A few areas need discussing at these siblings-alone times:

Who's in charge? Define, quite specifically, in front of all siblings, what being "in charge" means and doesn't mean. What are the rules? Who gets to hold the remote? For how long? Who gets dibs on video games? Ask for input on the rules that need clarifying before you leave.

If there is a problem between your children, have them write down their versions of what happened for you to read when you get home (writing should keep them quiet for a while). Sometimes an older child is left with a much younger sibling, who is not able to write (or write well) yet. That child can express the situation by drawing a picture and explaining it later.

Know your children. Be realistic about how they interact. Certain ages and dynamics are more combustible than others.

Childhood Friendships

Working parents have much less time to observe and nurture their children's friendships. The bosom buddies your kids make in preschool and beyond may not be weekend friends as well, so you may not know this person at all whom your child adores so much.

Children in child care spend a lot of time with their daytime friends, perhaps more than they would if they were at home and playing in the neighborhood. The relationships there can be intense and volatile, even with toddlers. A good day can mean a fun day with their best friend. A bad day may mean the two didn't get along.

There are ways parents can get to know these friends through their children's eyes. Encourage your child to talk about his child-care friends. Have him point them out to you when you drop him off and pick him up. Say hello. Chat a little.

The Importance of Friendship in Childhood

Even if a child has the two best parents in the whole world, three close-in-age siblings, four attentive aunts, five fun cousins, six swell uncles, seven Nintendo games, and a big backyard, he still needs friends. A special friend. And others.

Through friendships, children learn how to deal with different types of people, setting the stage for a well-balanced adult life. At all ages, friendships are a source of emotional strength.

Friendless children can become friendless adults. They may never learn how to be a friend or how to make one. They may feel a sense of living life on the periphery, of looking through the window at the party inside. Of being left out. These are strong statements, yes, and ones that may cause a feeling of anxiety in some working parents, who may have had their own difficulties with friendships in the past. Of course, if this is the case, there's all the more reason to talk about the roots of friendship. Working parents who have limits on their free time need to put a priority on friendship-making skills.

As a culture, we value friendship. We feel that strong, warm relationships make life richer. As a result, we like to see outgoing children who play easily with others. We often wish that introverted children would be more outgoing . . . more friendly. This is simply a cultural ideal in this country.

In examining the role of friendship in life, it is important to differentiate between friendship and popularity. We aren't talking about *how many friends a child has but the ability to make them.* For some children, one best friend is sustenance enough; others need to have a group of friends.

In helping children to build enriching friendships, parents must examine their own histories, their children's temperaments, needs, and skills, and the opportunities for friendship in their young lives.

Most people find some measure of contentment and stimulation in solitary pursuits, such as reading, working, or playing at the computer, and tinkering on projects. While these activities can be rewarding for everyone, they can also be a refuge for those who've never learn how to develop close relationships with other people. Reading (or computerizing) should be one choice on a full activity plate, rather than the only dish.

Babies have friendships much earlier than most people would suppose. Caregivers who work with the youngest age group witness the development of friendships very clearly. A baby responds to seeing and hearing another baby and often seems to miss that friend when he's not around. Special friendships develop between two babies that are different from the relationships that each have with the other babies in the nursery. They send off nonverbal cues that are very clear to those who tune in.

How do you know if your child has enough friends? Even a child with several strong friendships will say "nobody likes me" on a bad day. You may worry when you see that your child isn't finding instant friends on a playground of strangers on a Saturday afternoon, but she may nurture friendships slowly, and productively, in school. And some children have such volatile friendships that they genuinely feel bereft after a heated spat at recess.

Don't just rely on the information your child tells you. Watch for clues. Has your child mentioned the names of friends or does she only talk about solitary experiences in school? Parents can pick up these clues by observing their children with their peers in a relaxed setting. There's a lot to be learned by staying through the birthday party, dropping by in the middle of Sunday school, or walking or driving by the schoolyard on your lunch hour. End-of-the-day observations at child care may not be as revealing, or on the mark, as ones made midactivity. Ask caregivers and teachers about your child's friendships. They should be able to tell you if and when there are difficulties. A perceptive caregiver or classroom teacher will be able to notice areas that need working on: for instance, maybe your daughter is too quick-tempered or your son is withdrawn. She may also have helpful ideas to improve the situation.

One of the major tasks of the preschool years is to learn how to make friends and how to be one. There are, even at this young age, many elements to friendship, including genuinely liking another person, showing yourself in a favorable light so that person will return the feeling, and discovering which actions, attitudes, and words "work" and which don't. The ability to form friendships comes from a sensitivity to others and a willingness to share, whether it's toys or feelings.

Strong friendships in childhood are, in many ways, preparation for intimacy in long-term relationships and partnerships in adulthood. They are the foundation that teaches people to share, to care, and to support another person. They teach that relationships change from day to day, that it is beneficial to get away from someone for a while and then want to be together again, that it is possible to have a disagreement, flare up with feelings of hate, and then calm down. And still be friends. And still be married.

A lack of friends can be caused by such things as little opportunity, fear of rejection, or problems with social skills. Friendships formed during preschool or school hours are traditionally cemented with after-school get-togethers. However, many of today's children do not go to neighborhood schools, or they live where there are few children to play with after school or on weekends. Working parents do not have the time that stay-at-home parents do to help their children's friendships blossom. For today's children, who may not have many traditional connections, strong friendships, while not impossible, are harder to develop. They take more of an effort, often on the parents' part.

It is important for children to see how adult friendships are conducted. Parents can facilitate this by inviting friends over to visit, instead of just seeing them at work or in restaurants. They can talk about their own friends to their children, discuss why they like the people they do and what they have in common.

Parents can demonstrate how friendships begin: "I met a very nice woman at work today. It turns out she collects stamps, too. I think I'll invite her over for coffee next Saturday. It might be nice to be friends with her."

Children who have naturally absorbed the lesson that a little joking can be fun have a much easier time socially. It helps to be able to accept playful (rather than mean-spirited) teasing. Children who don't know how to joke may need a little help to recognize the positive aspects of teasing and to develop ways to cope with it. When one child calls another child a "baby," the teased child may be devastated. He may withdraw and cry, turning a relatively minor taunt into a major incident. Parents can help head off such situations by role playing beforehand. There are two ways to approach this. Sometimes the best response is for the teased child to speak from the heart: "That really hurt my feelings." This response may, of course, simply tell the teaser that she has hit her mark. Sometimes a child needs to be prepared with a quick retort that can be put into action almost as a reflex, before the hurt sets in. For instance, a child can easily deflect this kind of teasing with a comment like "If I'm a baby, so are you."

Children can be taught to pick up clues on how their own comments are received. Parents can help teach what facial expressions and body language mean by commenting on television and movie characters and pictures in books and magazines. They can discuss with their children how they might have reacted differently after an incident that seemed to drive another child away. Try, "Zachary doesn't like that. You can see by his face."

Children can make friends and then lose them. A best friend, someone a child has invested a great deal in emotionally, may move far away, leaving a deep sense of loss. Or your family might be the one to move. Some children protect themselves from being hurt again by such circumstances by not forming another close friendship. Parents need to acknowledge this loss and perhaps share similar losses from their own childhoods. They can talk about life as a backdrop for a series of best friends. Parents should also recognize that the fear of being rejected may be another factor that keeps children from making or responding to overtures of friendship.

Of course, there is a difference between forcing friendships on children and giving them ways to develop. Parents can suggest sleep-overs and outings with other children and create a warm, friendly environment during these get-togethers so that new friends will be eager to return.

Parents can't make friends for their children. But they can show them how to be a friend and to provide opportunities for cultivating friendships.

Three's a Crowd—or at Least Difficult

Does this sound familiar? Your five-year-old, Sam, invites his cousin, Josh, who's also five, to play in his room on a Saturday morning. Tommy, your son's best friend down the block, calls and asks to come over. His mom gets on the phone and says she's got to run a few errands. Suddenly the quiet twosome has become a raucous, contentious threesome.

Sam and Josh can play quietly together for hours. But when Tommy enters the picture, all hell breaks loose. The three go into Sam's room and in a few minutes, they are fighting, yelling, screaming. Sam and Josh gang up on Tommy. Josh and Tommy gang up on Sam. Sam and Tommy gang up on Josh. Or maybe one child remains on the outside for the whole morning. The dynamics of the threesome can be overwhelming to a young child just developing social skills.

A child who is sought after by two friends one minute can feel shut out from their attention the next. Sometimes it's the newcomer who is the center of attention. Two old friends compete for the new arrival's favor. "She likes me better." "No, she likes me better." A child can sense the sudden power she has and exploit the situation to her advantage. Such situations become a test of manipulation skills rather than a chance to play with two friends equally: *Can I get Yolanda to like me better? Can I get Sarah to turn on Anita? Just how powerful am I?* Threesomes give a child a chance to find out.

There are strategies that parents can use to diffuse these types of problems. Before a threesome sets out on a morning of play, parents can set the stage for increased harmony. In general, whenever three children play together, you should be alert to any signs of power-tripping and hurt feelings.

Older preschoolers and school-age children can understand when you talk about the possibilities of problems arising. "You and Tommy play together every day, and you've learned a lot of little fun things to do together. So when your cousin comes over, and you haven't seen him for a few months, he doesn't know the things that you and Tommy do. So he feels a little left out. It would make him feel better if you and Tommy showed him what you like to play." Ask your child to remember times he has felt like the odd child out.

Talk up the third child's assets. "Aunt Linda was telling me how Josh is getting very good at dominoes. Maybe he can show you and Tommy how to play." Having both friends arrive at the same time also helps to equalize the situation. The later arrival won't feel like he has to break into an already tight circle.

After they arrive, ask all three children to suggest what they'd like to do. Put out some Play-Doh at a table with three chairs. Or start off the get-together by doing something that gets everyone working and playing alongside one another. Have the threesome baking cookies, with each child getting an equal turn at stirring or dropping spoonfuls of dough on the baking sheet. Taking the threesome for a walk can (literally) put them on equal footing, as well as expend some of the boundless energy.

Encourage games that three children can play at the same time. Games such as checkers and two-person video games put the third child in the difficult position of demanding her turn. Chutes and Ladders or Monopoly work better. Or suggest a jigsaw puzzle, so each child can fit separate pieces into it.

If you're transporting three children in your car and plan to put them all in the backseat, oversee the seating arrangement. Put the newcomer in the middle. Otherwise, the two old friends may play and giggle together, while the newcomer sits to one side, gazing out the window and feeling left out.

There are some threesomes in which the chemistry just isn't working. And it probably will never work. In such a situation, it might be easier to avoid putting that combination of children together for an afternoon. If you find yourself with a threesome that just doesn't seem to respond to all your efforts to make playtime pleasant, the only solution seems to be to separate the three for individual play (such as coloring, Play-Doh sculpting) until one of the children is picked up.

Promoting Creativity

Supermom would make cranberry and orange muffins from scratch, set up fingerpainting at the kitchen table, help kids make all their own holiday gifts, play the piccolo, write haiku, and read the *New York Times* every morning.

But real moms doing all this? Yeah, sure. So how do you promote creative opportunities with such limited time, especially when much of your creative energy goes into dealing with work issues?

One of the most important things to consider about creativity is that it's not only for children identified as gifted or talented. A creative approach enriches *every* child's life and every day of that child's life. It goes far beyond arts and crafts projects or being able to write a poem.

There's creative potential in an eye-opening walk in the neighborhood in the early evening, playing thought-provoking waiting games, and keeping journals. Creativity is the approach—not the activity itself.

Don't ask yourself if your child is creative. All children are creative to some degree, and they can all benefit from an environment in which creativity is encouraged. Instead, ask yourself how you can create an atmosphere where this creative approach to life can flourish.

Yes, some children do have special gifts. They're born to play the piano or soccer or draw. But all children do—and need to do—creative things. Some experts feel creativity issues should be framed not around how to be creative with kids, but around how not to stifle the creativity that's already there.

Creativity thrives when children are allowed to be spontaneous, messy, and silly. It requires a spirit of playfulness. A creative family environment is one in which ideas are tossed about, unconventional responses are taken seriously, and the emphasis is more on the process than a slick product.

Experts in the field say that there are two criteria for judging whether a child is being creative: novelty and appropriateness. Are you noticing behavior that is substantially different from what your child has done, heard, or seen before? A child who plays with her shoelaces in endless experimentation and finds ways to tie them is being creative—even if she doesn't discover a way to keep them tied.

Babies are very creative. Every baby reinvents the world as the beginning of lifelong learning. You only need to continue nurturing this creativity as your child grows older.

A creative family is one in which it's okay to be inventive and have original interpretations of the world. Children from such families are respected as individuals, and the emphasis is on moral values rather than specific rules. Flexibility is the key. Within this family, there is a lot of activity, playfulness, and fantasy. New ideas are encouraged.

Some efforts may backfire, however. Rewarding or bribing a child for creative acts, for example, is the surest way to stifle creative expression. In research tests, when children were asked to come up with imaginative approaches to problems, such as how to get a teacher's attention, groups that were encouraged with positive reinforcement came up with significantly more inventive ways than those in groups who were promised specific prizes for their efforts.

Parents can destroy creativity by using coercion to achieve it or by evaluating ideas or projects too soon or too often. Making the creative process competitive or limiting choices, such as insisting that the trees be green when a child picks up the purple crayon, can kill creativity.

Creativity can be about turning a child loose in an arts and crafts store with a set budget and encouraging him to come up with supplies to make things. Such a strategy is much better than presenting that child with parent-selected supplies. Other projects that expand creative thinking include finding new ideas for food preparation, flower arranging, even something like inventing new clapping patterns. Throw new light on favorite old toys by encouraging different ways to play with them. Too often, parents inhibit creative play by instructing kids on the "proper method" of playing with each toy.

Creativity can be incorporated into everyday activities. If you and your child are waiting at an airport or train station, make up stories about the people around you (carefully, quietly, and with no pointing, of course). Imagine who they are and what their plans are. Is one a rock star? Another, a spy? Invent names for other diners in a McDonald's, like Mr. Brownsuit or Miss Giggles.

Even a walk around the block presents opportunities for creative expansion. Imagine who lives in the different houses. Or count the cats. Or rate the houses on their plants or paint colors. Look for the largest puddle after a rainstorm. Pick the home you'd most like to live in. Let your child pick a category for discussion.

Allowing children the freedom to be messy can be hard for many parents, but it is useful to save as much cleanup as possible for the end rather than tidying up during the activity. The clean-as-you-go method may work for adults, but it distracts from the creative process and gives the wrong message about what's important. Also, imaginative projects blossom more in open spaces than in crowded corners. Clear off tables or set up temporary ones that allow plenty of elbow room.

The first step to imaginative exploration can be simple: turn off the TV. Yes, some creativity can be fostered in front of the television (such as discussions of who the characters remind you of in real life and how you would have handled a similar situation), but most creativity begins when the set goes off.

Instead of simply offering a project to a child (for instance, handing her crayons and paper and them going off to read a report or do the dishes), show your interest by sticking around for a while.

Brainstorming—such a popular technique in work meetings—is also a valuable tool for developing creativity in kids. Ask your child how many ways he can think of to decorate his bedroom door. Start him off. Suggest balloons, candy wrappers, pogs, pictures of skateboarders. Encourage the wild flights-of-fancy ideas that could never be, such as sticking on marshmallows. Get silly.

Whenever my daughter and I would have discussions about up-coming birthday and holiday gifts, she would mention crazy things she knew she could never have. Like her own horse, even though we live in an apartment. I wanted her to stick to things that we could realistically buy her. It made me uncomfortable when she'd say she wished she could have her own pony and a stable and that kind of stuff. I felt I had to say that we couldn't af-ford it. But she knew that. Then I realized that she was just dreaming, like adults do about winning the lottery. It was fun. It was a great escape for her from her everyday work. So when she'd talk about wanting a horse, I went along with the dream. I'd say things like, "Yeah, wouldn't it be great to come home from school and ride every day?" She loved it. Later, when my younger child would say he wanted crazy things like a motorcycle for his seventh birthday, I didn't remind him that he was too young to drive. We talked about how fast he could go and where he would ride and how all his friends would want to ride on the back.

Parents who are independent and active and who seek creative solutions in their own lives are a great source of inspiration to their children. Creativity flourishes around role models. So next time you're stuck in rush-hour traffic, imagine how many ways you could decorate the hood of your car.

eleven

Time Off: Holidays and Vacations

IT'S not true that you stop having vacations and holidays when you have children; it's just that everything takes more planning. Do enough planning, and you may recover that sense of fun time that may seem like a casualty of parenting.

Holiday Child Care

The word *holiday* takes on new meaning for working parents. Whether it's winter or spring break or all those other days off, it can seem like every time you turn around, there's another day when school, preschool, or your caregiver is handing child-care responsibilities back to you. A few strategies:

Get information on child-care alternatives early. Sign up early. Pay up early.

Ask at your child's school or day-care provider if they know of any care that will be available when they are closed.

Check local community organizations (the YM/YWCA, YM/YWHA, Jewish community centers, boys' clubs, girls' clubs, recreation centers, church and temple groups). Some offer programs only on holidays, while others expand their daily program to full days when school is out.

Talk with other parents who are in the same proverbial boat. Ask them what they are doing for child care over the break. Maybe they are floundering, too, and together you can work out a plan, such as splitting the days up.

Some child-care centers will take school-age children on holidays or school breaks.

Local day camps and recreation camps may be open for holiday child care.

A visiting relative might be willing to take on some child care.

If your in-home caregiver wants holiday time off, perhaps another family has the same situation and some doubling up is in order. Your nanny might take both children for one week at your house, then switch off with the other nanny.

Put up a sign on the company bulletin board asking for child-care assistance: "I've got two children, ages three and seven, who need care during spring break. Any suggestions? Call Dot, ext. 123." You might get referrals for caregivers. You might find other families in the same predicament.

If a family you know is going away for the holiday, their nanny might be available.

Hire a high school or college student. They're probably on the same holiday or vacation schedule and need money.

Depending on your neighborhood, check with local school employment offices or put up a notice on community bulletin boards.

Hire a caregiver from an agency. This option will probably be more expensive than your usual care, but joining forces with one or two other families can help cut costs.

Managing the Holidays

For most families, December is a time to shift into high gear. From Thanksgiving until school begins again in January, it seems like it's life in the fast lane: speeded up, stressed out, hyped up, and not at all like you remember it was when you were a child. For working parents who still have a nine-to-five obligation to meet during this time, the holidays can be a dreadful season.

Parents and children can develop some incredibly high expectations for the season. Children get revved up by a supersaturation of commercialism on television and visions of an entire Toys "R" Us store wrapped up just for them. Parents, meanwhile, tap into a sentimental longing for life as it used to be, encouraged by endless reruns of *It's a Wonderful Life* on television. Reality check: You can't go home again, and hardly anybody gets the whole toy store. It can feel, on a bad day, like holiday fun is for everyone else. Another reality check occurs when you realize the full extent of the extra work of the holidays, on top of office work. To get a grip on the situation, take a long, hard look at the holiday season before it begins. What do you love about the holidays? What do you hate? Are there things that could be eliminated or at least fine-tuned? What hasn't worked in the past? What are your real needs and wants?

You *can* make meaningful changes in how your family celebrates the holidays. If you are a new parent, taking time to think about the holiday ahead can get your family off on the right foot for years to come. Make a master calendar for the entire holiday period. (Thanksgiving to early January). Use the same calendar we've suggested to plan one-day, school-holiday child care in Chapter 5. Make it a big family project. Each day should be represented by a big enough box so that several items can be written on it.

Then, working together as a family, make a list of everything that needs to get done. Be realistic. Do you need two nights at the mall to get your shopping done—or six? Write it down. A night to bake cookies. A night to wrap presents.

Fill in your master family calendar with everything you need to do. The day you'll buy the Christmas tree, or candles for the menorah at a temple crafts fair. When you'll get the tinsel and decorations down from the attic. Greeting cards. Postage stamps. And when you'll address and stamp the cards. When you'll buy presents for your boss and coworkers and your child's teacher.

The most important part of the calendar is to see that chores (a.k.a. "assignments") are evenly distributed. Everyone should have some responsibilities and consider the calendar a contract.

If the idea of a calendar seems too ambitious for your family, scale down the concept until it's workable. Maybe all you need is a list, with every item prioritized or assigned and posted in the kitchen.

Plan your store shopping like Ike mapping D-Day. You may decide to start well before Thanksgiving. First case the toy stores for ideas. Go through catalogs. Write down names of toys you think your children would like, so that when friends and relatives ask for suggestions, you've got the answers ready. Take advantage of extended holiday shopping hours. Do stores open on Sundays at ten o'clock? Stay open Saturday nights until nine? Many toy stores open at eight in the morning and stay open until midnight!

Early in December, make double batches when you cook dinner. Make two meat loaves and freeze one for use two weeks down the line. Two lasagnas. Two quarts of spaghetti sauce. A gallon of minestrone soup. Then, on those weekdays when you stop to do a little shopping after work, a home-cooked meal is just a zap away.

Children are just beginning to form their own beliefs and understand family traditions. Around holiday time, these issues can come to a head. When parents feel strongly about who they are—and it's different from the mainstream in their community—children need support in understanding why certain choices have been made. This is especially true if your children attend a mainstream school. Put yourself in your children's shoes and try to understand the conflicts they are feeling. Until you do, you will not be able to help them grasp the issues involved.

My husband and I had discussions before we had kids on how we wanted to celebrate the holidays—as little as possible. But it seems that we are frequently compromising. The simplicity we envisioned is harder and harder to maintain. A friend suggested that our two families rent a cabin for the week before Christmas and get away from all the pressure. We've done it for four winters. We've established our own family rituals.

Family Get-Togethers

Holidays with the family take on a new dimension once you have children. You may be seen in a new, more favorable light now that you've finally proven yourself to be more than a footloose member of the clan. Now you're adding to the family tree. If you're the first to have a child or the only one with a young child, everyone will have opinions on your parenting skills.

Children, in their unvarnished, unedited reality, can be a bit of a shock to the uninitiated—all that energy, picky eating, crying, demands for attention in the middle of adult sentences. It's just normal kid stuff to you, but to someone accustomed to a quieter, more controllable lifestyle, it's exhausting and overwhelming.

Let's assume in this discussion that your children's behavior is typical for their ages. Try viewing the tensions as a clash of cultures. You're the U.N. mediator whose mission it is to explain the attitudes of the two sides and find something both can live with.

Before the holidays begin, talk with any problematic relatives about upcoming family visits. Acknowledge the tensions of the past. Enlist their help in making this year better, particularly more relaxing and more fun. Ask them to tell you frankly what makes them edgy. Are they worried about things getting broken? Perhaps they can put away the more precious items before you arrive. Explain that their antique doll collection is just too much of a temptation for any two-year-old, and the only way to handle the situation is to put the dolls out of sight. Remind them that it won't always be like this. Your child is simply too young now.

Dinners at grandparents can be filled with tensions that evolve from different ideas on how your children are being reared. Your in-laws may be indulgent or they may seem too strict. Either way, you may feel that they are being judgmental of your kids at these holiday meals, and that reflects on your parenting abilities.

Children need to understand that whoever lives in a house makes the general rules of that house. They must abide by their aunt's or grandparents' rules when they are in those respective homes. Explain to them what those rules are. Tell them that your sister isn't used to having children around her house. Of course, you can't explain this to very young children—the ones who are most in need of a rational talking-to (alternate solution: have the dinner at your house).

The noise children make can be difficult for people used to tranquillity. One of the lessons of childhood is learning to modulate your voice (of course, there are plenty of adults out there who seemed to have missed learning this essential social skill). Tell your children beforehand about the need to keep the noise level down. Develop a signal you can use to remind them they are getting too loud. Make it funny, like a pull on your left ear followed by a wiggle of your nose, but explain that you mean business.

If the noise is partially a result of pent-up energy, get the energy out before you arrive. Plan an invigorating walk, a trip to the park, or a game of catch before you leave home. Save naptime for when you get to your dinner destination.

In many families, these holiday visits can last from early in the day to late at night. If your family favors extended visits, it's essential to plan some activity to break up the time indoors. Taking your children for a walk in the middle of the visit will not only expend energy, it will also give you time to be alone, just you and them. In the midst of a difficult day, that can be a safety valve for everyone. Tell your relatives about this plan soon after you arrive, so you can work out the timing together.

If your children's table manners are questioned, question them yourself. What's at issue—is it mainly a matter of development, such as the inability to master a fork yet? If so, explain that to your relatives. Perhaps they don't realize that three-year-olds cannot handle a fork well. The fine motor stuff just isn't there yet. On the other hand, there may be areas you can work on. Practice table manners at home, with special family meals during which everyone shows off their best manners. Explain to your children that special meals call for customs that everyday meals at the kitchen table don't require. For example, during kitchen dinners at home, it may be fine for kids to start eating before everyone has settled at the table. But at special meals, everyone begins together. And sympathize a little. These new customs are difficult to master.

Ask your children what bothers them about these get-togethers. Likely answers include "I have to sit at the table forever." "It's boring." "There's nobody to play with." "There's nothing to do." "Nobody talks to me." The complaints aren't usually about not being able to be noisy or having to wipe their mouths, because those are areas of negotiation. What they want, usually, is something to do, some attention, and not to be forced to sit upright for three hours.

You can provide your children with something to do if you take special toys and games from home or if your relatives keep some toys in a box or a closet (of course, these toys should change as they grow). You might want to make a gift to your relatives of a few games, so you'll be sure they'll be suitable for your children's ages and interests. Take along games you can play with your kids while also conversing in a reasonably adult manner with the grown-ups. Try pickup sticks or start a jigsaw puzzle on a card table. Pack a special video that's one of your children's favorites. And, most important, include children in some of the conversation.

When television viewing is a bone of contention as when your children want to shut themselves in the den all day, coming out to spend five minutes at the dinner table, make an agreement beforehand. Set limits on how much they can watch TV (or listen to Walkmans) and how long you expect them to stay at the table.

Involve your children in recording these holiday get-togethers. Take nonmessy art supplies and set them up on the coffee table, making sure you protect the surface with plastic sheeting, or on a card table, so they can draw everyone around them. Older children can take photos (Polaroids are great) or use video cameras. Not only do such projects keep them busy, but they also create a record of the event to share in the years ahead.

Finally, realize that part of your children's attitude depends on how you approach these get-togethers yourself. Children may pick up the idea that you're not so keen on the idea from conversations you have in front of them, resulting in less-than-perfect behavior once you're there.

Ideas for Summer Camp

Most working parents work summers. But once they start kindergarten, children have ten weeks of free time from June to August. Fun for kids. Desperation time for parents who must find child care for those days.

We've gone through a number of suggestions for occupying school-age children during the holiday schedule, but another option you might consider is day camp. Older children can stay home, probably unsupervised, although of course this becomes a source of stress for most parents. A third alternative is a mix of day camp, sleep-away camp, family vacation, and a week or two at relatives' homes.

Full-time day camp is an "easy" (but often expensive) solution. Go through local magazines, the Yellow Pages, or the American Camping Association, and *voilà!*: you've got plenty of possibilities to check out. Pick wisely to be sure that your child will be safe, comfortable, and stimulated.

Parents can be easily dazzled by a swimming pool or other fancy equipment, such as jet skis or state-of-the-art computers. Even an elaborate playground can capture a parent's attention. More important than fancy monkey bars, though, just as with child care, is the camp's philosophy and the people involved.

Here are a few topics to discuss with the director of the program:

What are the philosophy and values of the program? Some are more competitive in approach, while others avoid competitive sports, preferring to stress cooperation.

How many children are in the camp, and in your child's group? What are their ages?

What are the qualifications, experience, and special skills of the director and counselors?

Is it possible to change counselors if it turns out not to be a good match?

How will children be transported during the day; who are the drivers?

What kind of insurance do they have?

How is discipline handled?

If your child has a problem in a specific area (not good at tennis, doesn't make new friends easily), will the staff be able to deal with this on a caring and individual basis?

Will there be an opportunity to discuss your child's experiences with the counselor during the summer?

What is a typical week's schedule; will there be written schedules in advance? Is one activity emphasized? Is the day spent in a "home" park or camp headquarters or moving around the city? Some camps have permanent sites, while others float.

Are children allowed to choose activities? Is there free time?

Are lunches and snacks provided?

Is extended care available? Will the hours meet your work needs?

What are their emergency procedures?

The goal in choosing a camp is the same as in selecting child care or a school: finding the right match for your child. Whatever camp you select, it will be costly, one you might not even be able to afford for an entire summer. Also, some children find a highly structured day camp's schedule so much like school that they don't get a chance to really relax, which is the purpose of summer vacation anyway. You may decide to break up the summer and supplement the organized camp—whether it's day camp or sleep-away camp—with a homier change of pace.

We offer suggestions for two alternative camps. In one, parents become rotating counselors-for-a-week themselves. The other is run by someone hired by parents to be a counselor/teacher/guide/driver for the summer. As with more traditional camps, these situations are most suitable for children postkindergarten and older. Both work best for small groups (five or six children). Limiting the number that can safely fit into one car or van (if one is available) will expand the potential activities offered by the camp.

Depending on the needs of the parents involved, these camps can be organized to fill the entire summer or just a few weeks. Both offer a more relaxed approach, such as flexible schedules, last-minute changes, and time to relax and do nothing special at all. They combine the stimulation of camp with the relaxation of home, all while offering supervision. And of course both parent-led and parent-sponsored camps work best when the parents involved know one another in advance and share common values.

Parent-Led Camp

While parent-led camp is free (at least in terms of money), it calls for several families that can each offer their time for an agreed-upon number of days. For example, six families may decide to hold camp for six weeks in the summer. Each family is required to host camp at home and supervise for one week. This means that working parents must be able to take five days off from work, which may call for fancy footwork. You may take a week's vacation time, use up overtime, or take personal days. Two-parent families may be able to split up the week.

When it's your week, it will be one of the longest weeks of your life. The other five weeks are pure gravy. The advantage of parent-led day camp, beyond financial, is that children are able to enjoy leisurely days at their own homes and at those of their friends—a welcome change from highly structured days in formal camps. Schedules will probably vary with the creativity and energy of the hosting parent. There will be lively times and laid-back times. Maybe more television than you'd like. Maybe more trips to the park and library than you've been able to manage on your own. As a group, parents may decide to invest in a few items that can be moved from home to home over the course of the summer, such as water toys, art supplies, and puzzles. Sometimes, the host child can have difficulty sharing toys with so many friends at once. This scenario can, if handled gingerly, be a good learning experience.

Each parent brings his or her talents to camp, making it an opportunity for children to learn about things outside the world of their own families. One parent might turn the week into a cooking class, with campers making breakfast, lunch, and even snacks to take home and share. Another with a garage workshop might plan building activities. A third might decide to show the children a variety of museums and plan a different excursion every day. Parents should be encouraged to draw on their strengths and plan the week much as a teacher would.

I am an architect. I used a week of accumulated time to take my turn as counselor Mom for neighborhood summer camp. We had camp for five weeks, from the last day of school through July, for my son and four other kids, all second and third graders. I had a great deal of trepidation, because we live in an apartment with no balcony, no yard. I planned a major activity that took up much of the week. *The kids would make a three-dimensional model of the buildings on our street. They didn't build full houses—just facades that we glued onto a Fome-Cor [laminated panel] board, colored to look like our street.*

The first day, I talked to them about the project, and we took a walk around the block, talking about the buildings. The kids were trying to pick ones they wanted to include. There were a couple of front steps on the street where we gathered with our sketch pads to draw the buildings they chose. They were trying to make visual notes to expand on later.

The next day, we took a refresher tour of the block and then got to work at the dining room table. We worked together to decide on how big the buildings should be. I made them do preliminary sketches—no finished products allowed—varying the details each time. They added shutters where they thought facades needed them, changed colors. It gave me a chance to talk about artistic license. One boy put man-eating plants around his building, because the block's mean-old-man Leon lived there. Then I talked about how art is used for political statements.

The last two days, the kids were working on their final drawings, on heavy paper with markers. We then glued them in place for the parents to see when they picked up the kids on Friday after work. Afterward, I dismantled the street and gave the families their children's contributions.

I think the project was a great success and one most parents could do. We had a purpose to our trips in the neighborhood. The kids really thought about what was on the block and about the nature of art in a way that no lecturing could ever match.

To run smoothly, all participating parents should meet beforehand to plan the camp. Important issues to discuss include assigning weeks, setting hours, deciding how to handle food and drinks and emergencies. It's usually easiest if the children bring their own food, with host parents providing drinks. A well-run parent-led camp depends, in large part, on not taking advantage of the other parents. This means adhering to drop-off and pickup times.

Hiring Your Own Counselor

The other alternative is to hire a counselor and create your own camp. If there are several families who need summer-long child care, this option can be less expensive than regular camp.

There are many issues to be decided in a parent-sponsored camp. First, how many children? Answer: only as many as one counselor can safely and effectively handle. Four to six children is a good range, enough to make it financially feasible. If you're planning field trips to the beach, museums, and parks, you'll need to match up the number of kids with seat belts in one car or van. Check into insurance before you set out, and don't overlook the driving status of your counselor. A skilled counselor should also be able to handle five or six children on public transportation.

Hiring the right counselor is the most important consideration. Look for someone who is responsible and will make a firm commitment for the entire time period, who has experience working with children, and will be comfortable with six children all day and no fellow counselors for company. Start your search at local Ys, and put out the word that you're hiring for a full-time summer job. Try ads in local college newspapers and campus employment offices. Or look for a school teacher who needs extra money over the summer.

Interviews for likely candidates should be conducted by at least one parent from each family for an informal discussion on the interviewee's attitudes. Ask about background, special skills, how he or she would deal with difficult situations (name calling, hitting, too much noise in the car or bus). Will his or her interests dovetail with those of the children (swimming, art, computers)?

We have a very good after-school care program in our local school district, with many excellent teachers. They run a summer program on the school sites, but several of the parents were not thrilled with the idea of having their children at the same place year-round. The kids needed a break from the same four walls! So since the summer program uses fewer teachers than the year-round one, some teachers are on vacation, too. Five families got together, and we decided to approach one of the teachers whom we knew would be out of work during the summer. We asked her to help us put together our own informal camp for our kids. She loved the idea. The kids already knew her, and we knew how great she was with them. She knew just what they wanted to do. One of her best ideas was to use community resources. For example, she'd take the kids to the story time at the library, and when the parks department had a big outing to a water park, she signed up the kids. But most important was the time they spent as a group.

Issues that need to be agreed upon up front include workdays, holidays off, hours, salary, and deductions. Outline the responsibilities of the counselor and parents. A written contract or agreement should be drawn up. This needn't be a highly legalistic document, but it helps to have major issues worked out in advance, written down, and signed by all parties. It's crucial to have a contingency plan if one family drops out during the summer. Such a child-care arrangement—lasting only the duration of school vacation—falls into a gray area with regard to most state child-care licensing regulations, as there are exemptions in many codes for the June-to-September period.

Together, parents and children should prepare a list of potential summer activities. The counselor should also feel free to suggest places to go and things to do. Devise a schedule with flexibility in mind. If a trip to the museum, planned for two hours, turns out to be such a hit that everyone wants to stay another hour or two, the counselor should have the authority and initiative to change plans. This type of arrangement, after all, offers just such advantages over a more structured camp that gets everyone back on the bus at a rigidly adhered-to time set the previous March.

The budget for this kind of create-your-own camp includes salary, transportation (gas, insurance, bus fare), arts and craft supplies, sports equipment, museum fees, parking, and snacks. While most parents are probably concerned with keeping costs down, remember that it is important to offer a high enough salary to draw applicants who have skills, dedication, and maturity.

The site for this camp can vary according to the group involved. One group, for example, might decide to rotate the location among the families, while another may decide to use one home, apartment, or backyard exclusively.

Parents and counselor together can work out an emergency plan for fires, earthquakes, floods, and other disasters. Decide in advance where everyone will meet if an evacuation is necessary. Keep enough extra food and water on hand at camp headquarters to see campers through a few days. Review emergency plans with campers the first day.

For both kinds of camps, all involved families should have emergency cards for all children, listing names, ages, parents' work phone numbers, doctors' names and phones, emergency contacts, allergies (both medicine and food), and child's weight (for emergency dosages). Parents should be informed beforehand of all trips away from the home base. Parents should also sign a medical release form, giving permission for medical treatment in case of an emergency.

Family Vacations

Most working parents have a set amount of vacation time each year, usually two or three weeks. There are a lucky few who get the whole summer off or who can manage to take extra time off, but garden-variety working parents must make every day count.

Having a limited amount of time—and probably a limited amount of money—to spend puts a great deal of pressure on parents to have fun. A long weekend away may be more relaxing and lower-keyed than a full-scale vacation.

Staying at the right hotel or motel is a key factor in determining how well a vacation goes. Finding that place involves more than just paying the right price at the right location. When traveling with children, it's all the little things that can turn a merely acceptable place into what can seem like the Motel Paradiso.

The Paradiso, of course, has television, a small refrigerator in the room, a soda machine down the hall, reliable and reasonably priced babysitters, and a convenience store nearby.

Parents may have to make a few phone calls from work to track down the Motel Paradiso where they're headed. Often when you call a toll-free number for a hotel chain, you are connected with a central operator for the entire country. Your questions about a Holiday Inn in San Francisco cannot always be answered with authority by an operator in Denver, who has never seen the place and is working only from a short, written description of the property or a checklist. You may have to call the hotel itself for reliable information. When you get a knowledgeable person on the phone, here are key points to cover:

Sleeping arrangements for children. Ask about extra charges for children sleeping in the same room with parents. Many places do not charge extra, even though it means wheeling in a bed. Will the room be big enough to sleep all of you comfortably? Sometimes the third person's rollaway takes up all the walking space in a room. An on-site staff person can advise you on room size and configuration. Two-room suites can be a great solution for families: they usually have more floor space, as well as the privacy afforded by being able to close off a room. Rooms with upstairs lofts are great fun for kids and appealing to parents because they allow them a private area, often with a sitting room and kitchen.

Cribs. Unless you're bringing your own, ask the hotel to guarantee a crib. In some cases, the motel may have only one or two cribs for the entire place. If so, consider arriving very early in the day to lay claim to one of them. Families traveling by car have a little more latitude than air travelers, because portable cribs, stowed in a trunk, guarantee you a crib every time.

Optimum room location. Request rooms according to your child's age and behavior. When traveling with younger children, specify a room without a balcony. For families with babies and easily distracted toddlers, the best rooms may be the most remote. They're quiet for naps, and there are no activities to lure them until you're ready. With older children, it can be more pleasant to have a room near the pool or Ping-Pong table. As usual, what works for one family may not work for another. Weigh the pros and cons of all the hotel/motel's possibilities and make your requests accordingly. Most places won't guarantee a specific room, but they will note your preference on the reservation. Arrive at check-in time for the best selection. And don't just take what's proffered; ask to see a few rooms, then decide yourself.

Is there a refrigerator in the room? A small one makes snacks, breakfasts, and even full meals an easy and economical proposition. Even a minibar fridge stocked with beer and wine can be restocked for the duration of your stay with your own supplies of milk and orange juice.

Is there a self-serve ice machine? Room-service ice is not good enough. With easy-access ice in plastic containers, you can keep milk and juices cold if your room has no refrigerator. You can also cut expenses if you chill down drinks yourself, rather than running to the coffee shop or poolside bar all the time.

Is there a convenience store nearby? Or better yet, a real market? Can you walk to it or drive to it without dealing with a parking attendant or incurring a charge? What may seem like a prime location in the middle of the city is not practical if you can't run out for diapers, milk, or snacks without making a big deal of it.

Can management help arrange for a babysitter? Some places have a list of nearby residents who sit for their guests on a regular basis. Others know of maids and other employees who are willing to moonlight. Or they may refer you to an agency that has sent sitters to their guests. Ask the price in advance: you don't want to be taken off-guard with a ten-dollar-an-hour fee that some places charge, with the sitter getting less than half.

When my daughter was five, we went with three other families we knew from preschool for a weekend at a mountain resort. We rented two large adjoining suites. We all got along great. The one problem came when I suggested we hire a babysitter and go out to the local dance hall for their Oktoberfest. I called the hotel manager, and he gave me the name of one of the cleaning women who frequently babysits for their guests. One of the families was appalled that I would consider leaving the kids with her. I thought that she was a known entity to the manager and, I was told, had four grown kids of her own. That was enough for me. It was a very messy situation. Finally, we drew straws and two families went out and two stayed home (luckily, we went out). Next time, I'll make sure the issue is agreed upon in advance.

Self-service laundry. Are facilities available on the premises or nearby? Being able to do a load of wash midway through the trip can cut down considerably on the amount of clothes you need to pack.

Other tips. Pack individual serving sizes of packaged foods, like cereal. You wouldn't think of using them at home, but they are a real convenience on the road. Take powdered milk—an acquired taste best acquired before you leave home.

Plain Talk About Plane Travel

With visits to grandparents, summer trips, or family-friendly conventions, planes have plenty of children on board these days. When you're traveling with young children, there are ways to make the flight flow smoothly. Here are a few suggestions:

Fears. If you're nervous about plane travel, you can make your child fearful, too. You may have developed some rituals to distract you and help get you through a flight. Focus on these, rather than showing your fear to your child. And keep in mind all those statistics about airplanes being the safest way to travel.

Seating. There are several schools of thought here. Some parents swear by bulkhead seats, the first row in each section; the obvious advantage is extra room. There's usually more floor space, so it can seem like a mini-playpen. You also don't have to worry about bothering the people in front of you. The disadvantage is that the armrests in bulkhead rows are permanently fixed, making it impossible for children to curl up close to parents or to make a little bed out of two adjoining seats. Additionally, this area can be noisy; people congregate there, and it may be near the flight attendants' work station or the bathrooms. (Reservation agents and travel agents have seating diagrams for all aircraft, so they can tell you where the bulkhead seats are. But keep in mind that there are last-minute substitutions in aircrafts, so double-check before boarding to make sure you're still in a bulkhead row.)

Some parents try to book on flights that are unlikely to be filled up and then request a window and an aisle seat in the same row, hoping no one will be sitting in between. If someone does arrive, you can always offer him the aisle or the window. Who wouldn't take you up on such an offer?

The safest place for young children is in their own seats, not on parents' laps. It's very tempting to take advantage of the kids-under-two-fly-free deals that most airlines offer on domestic flights, but they're risky. For infants and toddlers to be as safe as you are, they should be in car seats fastened in their own plane seats. Airlines permit passengers to carry their own car seats on board, but they must bear a label stating they are approved for plane travel. Most seats made after 1985 are approved by the Federal Aviation Administration but some brands have failed safety seats. The FAA can tell you which brands are currently considered safe. If you go to the airport hoping for a free empty seat to put your child and car seat in and arrive to find the flight fully booked, the airline will stow the seat in the luggage compartment.

Preparing children for flight. When they are old enough to understand, explain the different stages of the flight beforehand: how everyone gets on and into their seats; buckling up; taking off; landing. Let them know that there may be some bumpiness, but it doesn't mean anything is wrong.

What to take. For infants and toddlers, carry on twice the quantity of food, bottles, diapers, acetaminophen, changes of clothing, and so on as you think you'll need. *Twice as much.* You could be sitting in a sealed cabin for two hours before takeoff. Bring warm clothes, even if you're traveling from hot weather to hot weather, as airplane cabins can get very chilly. Take along moist towelettes or a damp washcloth in a plastic bag for quick cleanups. Backpacks (the kind that carry babies and toddlers, not books) have advantages over strollers. They allow parents to keep their hands free, and they can be used for a "stroll" down the aisles during the flight.

Let older children assemble their own carry-on tote bags filled with books, travel games, and personal treasures. Favorite tapes and video games are great for whiling away the in-flight hours (but not during takeoff and landing). You might want to wrap up little surprise gifts (maybe a travel game or new book) to bring out when your child starts to get whiny.

Food. Many airlines offer special children's meals. They must be ordered in advance and vary from airline to airline, from burgers and finger food to spaghetti and peanut butter and jelly sandwiches. No matter how perfect the meal sounds, take plenty of your child's favorite foods with you. Pack Cheerios, dried fruit, and similar selections in plastic bags to save space. Meal service may not be timed to your child's hunger pangs. Take extra liquids and juices (boxed juices, with straws, are compact and easy); children get dehydrated on flights, too.

Naptime. A good night's sleep before a flight is important, but try to discourage napping until you're on the plane. A long sleep in the airport lounge can mean a raring-to-go toddler at thirty thousand feet.

Instead try expending some infant energy with a brisk walk around the airport before boarding.

Ears. Bottles of water or breast-feeding for babies and chewing gum for older children may prevent ear pain induced by air travel. Swallowing, which keeps the eustachian tubes open, should be encouraged during takeoff and descent. If your child has frequent earaches or colds, check with your health-care professional for further ways to relieve discomfort.

The trick to a successful vacation is to plan so well that you come home rested—not in such a stressed-out state that going back to work seems like a respite.

twelve

Working-Family Issues

When Both Parents Work: Sharing the Burden

EVEN if you've been married for ten years, even if you think your spouse is your best friend and you know everything there is to know about each other, being parents will change your relationship. You may have shared incomes, chores, and errands in a manner that was more-or-less acceptable to both partners. But sharing the responsibility for a child's life will be like nothing else in your life. It is the deepest kind of sharing—at times the most exasperating, but also the most rewarding.

In the traditional marriages of the past, each parent had well-defined responsibilities. Both mother and father knew what the other, and society, expected of them. Such responsibilities didn't necessarily make anyone happy, but they knew which chores they were expected to do. Today's families, with two working parents, are forging new ground. In the past few decades, working mothers have reshaped the domestic agenda. Couples find it no longer acceptable for one parent to shoulder an unfair burden (except in emergencies). Our theoretically enlightened society accepts the fifty-fifty concept. But in practice, out there in the homes of the working families of the world, theory takes a backseat to everyday practice. Many parents harbor strong feelings of resentment over unfair and unequal situations, in which good intentions are never fulfilled. Whether or not you find yourself in such a situation, issues of sharing the burden must be discussed openly, calmly, and frequently.

In *The Second Shift*, author Arlie Hochschild revealed her findings on the dual working parent family of today. Among them were the facts that women do most of the daily chores (meal preparation, for example), while men are more focused on periodic chores (lawn mowing, car repair); women often do two things at one time (e.g., cooking dinner and supervising children), while men are more likely to do one thing (cook *or* supervise kids); and women's responsibilities tend to be more maintenance-oriented (e.g., food shopping, laundry), while men's are more play-oriented (play catch). Another key finding was that women tend to be the organizers in families: they are responsible for keeping on schedule. Sound familiar?

A preliminary discussion of the new responsibilities that lie ahead should take place early in pregnancy. A "how are we going to handle the extra load" musing is beneficial. Who will take care of what? And what task will you share? Soothing. Diapering. Bathing. Feeding. Visiting the doctor. Shopping for supplies and clothing. Finding child care. Driving to and from child care. There's no way you can get a firm grip on how either of you will feel about these tasks or how adept you'll be at completing them. Nevertheless, it is important to put these issues on the table in a tentative way.

During pregnancy, sit down with your partner and take an inventory of all the chores (daily and periodic) and who does them now. Which ones are yours? Which ones are your partner's? How flexible are the two of you about assuming each other's chores? Does one of you habitually nag the other to do his/her share?

You may think of your spouse as a very enlightened, progressive person; your relationship has proved this to be true. Sometimes a baby can change that. You may find your partner pulling away from the baby and all the new responsibilities involved in parenthood.

Some fathers feel left out of the strong bond between mother and child. These feelings can begin in pregnancy. They feel shut out. And then childbirth. And nursing. They feel like they've been demoted. They watch the two people they love most cuddle and coo and they feel, sometimes, like an outsider, an observer. It takes work to make sure these feelings don't go unchecked, but if they do, they may lead to a retreat into work or other things. A further consequence may be an unwillingness to do a fair share around the house. Both parents must work at preventing or solving this problem. Mothers need to be sensitive to this nose-pressed-against-the-window feeling, and fathers need to work on ways to be a full participant.

This generation of mothers and fathers is breaking new ground. Their parents' relationships may have been very traditional, and they may have had stay-at-home moms. Probably their dads didn't change diapers or do dishes. Few working couples grew up with role models for these new ways of doing things. So remember that the notion of this equal parenting is new territory.

I don't remember my husband and I fighting much about chores before Justin was born. When he was a baby, I was home for nine months, and so I did most of everything. But when I went back to work, we started having serious problems. It got worse as the years went by. I wanted my husband to be a fully involved parent in the raising of our son. But he always seemed to do the minimum. If I had to work late, he wouldn't make a real meal for Justin. He'd let him go to bed without a bath. Then I'd get home and have a fit. If I had to leave for work early and my husband would have to get Justin ready, I would have to pick out clothes, because I couldn't trust him to get him dressed warmly. I felt like I had two children, which was very depressing. Luckily, my sister, who is very wise, pointed out to me that I was treating my husband like a child, so he was acting like one. Bingo! A lightbulb went on. She said I'd have to back off and let him do it his way. Now, that was really hard. I was used to running the house like a drill sergeant.

Many spouses feel like assistant parents. They wait for work assignments. They act more like an employee than a partner. They may or may not be aware of feeling this way but either way, the result is a day-to-day arrangement in which neither partner is happy. In order to have a relationship in which both partners assume their fair share of the work, both must feel like adults with equal footing. There's never room for two drill sergeants in a family. (And probably not even for one!)

The person in the sergeant role will often try to explain the situation with an excuse such as "But he doesn't do a good job with . . ." or "She never remembers to. . . ." The drill sergeant must resign herself to some things not being done to her high standards. Sometimes, minimal standards just have to do.

> I used to grab the baby food away from my husband and show him the proper way of feeding Abigail. I used to push him out of the way and say I could do the diapering faster. I used to tell him he didn't put the right amount of detergent in the washer.

Once you and your partner have made a list of all household chores and are ready to split up the work, consider assigning by strengths. One of you may be better at cooking; the other at vacuuming and dusting. One may be a morning person; the other an evening person.

One way to balance out the load is to alternate take-charge times. One parent may be responsible for dinner and cleanup on Mondays and Wednesdays; the other on Tuesday and Thursdays. The same goes for children's bedtime rituals. One may get to sleep late on Saturday; the other on Sunday. Or on alternate weekends.

When one parent makes more money than the other or has a more prestigious job, it can have a big effect on how the division of chores and responsibilities is viewed. If a wife makes significantly more than her husband, it has probably been an issue, whether spoken or unspoken, for as long as the situation has existed. Both can have full-time jobs, or the husband might even be underemployed, yet the wife may still be doing the lion's share of chores and errands.

When a husband makes significantly more than his wife, it can be an easy excuse not to share the chores and responsibilities equitably. The excuse might be expressed in statements such as "I have to put my all into my work. After all, it's what we live on."

How do you discuss the inequitable distribution of household chores and responsibilities in your family? Gently. Not in the heat of the moment. Speak after careful thought to your words.

> I make thirty thousand dollars working full time as a lab tech; my husband makes a hundred thousand as a medical equipment salesman. We both work approximately the same number of hours. Although we have household help one day a week, I do most of the day-to-day chores—the marketing, cooking, loading the dishwasher. My husband reads to our two-year-old before

bedtime. I take her to and from child care. I'm getting angrier and angrier about these things. When I've tried to discuss it, I've gotten nowhere. Sometimes he says, "I'm making the money here. My job is very stressful." Sometimes he says, "You like all the things my income buys us." And sometimes he says, "You're the one who wanted this kid." You must admit, he has a knack for cutting off a conversation he doesn't want to pursue.

Nevertheless, such a conversation is important to pursue. Acknowledgment that each partner's work is valuable and that salary should not indicate value is essential. One tactic might be to ask if your recalcitrant partner wants to have this fight for the next twenty years? Or how he'd feel if salaries were reversed. Finally, the overburdened parent may simply and forcefully state, "I physically can't do all this."

I dragged my husband to a class for parents. The psychologist was talking about sharing the load. He asked everyone to think about what they knew about their own children. Did they know their child's teacher's name? Pediatrician's name? Shoe size? Which parent went to the last school meeting? The last doctor's appointment? Who organized the last birthday party? It was a real eye-opener to Bill what he didn't know about his own son. And he wasn't alone in that audience. I thought it was a very effective way for the psychologist to get into a discussion of what it means to be a parent.

Sit down and analyze all the chores and responsibilities in the household and who is currently doing them. Is there a way you can hire someone to take over some of those tasks? If the major fight is over who has to stop working to pick up your child at the day-care center, then perhaps you can hire someone to complete that one task. If you can't afford to hire someone, make a schedule, alternating days or weeks.

Human nature being what it is, forcing people to do things can cause them to react in rebellious ways. Force a parent to change a diaper, and he can do it roughly. Force a parent to take a child with her on errands, and she may jerk the child by the arm. Refuse to pick up your child at the center because of a work emergency, and you may wind up with a panicked toddler who is a pawn in a power struggle. It's scary, yes. It's abusive, yes. But sometimes, people react this way. They take the partnership issues out on the child.

In the end, like all things, sharing the burden comes down to respect between parents, communicating problems, and working on them until you've reached a mutually agreeable solution.

The Sandwich Generation

Giving birth at an older age, as the new generation of parents is doing, has many ramifications. One of them is older grandparents. Parents in their late thirties and forties, focused on raising young children, can also be faced with their own parents' problems of aging.

We went out for Mother's Day: my husband, our two kids (ages three and six), and my mother. She's eighty-two and has been in poor health for several years, especially since my father's death four years ago. It wasn't a great day. The low point came when I realized that I was treating my mother in the same way I was dealing with my kids. I had to remind all three of them to wipe food off their faces. I had to tell all three to lower their voices. Then— this was the clincher—I asked my mother as we were leaving if she had to use the rest room, because it was a long ride home. Just like I do for my children. It wasn't an inappropriate suggestion. We've had to make several emergency pit stops when we've been on other outings. When did I become my mother's mother?

The sandwich generation has to take care of two generations *and* work. And you don't have to be dealing with a full-blown case of Alzheimer's disease to feel squashed. Anytime parents ask for (or show signs of needing) help in areas that were once their own domain, it's disconcerting at the very least, and more than likely, very draining for everyone involved.

Sandwiched parents may recognize similarities between the ways in which they must help their children and their parents. Body functions. Safety. The elements of care are often the same. But the extra issue with parents is caring for them and preserving their dignity at the same time. You can't diaper or wipe an eighty-three-year-old the way you can a two-year-old.

While the Family and Medical Leave Act is meant to provide some help for those families with elder-care concerns, it's only the first step in finding a solution. First of all, as with unpaid leave to care for children, this act affects only workers in companies with more than fifty employees. And while it's a struggle to get employers to recognize that they need to address the issues of working parents and their children, it's an even harder sell to get some action with regard to elder care. A recent study by a Chicago-based benefits consulting firm revealed that, of the thousand companies surveyed, 78 percent offered some sort of child-care assistance, while only 20 percent offered any elder-care help.

In another unsettling survey, conducted by the Older Women's League in Washington D.C., statistics reveal that the average senior citizen will need eighteen years of special care. *Eighteen* years. That duration corresponds directly to the length of time necessary to raise a child from birth to high school graduation.

If you are beginning to see signs of your parent or parents needing such care, it's important to get as much assistance as you can as soon as you can. It's tough enough trying to raise young children.

If you find yourself in the all-too-common predicament of caring for both young children and older parents, remember that you don't have to respond to everyone's needs immediately. Take time to think them over. Learn to say "no" and "maybe."

When you don't have the energy for miniature golfing with the kids or a shopping trip with your mother, say so. They'll survive. Plan the outing for another time, another week. Both children and older parents will find it easier to put something off now if they have something special to look forward to later on.

Sit down and talk with your family. You might want to call a family meeting to discuss the issues and how you see the situation resolving. Tell your family that you need help. When the demands of children and parents seem to overwhelm, speak up. Compromises can be made that will be better for all involved.

Family Meetings

Yes, we know you may have all the meetings you think you can stand during the workday. Why would any working parent suggest or even agree to a family meeting? Because families have day-to-day business that requires attention. You could conduct it on the fly at breakfast or driving to the cineplex, but the more businesslike approach is really more efficient.

You might think this method is too official, too businesslike to actually work for *your* family. A three-year-old seconding a motion? Well, let's not get carried away. But meetings are a signal, even to a preschooler who has yet to see the inside of a meeting room, that what you talk about with them is important and that everyone's input is required.

The purpose of family meetings is to provide an opportunity for everyone in the family to participate in decision making. This arrangement works best in families that are somewhat comfortable with the democratic, rather than the autocratic, approach to family life. Decisions can range from the best way to get the leaves raked up on a regular basis to how to spend a holiday weekend. They can cover issues such as cleaning rooms, respecting other people's space, and when and where it's okay to play music—even if it's *Little Mermaid* songs and not heavy metal—on the boom box. If there's a little extra money in the budget, a family meeting can be the forum in which to decide whether to buy a new barbecue or go to a water park.

Families, or rather parents, often decide to start holding meetings because of thorny issues that have gone unresolved. Meetings are an opportunity to discuss subjects calmly rather than in the heat of "battle." Meetings are also a good way to make rules clear. Sometimes the same old stuff about coming to the table with clean hands or the acceptable way to answer the phone can be dealt with efficiently by putting it on the meeting agenda. Working parents, with limited time and most likely two different schedules, can use the meetings to deal with issues and problems that the whole family needs to address as a unit.

There's no one right way to run a family meeting. The most successful ones are tailored to a family's individual ways. The structure is a matter of what feels workable. Some families like a fairly formal atmosphere; others like the "ketchup" time-with-french-fries approach.

Here are some suggestions to get you started. First, suggest a time, date, and place for the first meeting that seems workable for everyone. Someone in the family may not be too keen on the meeting idea, so set rule number one from the start: Everyone attends; no excuses. Some families meet on a regular basis, while others call meetings as needed.

How the first few meetings go is crucial. Set a time limit before you begin. Don't be too heavy-handed on the chores. Strive for a balance of work and play issues. The essence of the meetings is the family's shared decision making; they shouldn't be used as a thinly disguised vehicle for parents to impose their will. Similarly, it shouldn't be viewed as a chance for three kids to outvote two parents on a so-called issue such as whether to have ice cream sundaes for breakfast. The goal is to facilitate decision making that is age-appropriate through consensus. Think of the family panel as an advisory committee, not a board of directors.

Issues, from allowances to pet maintenance, are best presented as challenges that require solutions solicited from all in attendance. Parents should hold back from expressing their solutions until young members have had their chances to mull over the problem and come up with ideas.

> After our second child was born, our four-year-old, Lucy, started refusing to eat at the dinner table. She'd say she wasn't hungry, but of course, she was always starved an hour later. We tried all sorts of ways to get her to eat. Finally, in desperation, we called a family meeting. Our six-week-old was in his seat on the table facing the three of us. We told Lucy that we were worried about her eating habits and that we really enjoyed having her at the dinner table. Her father said that we could no longer permit her to eat by herself later in the evening. Then we asked her for her ideas on how to solve this. She said that it might be easier for her to be at the dinner table if her favorite doll sat with her. Well, that idea had eluded us. She felt so good about coming up with the solution herself.

The emphasis at these meetings should be on problem solving—not griping. Whether it involves handling chores or settling conflicts, the approach should be in the fixing, not in mere complaining.

Some families begin or end each meeting with a round of compliments. Siblings who might be unaccustomed, shall we say, to saying something good about a brother or sister might be a little bewildered (and slow!) at this. But it gets easier.

Successful family meetings take work. The first few sessions will probably seem a little confusing to everyone. Parents will struggle with the ramifications of living up to the notion of decision making by consensus rather than by fiat. Children will also need a little time to understand that their ideas are valued but must be worthy of that consideration. Stick with it. Family meetings can help make life more comfortable and become a warm, anticipated tradition.

Family Finances: How Much to Tell Your Children

Do your children know how much money you make? If your nine-year-old asked how much you earn, would you tell her? Most parents cringe a little at the thought.

> *Once, when my daughter was seven, I took her to the bank with me while I deposited my work check. As we were going into the bank, she asked to see the check. I froze. I think she just wanted to study what a check looked like, but instantly, I knew she would see the amount and maybe know that meant how much money I take home. I got real uptight. I tried to divert her attention, but she asked again. I tried to laugh it off, saying "Checks aren't very interesting," something silly like that. She persisted, so I simply said "enough," with an end-of-discussion tone.*

Most parents, even those who consider themselves very open, find it difficult to discuss family finances with their children. They may encourage discussions on difficult subjects such as AIDS, sex, and racial bigotry, but when their children want to know how much money the family has, the most open-minded parents have been known to stammer and dismiss the thought with a statement such as "What do you need to know for?" or "As long as you have food and a roof over your head, you don't need to think about those things."

Why is it so hard for parents to talk about this? A few reasons:

1. You worry that your child will not understand that you don't want the whole world to know how much you make. She may tell her friend, who'll tell her parents, and soon the whole school will be privy to your personal finances. For young children, salary figures have no meaning. Your salary is really either "enough" or "not enough." Giving them a dollar amount may make them feel good, privy to inside information, but they can't put that information into context. They might tell the

other children in child care; maybe the child-care provider; or their teacher. If you instruct your child not to tell anyone, she may ask you if it's a secret. And then what do you say? One suggestion we can offer for this and other not-for-public-consumption issues, is simply to say, "We like to keep that information in the family."

2. You're concerned that your child will not understand that how much people earn is not a measure of their value. Young children are not ready to understand all the factors that go into what kind of work a parent does. They may think that salary is the only way to judge success in life. After all, isn't that how society in general works? Until you feel your children can comprehend the issues of job satisfaction, working conditions, and even the difficulties of finding jobs, you may prefer to sidestep the issue.

3. You don't want older children second-guessing how the money is spent. A twelve-year-old who pines for a CD player might analyze where every penny of the family budget is being spent, ask for an accounting, and insist that there is indeed money for his equipment. Since a child can have very independent ideas about how the family's money should be spent, you may feel that the only way to head off these discussions is to refrain from revealing how much money is coming in.

4. You don't want them to worry. There are enough issues for children to deal with as they grow up. Supporting the family is your responsibility.

Before you answer the "How much money do you make?" question, ask your child why she wants to know. Don't assume you know your child's motives. She may not be expecting the financial equivalent of the "birds and the bees." A simple "enough to take care of our needs" and a reassuring hug may be all she's after.

Ways to Involve Children

There's more to family finances than knowing how much parents earn. It's also how you spend it. Children benefit from observing how their parents handle money. How priorities are made, for example, or how much money is gobbled up by necessities—especially the boring, nonmaterial expenses (insurance, utilities) that no one wants to spend hard-earned money on.

Children who have some knowledge of family finances and budgeting learn important lessons, such as not every dollar is for treats. To children, a trip to the grocery store can seem like nothing more than an exercise in throwing food into a cart. When children are old enough to understand, parents should let them know that when they shop, they are working within a budget. That sixty, eighty, or one hundred dollars must pay for everything. Show them what sixty dollars buys. Make a few trade-offs. For instance, if you buy a half gallon of fancy ice cream, you'll have to put back two boxes of granola bars. A cheaper carton of ice milk and one box of granola bars might be a workable compromise. Or putting all the money toward buying a box of big, juicy strawberries.

When you save money by using coupons or going to bargain movie matinees, point how much money you've saved and what that could buy. The money saved on movie admission can go toward snacks. A double coupon on shampoo might mean an extra two dollars for school supplies.

The more children see these tiny building blocks of family budgeting, the stronger their base will be for dealing with the big picture when the time comes.

Parents who discuss possible ways of spending their money in front of their children are showing them how people make financial decisions. If you buy a new computer, what will that mean? It might mean fewer holiday gifts or putting off replacement of the old washer.

When There's a Reduction in Income

Sometimes children only hear about family finances when there is a drastic change—when there's a loss of income, full or partial, and suddenly, money becomes an issue. The price of everything is noted. Choices are debated. Cutbacks are analyzed.

How children handle this situation depends to a great extent on how you present the problem. You may decide to hide the income reduction for as long as you can, not wanting to make changes in your child's lifestyle, even though yours is being curtailed. Or you may decide to explain that income changes require spending changes. Ask them to decide on their priorities. Which expenditures could they forgo for a while?

Handling money well is a skill that parents can help their children acquire, beginning when they're school aged. No pun intended, it's a priceless gift.

Allowances: Why, When, and How Much?

Children benefit from receiving an allowance—a little pocket money to do with as they wish. And while it may seem, on the surface, that allowances just turn into arcade games, toys, and Slurpees, they really address much more important issues, such as financial responsibility, short- and long-term priorities, saving, and giving. For parents, allowances can represent the relinquishing of some control, because they allow their children to make financial decisions.

Allowances can open up discussions about money on a level that children can understand. They will learn the value of five dollars much more quickly when it is their money.

A child who gets a regular allowance may be a step ahead. He is being prepared for life in the real world, where handling personal finances wisely is crucial to living a good life. A child who is told to ask for things as he wants them may remain in a state of dependence, rather than developing independent living habits.

A child without an allowance can brag to friends that he can "get anything I want just by being nice." Such a child may be learning to manipulate his parents to get money, a proclivity which should clearly be discouraged, rather than encouraged.

According to a recent article in the *Los Angeles Times*, a survey by a marketing research company that monitors youth behavior found that children ages six to eight received an average of $2.79 a week. Teens of fifteen to seventeen average $15. How much money a child gets for an allowance depends on family resources, the child's age, and what the allowance is meant to cover. You decide what works for your family.

The amount appropriate for very young children may be so small that it precludes buying much more than a small trinket. Since preschoolers are often easy marks for those twenty-five-cent doodads in gumball machines in supermarkets, let them spend *their* quarters on them. Even if the amount is small, it may still be important to them to get a regular allowance, especially if they have older siblings.

If you decide on giving an allowance to your preschooler, vary the combination of coins, whether the allowance is twenty-five cents or a dollar. Offer a quarter one week; twenty-five pennies the next; then two dimes and a nickel. This exercise teaches math as well as money value.

As children get older, an allowance can start to cover a few basics and treats, including snacks, small toys, games, savings, gifts, and extra video and game rentals. Learning that they do not have enough money for all the treats their hearts desire may be as much a financial lesson as children this age can absorb.

Regardless of a child's age, there should be a clear understanding of what items the allowance is meant to cover. Younger children are better off handling smaller amounts and narrower guidelines. As they get older, they understand just what five or ten dollars will and won't buy. It may take a young child weeks to save for a special toy or CD.

Sit down and explain what you expect the allowance to cover and what you will pay for out of your money. Who pays for movies, videos, frozen yogurt, school lunches, school supplies, video games, koosh balls, holiday presents, gum?

Most parents do not expect allowances to cover clothing or school supplies. But an allowance might be used for "upgrades." You'll buy a new backpack from family money, but if your child wants a very fancy one, that's when her allowances kicks in. Set the amount you're willing to pay for a decent one. Then, if your child has her heart set on a special brand that costs more, she can use her allowance to make up the difference.

When my son's boom box broke and couldn't be fixed, he had his heart set on a superfancy replacement—the same $200 model that his best friend had. He was only twelve years old, but he talked about the boom box day and night. I told him that we did not have the money for an expensive one and that we were willing to buy one that cost about the same as the old one, which was about $125. If he wanted an upgrade, he'd have to figure out how to do it. Maybe he could put it on his Christmas list if he didn't want much else. But it was September, and he couldn't wait. He asked me how to use the phone book, and the next night, he called every electronic store in the Yellow Pages, asking if they had that model and how much it cost. He found a store that sold that model for $180 and then one for $165. He was willing to use *his own $40, and since he'd done so much consumer research, we went and got it.*

Setting Financial Priorities

A child should understand that his allowance is his to spend as he wishes (common sense, decency, and legal niceties prevailing, of course). But that doesn't mean you can't offer a few suggestions. Just as long as they stay *suggestions*.

Children need to learn how to handle money to their best advantage. For example, you may have a family routine of letting your child pick one video to rent on the weekend. He may want two. Should you let him spend his allowance on the second one? It may not seem like a great idea to you. Half of his week's spending money on a video? At first, he may have a hard time realizing that he is making a choice. A Friday night video means he won't have that money for arcade games on Saturday or be able to buy a skateboarding magazine. If all these expenses are labeled allowance purchases, not something *you* buy, he will soon learn what's most important to him. He may decide to save his money for a toy—or realize that he really does like renting second videos on the weekend. Before he actually makes his decision about how to spend his money, you may point out a few alternate possibilities for the week (playing arcade games, buying comic books) and what his choice will preclude. But abide by his decision (of course your guidelines concerning suitability still count).

Learning to Save

Children should be expected to put some—but not all—of their allowances away for long-term goals (like boom boxes). A child who is coerced into putting all of his allowance into a college fund, for example, is not really getting an allowance, just a savings account. He is not learning anything about prioritizing expenditures.

Learning to Give

Children are often deeply affected by the difficulties of other people's lives and want to help them. They may give some of their allowances to the homeless or want to send it off to telethons. It's important to take these gestures seriously. You might suggest that your child put aside a regular amount each week, to be saved in an envelope and then mailed to a special charity your child selects. And even if a child impulsively gives her entire allowance to a family on the street or a solicitor at the door, it's important to support that gesture. Most likely she won't do it every week, and her genuine response to other people's troubles should be viewed as a caring, rather than frivolous, act.

Tying Allowances to Chores

Most child experts feel that allowances are not payment for house-work. Basic chores and weekly allowances are two different areas. Children are expected to help around the home because that's what all family members do—not to earn money. No one pays you to do the laundry or make dinner. However, paying for car washing or cleaning a barbecue, if these are not regular chores, is analogous to earning over-time, and that's a completely different issue.

Give allowances freely and regularly, with no strings attached. Decide on a specific amount. Children can expect to have their allowances raised every year or so, perhaps on their birthdays. An allowance also points out to parents areas in which a child might have problems. Does he borrow against future allowances and then never pay it back? Does he hoard his allowance and then cry poverty? Does he blow it all in the first thirty minutes on junk food?

An Allowance When Money Is Tight

Even in financially difficult times, a small allowance helps to bring home to a child how much things cost. It may be only a very token amount, but it gives a child a chance to handle money and a little responsibility.

I am a single mother raising my son on a limited income. His allowance is a gift from his grandparents. It arrives every month, increasing as he gets older, and I give it to him weekly. But it is always clear that it's a special gift from his grandparents and one that I have appreciated greatly.

A similar arrangement might work with an aunt, uncle, godparent, or close friend.

Living with Television: Childhood Unplugged

Television. Can't live with it. Can't live without it. Like cars and computers, TV is part of our lives. And it's here to stay. But TV is a mixed blessing, especially for working parents. It can entertain children and even teach them. But it can also expose them to undesirable ideas and values. It keeps children busy while you're busy. But, parents need to know, as they would with any "babysitter," who's minding their children.

The Concerns About TV Watching

There are really two main concerns about children and television watching: the loss of time not spent in real childhood activities, and the values and ideas children get from the shows they watch.

If your child is typical, she is watching television more than twenty-two hours a week. That's twenty-two hours when she isn't doing other things, like having a childhood, playing with imaginary friends, playing with real friends, playing with you, building castles, reading, running, dreaming.

At its best, TV can expose children to high ideals, such as people caring for each other, telling the truth, doing hard work. But there are other less desirable attitudes on the tube, side-by-side with noble ones, such as solving problems with violence, lying and laughing about it, and meanness—lots of meanness. Children sit there, absorbing it all. The challenge for parents is to find those programs that expose children to their own good values and to say no to the mean ones.

Living with television requires parents to ask, "Is my child watching too much TV?" And "Is what he watches age-appropriate and consistent with our family's values?"

The only way a parent can know what a child is watching is to watch with him or *before* him (you can tape a program and watch it late at night). You don't need to watch every episode, but enough to know the basic elements and attitudes of the program. Some Saturday morning cartoons can be too violent for young children. Some sitcoms can champion negative values.

Parents will differ on what they consider appropriate. Some may find *Roseanne* warm and loving, while others may see it as too smart-alecky and cynical. But since TV offers shows that are surely inappropriate for *all* young children, parents have to make the effort to know what their children are tuning into. After all, children aren't simply "watching TV." They're being exposed to what's on the tube.

For example, it's 6:00 P.M. Do you know what your child is watching right now? Is it *Married with Children?* Or is it a *The Cosby Show* rerun? Don't assume that all dinnertime or family-hour shows are suitable for young children. Don't assume that all sitcoms are the same. On *Married with Children*, the teenage daughter is portrayed as the town bad girl and the parents pound each other with cruel insults, egged on by their children.

Once you've watched a few episodes of a show, you'll get a feeling for whether you want your child to watch it. If you decide that it is not right for your child, explain why. Of course, there remains the danger that the show will become forbidden fruit, all the more tantalizing. A compromise might be to watch it with your child, then make time to get your point of view across.

Changing TV Habits

You could pull the plug. Cover the set with a tablecloth. Move it to the attic. And believe us, some parents have taken these drastic measures. Of course, such actions affect the parents as well as their children. The TV stays unplugged for them, too. It's kind of like a babysitter quitting. A dreadful thought? Maybe the best place to begin figuring out how to handle your child's viewing is to assess your own attitudes toward TV:

How much time do you spend watching television?

Do you turn it on for background noise?

Do you watch a favorite program and then turn it off?

Do you sit for hours channel surfing with the remote?

Do you consider eight to eleven o'clock every night sacred TV time, whether there's something interesting on or not?

Do you plan your life around television programs?

How you feel about the role television should play in your child's daily life is being imparted by your relationship to the tube. Are you demonstrating to your child that TV is *very* important while you tell her the opposite? Or are you telling her that while TV can be entertaining, informative, relaxing, and fun, it has its place and is only one part of a stimulating life? While other people in your child's life (caregivers, teachers, relatives) will also pass on their ideas about TV to your child, it is your attitudes that are crucial. Once you've set the tone, remember to tell babysitters and anyone else who cares for your child what your TV-watching rules are.

Setting Limits

The earlier in your child's life that you set TV guidelines, the easier it will be for you to maintain rules. Setting limits for a two-year-old, before he has come to think of television as a way of life, is easier than changing the habits of a five- or ten-year-old. But five- and ten-year-olds *can* change.

If you feel a change is necessary, set aside time to talk about your concerns with your child. A family meeting might be the appropriate forum. Explain to your child why you have decided to cut back on television watching. Talk about some of the values discussed above. Admit to your own weaknesses. Explain that the changes you have in mind are beneficial to the whole family and require changes in your life as well as your child's. Set limits for yourself as well. You might decide that you are in the habit of tuning in news programs as background when you should really be watching a half hour attentively and then switching off the set.

Here are some things to think about:

1. Many experts suggest limiting television to one hour on school days, two to three hours on nonschool days. That may sound either drastic or indulgent, given your current habits, and if you decide to limit your family's viewing, cutbacks might be best done gradually. If your child is watching five hours a day, cut down to four for a week, then three, etc.

When you set rigid limits with children, they often spend a lot of energy finding ways to maneuver around them. Questions will arise. Your child might inquire, if he only watches a half hour on Monday, can he watch for an hour and a half on Tuesday? If you're watching *Home Improvement* and he's doing his homework in the dining room and only watching a little bit, does that count? Time limits may call for occasional exceptions. For example, the World Series might not "count." And favorite shows can be taped for viewing at another time.

2. Busy working parents may be reluctant to restrict TV watching, because doing so will put demands on their time that they can't meet. But realize that children can and will find other activities to keep them busy. Turning off the TV doesn't necessarily mean that you will have to fill every newly freed-up minute of their time by playing checkers with them. It might take a few weeks, but they will find other interests—reading, coloring, building projects, playing the piano—to keep them busy.

3. Discourage channel surfing. Make TV viewing a planned event rather than a filler of time. Consult the TV listings, put on a specific show, and then turn the set off when it's over.

4. Be aware that news programs can be very disturbing to children. These broadcasts can move from a sports report to an upsetting and graphic story about a murdered child in seconds. Be alert for any signs of distress during these programs, and encourage a discussion of the story. Some parents switch to viewing later evening newscasts on their own to avoid problems.

5. Resist the pleas for a television set in a child's bedroom. Yes, of course your daughter's best friend, Jessica, has a TV in her room. In fact, just about everyone she knows does. And it works out so well, your daughter assures you, because then Jessica and her parents don't fight over what to watch. Of course, they don't interact, either—Jessica's holed up in her room, alone, watching sitcoms.

Restrict TV watching to the living room or family room, where there's an opportunity for family viewing, discussion, and camaraderie.

6. Instead of using TV as background noise, play music.

7. Parents and children have been debating the subject of doing homework while watching TV ever since *American Bandstand*. There is no one answer for all children. The issue is getting homework done, and done well. Every child does homework in a different way. Some can do

math with *Tiny Toon Adventures* in the background, while others can't deal with distractions.

You know your child best. Establish limits and watching times that work best for your family.

And a Few Words About Videos

Watching a video is basically the same as watching a TV show. The same issues of values and nonactivity apply. Preschoolers often get "hooked" on a favorite video even more than actual TV shows. They are comforted by watching Hap Palmer's *Baby Songs* or *Winnie the Pooh* over and over—twenty, fifty, even a hundred times. Such preferences are a lot like asking to hear the same bedtime story night after night. A favorite video can be calming. While responding to the need for comfort through repetition, parents need to be cautious about the content of the videos and overrepetition. The first time your child watches a video, sit down and watch it with him. There may be something, even in a seemingly innocuous cartoon, that will alarm him (remember *Bambi?*) Understand your young child's need to watch *The Little Mermaid* again and again, but remember the need to strike a balance between video viewings and real-world activities.

Peer Pressure

Short of home schooling and cutting off access to all electronic devices, there's very little chance of totally avoiding the media hype, consumerism, and peer pressure that are part of childhood these days.

These three combined elements are very powerful, involving competition, self-esteem, value systems, and the conflict of family and culture and finances. Having and showing off a new Barbie doll, wearing Nikes or lipstick, or being allowed to see *Die Hard* movies are all part of peer pressure. Children feel pressure from their friends because of their need for a sense of belonging—a need that develops early in life. It's healthy to want to belong to a group. It's unhealthy when this need becomes too important.

Parents dealing with these issues must do so in the context of our culture. And it is a peer-pressure culture, even for three-year-olds.

Hang out at a preschool for a few mornings if you don't believe it. It's a big part of their world, just as it's a part of yours. Fitting in with the larger group is usually a lifelong pursuit. We want to feel our kids are individuals, that they have flair and their own opinions—but we also want them to fit in. We are social animals.

When does peer pressure begin? These days, probably with *Mighty Morphin Power Rangers* or models of Aprica strollers. A two-year-old can be as concerned with showing his Power Ranger toy to his friend as he is in actually playing with it. His friend's reaction is eagerly sought, and a mix of envy, respect, and awe is the perfect response. Peer pressure is off and running for a lifetime.

Cultivating consumer pressure has been honed to a fine art in Saturday morning commercials. Ads don't simply show children playing with toys; they also depict them showing off the toys to their friends. Kids learn this show-off behavior, this one-upsmanship, on TV.

So what do you do when your child begs, pleads, and wheedles for a fancy pair of power-pumping athletic shoes, top-of-the-line Reeboks, or expensive Guess? jeans that you know will be outgrown in a few months? Typically, his main argument is that everyone has them. His desire for ownership has nothing to do with fit, comfort, or even true admiration of the item. And it certainly has nothing to do with cost.

If you feel you can't afford something, say so. If the desired item is simply too expensive or of dubious merit, say so. It may be the end of the discussion or the beginning of a creative, and heated, conversation on the subject. For example, you may conclude that your child can find ways to help pay for the oh-so-necessary object.

When your child pines for an expensive item, ask hard questions. Calmly. Who has those shoes? Have your feelings toward your friend changed since he got a pair of them? What makes you think he will think better of you if you get them? It may take a few tries to get these types of discussions going. Timing is everything. Be persistent. These may be questions he will not ask himself but is able to explore at the right time with appropriate prodding.

On the flip side, there are also hard questions for you to ask yourself. Are you giving in to peer-pressure demands simply out of guilt? Working parents often feel bad about not spending enough time with their kids, so they make up for it by buying them whatever they ask for. Divorced parents can be especially susceptible to these feelings—or be drawn into competing with the other parent.

Resisting peer pressure by blaming parents is a typical ploy children use—and often it works. "My mom says I can't watch *Die Hard 3* because of the violence," your child may lament. His friends will surely commiserate over the problems with hardheaded parents.

Sometimes kids will even use the "My dad won't let me" excuse when they themselves want to get out of a delicate situation. Maybe they themselves don't want to see *Die Hard*, but they don't want to admit it to their friends. In terms of keeping up appearances, it's better to be seen as "not allowed" than scared.

When you refuse your child's request for a peer-pressure item, it's essential to explain your reasons. Maybe you can't afford it. Or you think she's too young for it. Or you think it's dangerous or mean-spirited.

Since peer pressure is imposed by the outside world, sometimes its direction goes against a family's values. Parents have to know who they are and where they draw the line, then explain their position to their kids. While family identity may drive children crazy when it conflicts with peer identity, it is still a very strong force in molding a healthy adult.

thirteen

Difficult Times

Worries and Fears

THESE days, parents' worries and fears seem to focus on the safety and healthy development of their children. In this chapter, we will address issues of particular interest to working parents, because they're not able to spend as much time with their children as parents who stay at home.

Feeling Safe in an Unsafe World

A basic instinct in all parents is to protect their children from harm—and from the worry about being harmed. We want an idyllic life for our children. Working parents, who are away from home so much, can feel helpless in protecting their children from the world's troubles.

Every generation seems to have its own particular fears and worries. Children in the 1930s had the Depression. In the 1940s, it was World War II. For children in the 1950s, it was the A-bomb and polio. Everyone grows up with some scary sights, thoughts, and events, whether it's breadlines, bomb drills, or hurricanes.

But today's children seem to be exposed to so many unsettling things, all at an earlier age. And it's getting more difficult for parents to protect their children from the harsh—and increasingly harsher—realities of the world. What life doesn't bring to them, television does, not to mention older children or "worldly" classmates all too eager to explain the horrors of the world to a child whose parents have tried to shelter him from such realities.

Modern times can be very fear-provoking for children. Bomb drills in grade school may be a thing of the past, but, in some schools, they've been replaced by drop drills to train children to drop to the floor in the event of a drive-by shooting.

Families stopping at the video store or the yogurt shop are confronted by disheveled, distressed people asking for money. These images can prompt even very young children to ask "What's wrong with that man?" or "Why is that woman asking for money?" And then they may wonder—out loud or to themselves—if the same fate might be awaiting them.

Until fairly recently, children who were not subjected to sexual abuse usually didn't know that such a thing existed. Now, in an effort to protect them from abuse, adults make them aware of its existence at an early age. But while the open discussion and practical preparations seems like a step forward, in the process, children are given something else to worry about. The alert child is safer, but also carries a new worrisome burden and responsibility.

Today's children worry about becoming homeless, getting AIDS, being shot on the way to Burger King, and being abused, as well as all the other fears that childhood involves from floods to hurricanes to earthquakes to their homes catching fire.

Can parents help their children feel safe—or at least safer—in this unsafe world? Yes, by understanding what causes fears and creating safety nets around their children, parents can lessen fears and let children get on with the business of being children.

Fear is rooted in a sense of helplessness: a lack of control over events, other people's actions, nature, disease, disaster. We worry about getting sick, being shot, losing jobs, dying, all things we don't have complete control over.

A word of caution, however. Don't precipitate a problem. Be sensitive to your child's exposure to fearful issues, and time your discussion as a response to that exposure, rather than saddling a child with worries that may never have occurred to him.

Begin by letting your child know that everyone has fears, adults as well as children. There are things *you* worry about. But you've learned to manage your fears by taking precautions, and you can help them to manage theirs as well. Children have to learn to work through their fears one by one. It takes a while, but once they have some sense of control, their fears will lessen.

Let your child know that there are often things people can do to take some control over how they live their lives. Again, wait for a receptive time to have these discussions. Explain that fear has a positive side. It gets people to act safely and be alert to danger. Fear of being in a car accident, for instance, leads to the preventive measures of buckling seat belts, driving within speed limits, and driving only while sober. Similarly, a child's fear of being hit by a car leads to her looking both ways before crossing the street.

Parents can lessen children's fears by helping them feel safe and protected. Emphasize to your child that one of your jobs as a parent is to be a protector. "It's my job to take care of you. Even when I'm not with you, I've made sure than wherever you are, you are safe and whoever you are with will take good care of you." The notion that someone is watching over them is a very comforting thought to children.

Should you promise that nothing bad or scary will ever happen? Be realistic. Never promise what you can't deliver. You can't promise that you will never have a fire in your house. But you can explain how unlikely it is that your house would be destroyed by fire. You can say that it hardly ever happens in your neighborhood. If you've never known anyone whose house has burned in a fire, share that thought. If you do, point out a cause that comforts, for example, "The fire started because Harry's grandfather was smoking in bed." Explain that you have a very safe house and that many of the problems that start fires are not present. Point out the smoke alarm and let your child hear how loud it sounds. "See? That will wake us all up, won't it?" Point out the fire extinguisher. Give your child a sense of control by running through a few what-to-dos. Plan exit paths. How to call 911. Tell him that he can also help by not doing anything risky, like playing with matches or poking sticks into pilot lights. Similar steps can be taken with regard to earthquakes, hurricanes, tornadoes, and so on.

It's not good enough to *have* emergency plans; these plans need to be discussed with your children. Double-check that all caregivers have workable emergency plans and supplies, and tell your child about them, too.

Dealing with crime-related fears are trickier, but the same principles apply. Discuss the steps you've taken to keep your family safe from crime, such as always locking doors and using alarms, and how children can do their part. Again, make no promises that there'll never be a robbery or burglary at your house, but do discuss your anticrime measures and plans. Let your child know that you've taken measures to keep your family as safe as possible. She doesn't have to worry; the responsibility is on your shoulders.

Then there are the classic childhood fears—the bogeyman under the bed, the monster who chases your child in her dreams. To children, such fears are just as real as their fears of the house burning down, and they should never be dismissed as silly or inconsequential. In a child's perception of reality, they are *very* real, and these fears need to be acknowledged seriously.

Here too, you can take control together. Look under the bed together. Make sure nothing is lurking in the attic. Employ the services of a very special stuffed animal who can watch over your child while he sleeps. These seemingly small actions help children take control of the situation—until the next under-the-bed check is needed.

While all children have fears, they don't all express them in the same way. Worrying about being kidnapped after an incident in the news can cause one child to talk about it incessantly, while another child, equally bothered, might become extremely clingy and afraid of strangers, refusing to let his parents out of sight.

It takes very little to invite worry in a child. A casual remark or a split-second image on TV can stay with a child for a long time. An offhand comment at the dinner table or in the car about having fewer customers at work can plant the seeds of a fear that your family might soon be homeless. Children can spin whole scenarios with very little to work with. If you verbalize—in part or completely—a scenario, the problem can be compounded. For example, you may be watching a homeless family on TV and say off-handedly, "If business doesn't pick up soon, we could be living out of *our* car." One child may not give that remark a second thought, while another might develop acute anxieties.

You know your child best. Parents need to be alert to any changes in a child's behavior or mood, which can be a signal to explore a situation further by asking more questions and offering reassurance.

Parents can take steps to lessen the feelings of helplessness that fuel fears. Parents who take active roles in their community, working to alleviate the causes of these fears, can help to instill a feeling of security in their children, because they, again, are doing something to take control of a potentially worrisome situation. You might consider participating in an AIDS walk, collecting money for cancer research, or working at a church or community food bank. Join other families who are working on human and social issues, and make it a family activity.

Car Safety: Making Every Trip a Safe Trip

For working parents with cars, out-of-the-home child care means a minimum of two car trips a day with the kids. Plus, on the way home, you might make a few stops. Buckling up every time is time-consuming, but absolutely essential. Despite the mandatory use of safety seats for young children, car accidents are still the leading cause of death among children, and injuries from car accidents are the major cause of permanent brain damage and epilepsy.

Imagine your child enduring a lifetime of epilepsy because it was too much trouble to buckle up for a quick trip to the market. Fully 75 percent of all crashes occur within twenty-five miles of home, some during routine trips to buy diapers, drop a child at the day-care center or a friend's house, or go to the pediatrician.

Using seat belts and safety seats and driving safely can keep your child from becoming a statistic. *Never* let your child talk you out of using a safety seat and seat belts. Make it clear that this is not a negotiable point. Let her know that you sympathize with the discomfort, but that you must put safety first every time.

One-fifth of all children are still not being consistently buckled up. The use of restraints decreases inversely with age. According to recent studies, 84 percent of children up to age four are buckled up. But the number drops to only 57 percent for children five to eleven and 29 percent for children ages twelve to eighteen. Studies also show that parents who do not use safety belts themselves are less likely to use restraints for their children.

Car Seats

Safety seats are only safe when they are installed properly. Unfortunately, this process is not always as easy as it sounds. There are seemingly limitless combinations of seat belts and safety seats, and they aren't always compatible. There is no way to tell if a specific seat will work safely with your car's seat belt system until you try it out. Resign yourself to the idea that it may take a few tries to find the right seat.

Buy your safety seat at a store that understands this necessary process of trial and error and allows you to exchange seats so you can find the right one. Read both the safety seat instructions and your car owner's manual carefully before you install the seat. You may want to do this in the store's parking lot after buying the seat, so that, if it isn't the right fit, you can immediately return it and try another.

Don't try to save money by picking up a safety seat at a yard sale. You need both the instruction manual and the recall history of the seat, items rarely available when you make secondhand purchases. If you do buy or borrow a used seat, it is crucial that you take responsibility for calling the manufacturer for instructions and recall information. Also, car seats age badly. After five years, the plastic starts to deteriorate and develop hairline cracks.

Ideally, once a safety seat is installed, it should be left in place—not moved around in the car or to the family's other car. Two-car families should have two safety seats; moving a car seat from place to place invites trouble. Each time the seat is moved, it must be attached as carefully and securely as it was the first time. It is all too easy to forget a buckle and attach a seat belt sloppily. The new built-in seats eliminate these problems and have been shown to be very safe in crash tests.

There are three basic types of safety seats: infant-only (rear-facing) seats, convertible seats, and booster seats. Infants under twenty pounds should ride in rear-facing safety seats—either an infant-only seat or a convertible one. As infants reach the twenty-pound weight, it may seem unfair to make them face the back of the car when there is so much more to see in front. But don't be tempted. In the event of a crash, the back-facing seat will offer much more protection to the infant's fragile neck than front-facing seats.

Many new cars have factory installed, passenger-side air bags. Rear-facing infant safety seats may *not* be used in the front passenger seat if there is an air bag for that seat, since the rapid inflation of the bag forces everything in its way against the back of the seat.

Children weighing twenty to forty pounds should ride in the backseat facing forward in "convertible" seats. When they outgrow that seat, a booster seat is safer and more comfortable than seat belts alone, as they're still not large enough to obtain a snug fit. Booster seats also allow small legs to bend easily.

Parents of children who are small for their ages (over age four but not yet forty pounds) may find it's psychologically preferable for their children to move to booster seats to keep up with their peers. If so, make sure the straps have been carefully adjusted for a good fit.

If other people (grandparents, caregivers) will be using your car seat, make sure they know how it works. They can be puzzling to the uninitiated, and the temptation is too high to forgo using it "just this once."

Where to Sit

The safest place to sit in a car is in the middle of the backseat. Head-on crashes are the most common and the most serious, and in this location, a restrained child is the most removed from the collision's impact.

If there are two lap/shoulder belts in the backseat and only a lap belt in the middle, let the older children ride using the shoulder straps and put the child who is still in a car seat in the middle.

A newborn should ride where an adult can keep an eye on her, especially if the baby was premature or has a medical problem. Positioning such a baby presents a dilemma, since the front seat is more accessible but not as safe as the middle of the backseat.

Never buckle two children into one seat belt, even though they're small enough to fit. In a crash, they can injure each other.

Distractions

The driver's full-time job is to drive the car safely—not to talk on the phone, find the right page in a map book, eat, or mind a child. If a child is behaving in a distracting manner, trying to deal with it at thirty-five miles an hour invites disaster. Pull over to a safe place and deal with the situation, or ignore it if it's not life-threatening. That may sound harsh, but a car crash is harsher. If a young baby has lost a toy or pacifier and is frantic and inconsolable, pull over. If older children are hitting each other, pull over.

Children also have responsibilities as car passengers: their behavior must not hinder car safety. Make rules for them, beginning at an early age. These rules will eliminate distractions such as children throwing things, fighting with other passengers, or screaming. Let your children know you mean business.

Loose Objects

Any loose items in the passenger compartment of your car can turn into dangerous missiles in the event of a crash or sudden stop. A pair of scissors left on a dashboard. A fork. A boom box. Whatever is loose will travel forward at a force of ten times its weight. For example, a ten-pound radio in a thirty-mile-per-hour crash will hit your child with a force of three hundred pounds.

Whenever possible, keep all heavy items in the trunk. Don't keep items on the "package shelf"—that ledge behind the backseat in sedans. If there is no place but the passenger compartment to transport items, place them on the floor of the vehicle, the lower the better. Sharp items such as scissors, knives, forks, and pens should be kept in the trunk. Some new open-shell cars, vans, and sport utility vehicles have heavy-duty mesh that fits over the trunk area to keep items from flying on impact. If this feature is not available in your car, keep loose items in containers with strong clasps. The best containers for all items are soft ones, such as backpacks. Another safe receptacle choice is a string pouch that hangs backward over the front-seat headrest. Avoid all items with pointy or hard corners.

While they can keep children occupied during car rides, drive-time toys should be chosen carefully. Stuffed animals and soft books are the safest. Again, stay away from sharp edges and hard stuff.

Food for car trips should also be chosen carefully. Avoid lollipops, hard candies, and other foods that could cause choking during a sudden stop. Bottles, whether for milk or soda, should not be glass.

First-Aid Kits

A first-aid kit is a smart addition to every family's car trunk. It should be kept in the trunk or other secure place where it cannot hurt any passengers. The concept of first aid extends far beyond the confines of the standard kit. For example, families should always keep on hand supplies that will help them get home if they are stranded several miles away, including jackets or sweaters, walking shoes (for family members who wear high heels or loose sandals), a thermal blanket, flashlight, pocket knife, street map, quarters, radio with fresh batteries, scissors, water, and snacks.

For More Help

SafetyBeltSafe USA is a nonprofit organization that can provide more detailed information on safety seats than we are able to include here. They have up-to-date information on recalls, and tip sheets on the installation of safety seats, belts, and harnesses. You can reach SafetyBeltSafe USA at (310) 673-2666.

Problem Friends

In child care, in school, or in the neighborhood, sooner or later you will encounter "problem" friends who enter your child's life. We define a "problem" friend as a child who is a poor influence or who does or says things that are distressing in a way that goes beyond the natural give-and-take of childhood friendships.

> When my child was three, I took him grocery shopping with me one day after work. I was standing in front of the soup section, and he was getting irritable and wanted out of the cart. Just as a very proper, dignified, older man walked by, my son turned to me and started screaming a foul name, a variation on the usual "M——f——" but one phrase that, in thirty-five years, I'd never heard before. I was stunned. The old man turned to me and, without saying a word, made it clear that I was an unfit mother in his eyes. I had never heard, much less used, this term, but he was not about to believe it.
>
> When we got in the car, I said, trying to be calm about it, "That word is a new one for me." My son said, "Timmy told it to me"— naming the four-year-old son of the district attorney, a famous man in our city—who was in his preschool. I explained to him that it was not okay for him to use the word.

You may be faced with a four-year-old who is foul-mouthed or very destructive with your child's toys, or a ten-year-old who is extremely manipulative and can convince your child to lend him expensive games that are not always returned or are returned damaged. The goal in dealing with these kinds of situations is to empower your child to handle his own friendships as constructively as possible.

The first step involves expressing your concern to your child and creating an environment in which he can understand those worries. Make it clear that while there may be some things that you can live with in terms of how he manages his relationships, there are other things that you take very seriously. Tell him exactly where you draw the line. Explain what behavior makes you worry or "drives you crazy." Reiterate family or house rules.

You can set limits more easily if you're dealing with a destructive four-year-old than a clever ten-year-old. Explain to your child that you are concerned about his friend's behavior and that you feel you need to do something about it. Before the friend arrives to play, put away easily breakable toys.

My son Lewis was wild about his new kindergarten friend Theo. He loved having him over to play on the weekend. At least he loved it before Theo arrived and then for about half an hour. Then the same thing would happen every week. Theo would get rough with Lewis's toys. He was much more physical than Lewis. He'd knock things over. He'd try to play catch in Lewis's room, even though he knew it was against our house rules. I could see Lewis was very frustrated, but he didn't want to make Theo angry. There was no way Lewis could confront his friend. So one Saturday before Theo was due to arrive, I sat down with Lewis and we talked about what usually happens when Theo comes over. He admitted that it did bug him. I asked what he thought of putting away some of his special toys and all the balls. He liked that. I asked him if it was okay for me to tell Theo our new house rules. Lewis nodded.

I talked to both of them and both boys seemed relieved. It helped Theo to have the limits clearly set out for him. Of course, I had to review the rules periodically.

Children's friendships are affected, to a great extent, by their parents. Not only do the parents do the transporting, but they also control whom their children see. If you like the new friend your kindergartner has made in school and think your child would benefit from the friendship, you're more apt to make an effort to drive your child to the new friend's home. You're quicker to extend invitations to your home and be more hospitable to a likable young guest.

Assess both your feelings and your child's feelings about a difficult friend. They may be in accord, or they may not. Your child may have concerns but still need help articulating them to you—and himself. He may manifest his unhappiness with the situation in nonverbal ways, getting cranky or behaving in atypical ways after the friend exhibits behavior he can't handle. Or he may not be upset at all by a child who drives you up the wall.

For example, a friend of your daughter's may be in the habit of trying on your daughter's clothes. While this may seem like an improper invasion, your daughter may in fact find it fun and flattering while *you're* the one who feels there's been an invasion. Explain how you perceive things and compare it to your child's take on the situation.

Should you tell another child's parents if you don't approve of certain behaviors? Ask yourself if you would want to know if your child were acting out at another child's house. Also ask yourself how you'd like to be told. How could the information be presented so that you wouldn't react defensively?

Let's go back to the example about the friend who breaks toys. When the friend's parent arrives to pick him up, mention that you had a discussion about the issue at hand. "I told the kids that I will go in when I think things are getting out of hand. I think it's going to be fine, but I wanted to keep you informed. I hope you would talk to me if Lewis did something you weren't happy with."

Before you take action with your child's friends, consider turning to teachers or child-care providers. They may see your child and his friend in different settings—a different light—and be able to offer a few insights into the relationship. Use a neutral phrasing to ask a question such as "How does my Marcia play with Lisa at school?"

Dealing with problem friends of older children gets more complex. For example, your child may not be aware he's being manipulated. He may have a slight suspicion but doesn't really want to deal with it because the friendship is very important to him. He may feel that any discussion or refusal to be manipulated will send the relationship down the tubes. Draw the line at behavior that is truly humiliating, unsafe, or hurtful, but allow your child to make his own decisions after he hears you out. Also be aware that when you share what bothers you, it may work against you. You are in essence giving your child power, because he now knows what bugs you.

The most effective way to handle these kinds of problem situations is having quiet, reflective talks with a child. Explain how you see the friendship. Tell him why it bothers you, and ask if it has bugged him, too. Acknowledge the strong bond between him and his friend and that you hope it will continue. Talk about how the friendship could be more positive, and your child could feel better about himself if it were more balanced. You may in fact be bringing up a problem that your child has been unable to resolve by himself.

Give your child time to handle the problem on his own. If it's more than he can deal with, then you may need to step in. If your intervention requires your talking directly to the problem friend, recognize the potential for your child to go ballistic. He may view your involvement as seriously jeopardizing the friendship (also known as "ruining his life"). Talking directly to the problem friend or turning to the last-ditch resort—talking to the friend's parents—are drastic measures.

On the other hand, if you say and do nothing, the problem may continue to create an uncomfortable situation. To avoid unpleasant confrontations for you, your child, or both of you, you may decide to resolve the problem by simply not inviting the child over anymore or not allowing your child go to the friend's house. Like speaking to the friend's parents, this option should be viewed as a last resort only.

Helping your child deal with poor influences should begin early, for example, when troublesome issues are on the level of breaking toys or not sharing. Talking with your child now about the nature of healthy relationships and how to improve problematic ones will prepare him for even rockier, and potentially more troubling, preteen and teen relationships.

fourteen

Finding Time for Yourself

A WORKING parent's own needs can—and often do—get lost in the reshuffling of priorities that comes with having a child. But they mustn't. For you to be a good parent and a good worker, you need to feel you have time for yourself.

You will not be able to find time for yourself in the large chunks—a whole day or weekend without responsibilities—as you once did. For the next several years, your time off may have to be enjoyed in smaller increments: a half hour here, a long dinner there. Look for such opportunities, and take them without guilt.

New Priorities

No matter how much you love your child, there will be times when you simply need time to yourself. Being a parent means being "on." When you are with your child, you tend to their needs, their emotions, their rhythms. Sometimes it feels very natural. Other times, it's an effort. You might love reading *Runaway Bunny* at night—at the same time you're wishing you could be snuggled in your own bed with a new Sue Grafton mystery. Even Mother Teresa and Mia Farrow need time alone. Nobody is that selfless.

If you were to write down all the time that someone is making demands on you (commute time, two hours; work, eight hours; child care, four hours; housework, four hours; sleep, seven hours), it may seem that you still owe time somewhere. It's a struggle to get it all done, much less think about relaxing and being alone.

If you're a morning person, getting up fifteen or twenty minutes early and having a solitary cup of coffee with the newspaper may be an upper that starts the whole day on a good note. If you're not a morning person, such a suggestion may sound like torture—but what about setting aside the same amount of time during the evening? And if you're not able to find alone time during the workweek, then it's essential to carve it out of the weekend.

One way to carve out time is to simply say no to requests for your time and energy. You can say no to a spouse, committee assignments, other parents. And you don't have to offer a "good" excuse. Many times a simple "I'm sorry, I won't be able to" is enough.

When it comes to the family's demands on your time, you might want to call for a family meeting. Make a plan to find solutions; don't just dump your frustrations. Tell your family that you simply can't do it all and that you need help. Then search for compromises.

Sometimes it's possible to do two things at once: pay bills while waiting for a doctor's appointment; fold laundry while you supervise homework. Commuting time also offers possibilities for both relaxing and accomplishing tasks. Drivers can listen to tapes. Bus, train, and van riders can catch up on work, read, write letters, keep a journal.

But here's the flip side: You don't always have to be doing something. We often think that a Saturday afternoon with a child should be spent at the zoo or the beach. But sometimes, the very best thing is to hang out at home. Many children are at school and child care all week, and an afternoon at home with no plans can be a welcome change for them.

Finding time for yourself requires becoming aware of what relaxes you. It may be listening to a Tina Turner CD or reading poetry. Reading cookbooks or planting bulbs. Closing an office or bedroom door and doing five minutes of stretching exercises. One person may find the fifteen minutes in a doctor's waiting room "wasted," while some patients arrive early on purpose to have some quiet time or browse through magazines.

If you don't make time for what's fun to you, then you may just fill up time with obligations, with the end result that you collapse and spend what leftover time you have exhausted, instead of enjoying yourself. You must take control of your time; there *are* choices available to you, even in a very busy schedule.

Maintaining Friendships with Non-Parents

When a woman has her first baby, her friendships with other people change. To other mothers, she is now welcomed as a member of the club. She understands the shorthand, the code words, the fatigue. The highs, the lows. Other mothers understand the strong emotions that parenthood brings. They nod knowingly when you say you didn't really know what life was about before you became a mother. It takes another parent to understand what you mean by "reaching a new depth of emotion" or having an intense identification with a child. Non-parents usually do not wish to be told that they haven't plumbed the depths of life's emotion. Save that discussion for someone who is seriously deciding whether to have a child and solicits your ideas.

When you're pregnant, a lot of childless friends will show real interest in your pregnancy. They'll want to know what it feels like, and so on. You're now an expert. But this interest may not necessarily continue after you've had your baby. The blow-by-blow minutiae of new parenthood will not be the most thrilling subject to someone who hasn't been there.

To non-parents, your new role can be threatening. It can mean that you no longer have as much time or energy to put into your friendships, or it may tap into deeper issues. The reason your friend is a non-parent will affect her reactions. The same issues that we addressed about pregnancy, parenting, and the workplace arise in personal friendships as well.

First, there's the "old" parent category. These friends are real parents—perhaps they even have four or five kids. But their kids are grown, or at least are teenagers. Their parenting issues are very different from yours. Their memories of postpartum problems are a little fuzzy. They usually view a new parent as a new member of the club—a club of which they are emeritus members. They enjoy hearing stories about life with a six-month-old, but they may react in different ways. Some will feel great relief that their kids aren't babies anymore. Others will be hit with a sense of loss, recognizing how sweet the baby moments are and knowing they'll never experience them again. Overall, these experienced parents will probably be supportive.

Then there are the friends who have no intention of ever having a baby. Of course, they may change their minds down the line—it's been known to happen. But right now, the thought of caring for a baby gives them chills. It's perfectly fine for you—they want you to have what you want. But please don't expect them to understand your starry-eyed adoration of the little tyke. Expect benevolent smiles. Toleration of stories of cute things. But don't go on too long. There are other important things to talk about: a new lover, the possibility of a transfer to London, a corporate shake-up.

The best way to maintain these friendships is to do it on neutral ground. Someone who's never been a mother will not understand the day-to-day workings of life with a recalcitrant two-year-old. Better to meet for lunch at a restaurant—without your child.

These friendships *can* be maintained and provide an oasis from your new, demanding life. A respite from parenthood. And you need that. Welcome the chance not to talk about your baby's bowels. You can be your old self with this friend. Talk about birth control. These friends can help you from becoming swallowed up by your new role. You can keep up with their lives, single or married. You can talk about those things you always had in common or spend some time reminiscing about the past.

Remember that anyone who is obsessed with one thing is a bore. A Joanie-one-note. Someone who talks about her baby all the time is as boring as someone who talks, talks, talks computers or baseball. Determine that you will show some concern about world events or social problems. At least be able to comment on something you saw on TV. You may be thinking *baby-baby-baby* twenty-four hours a day, but get a grip. *Pretend* to care about the universe until those feelings kick in again. (Helpful hint: It's your baby's universe, too.)

There are, of course, other friends you'll probably run across—the friends who are trying to get pregnant and haven't been successful. Seeing you with your baby may be extremely difficult for them to handle. Accept that. Be sensitive to how much baby talk they can handle. Let such a friend know that you understand her pain. And realize that maybe she will pull away—at least for a little while.

My best friend since college, Ilsa, is single and thirty-five and is in a panic about not having a baby. So she had mixed emotions when Jake and I announced we were having a baby. Happy for us, but every friend who joined "the fraternity of man," as she calls it, meant more isolation for her. Before I got pregnant, she was already making remarks about our friends who had babies and how spoiled they are. Never a good word. Complaint after complaint. Ilsa brought flowers to the hospital and cooed over little Max. But then I didn't hear from her for six months. I decided to write her a little note saying that I understood how difficult the new changes in my life must be for her, but that I treasured her and wanted us to work at staying friends. I said that I needed her to remind me that there was a real world out there.

Aside from your friends' position on babies, relationships can also be tested by a new parent's suddenly tight schedule. A sense of unavailability looms over the friendship. You're not there like you used to be. You have a new and serious responsibility. You've lost your spontaneous, carefree persona.

Listen to your conversations. Are you sounding self-important? Are you a know-it-all? Tailor your parenthood banter to the right audience.

Non-parents may also have had little experience around children, which may make them uncomfortable around your baby. They don't like feeling so "out of it." Babies can be disconcerting because of their fragility; toddlers, because of their unpredictability and trying behavior; and older children, because they "say the darndest things." Your non-parent friend may find the intimacy of your breast-feeding too much to handle, may not understand that every two-year-old in the world pulls at her mom and gets whiny, and worry that a four-year-old will say something embarrassing to them like, "Why do your ears stick out?" These fears often create a tension—which then leads to criticism. Taking a cut-'em-off-at-the-pass approach, they think, *I'll reject the child before the child rejects me.*

Help your non-parent friends by not forcing your most intimate parent-child moments on them. If your child is there, explain the rudiments of child development as they seem applicable. Tell them what you've read about typical two-year-olds, so they'll know that your child is just being normal and not exceptionally bratty.

Your friendships with non-parents can survive if both parties acknowledge the changes and work on compromise and toleration. Such a compromise calls for your friend's putting up with your baby stories, but both of you should recognize when you've reached the "that's enough; let's talk about other things" point in the conversation.

Making the Most of Your "Chauffeur" Time

You don't need a stretch limo to be a chauffeur. Parents are de facto chauffeurs: one of their major jobs is to take children from place to place. To school. To play dates. To parties. To gymnastics. Sometimes you get to go inside; sometimes you have to kill time until pickup. It's never going to be swell. But you can put this chauffeur time to good use with a little advance preparation.

The simplest advice is to always keep a good book handy—in the trunk of your car or in your bag if you travel by public transportation. And we mean a *good* book. Something you can pick up off and on (forget mysteries!). And definitely something you'll really enjoy. Or keep a stack of unfinished *Vanity Fair* magazines or *The New Yorker* in the trunk. A few other suggestions: take along crossword puzzles and a pencil, stationery and a pen, knitting, needlepoint, a self-help book, or nonperishable snacks. Also keep a favorite cassette available so you won't have to listen to Barney (or worse, Metallica!) on your own time.

Take along your own refreshments, such as a soda or bottle of water, in an insulated bag. Or invite a friend along—a low-key, good, old friend who knows that sometimes getting together with working parents must be sandwiched in wherever possible. Someone who appreciates forty-five minutes of "found" time.

How to Start a Babysitting Co-op

At first thought, babysitting co-ops may sound like some 1950s suburban setup for stay-at-home moms to get away for a few hours. Maybe at one time that's exactly what they were. But for working parents who are spending hundreds of dollars a month on day care, babysitting co-ops are one way to avoid expensive Saturday-night sitters. You may put so much of your income into child care that you just can't justify paying a sitter for a night out. But wouldn't it be grand? And don't you sometimes feel like a weekend prisoner?

A babysitting co-op is a group of families that agree to sit for each other's children without charge. Beyond that, it can be whatever the members want it to be. You can call whomever you want to do the sitting or be required to call the member who has done the least amount of sitting recently. You can use a ticket system, have a secretary keep track of hours, or devise some other method. Once you set it up and shake out the inevitable kinks, it can be a godsend.

Fine . . . but what if you need a sitter for this Saturday night—which is tomorrow? It takes time to get a co-op up and running. The answer is to begin with the simplest cooperative arrangement of all: find one other family, ask if they'll sit for your child with the promise of reciprocation, and build from there.

> *When Norman was four months old, I asked a family in the neighborhood if they would consider watching him for two hours while my husband and I went out to dinner, and I would be happy to do the same for them. Consider! They jumped at the chance. They had a one-year-old. We just went out for pizza and then we browsed around Home Depot. Not exactly an exciting evening, but it felt so liberating. I needed that time away. It was only two and a half hours, but it recharged my batteries.*

Starting or joining a babysitting co-op may be one of the best things you can do for your child—and yourself. For children, it's much more enriching and fun than having an adult or almost-adult sitter. For parents, it's free—and offers the potential of building friendships with other parents, plus that rare commodity, a sense of community.

Children often form close and lasting friendships through babysitting co-ops. While child care and schools may change, the friends children made in a long-standing co-op can be an anchor. They may even begin to insist that you go out so they can go over to be "sat" by a friend's parents.

> *The first few months in day care, I felt I could never manage to make real contact with the other parents. Everyone was in such a rush to get home. Then the center offered a parenting class at night. Nine families signed up, and we got to know one another very well. By the end of the six weeks, we decided to start a babysitting co-op. It lasted for five years and was one of the richest experiences of my life. I became good friends with about four*

of the parents, but I felt comfortable leaving my daughter Judith with all the families. For those five years, I never had to pay for a sitter and I never had to decline an invitation because I couldn't get one. My daughter loved her "co-op friends" and was eager to have them "visit" her and to go to their homes.

One of the simplest co-ops is a Saturday-night co-op, in which four to five families agree to rotate babysitting chores on Saturday nights. One Saturday, one family welcomes all the children over for the evening, and the other three or four Saturdays after that, they have free and reliable sitting. With a schedule set up a few months in advance, it's easy to plan when you can go out. As the children get to know each other, their Saturday nights can seem like a club of their own.

Issues to discuss in this type of co-op are earliest and latest times for arrival and pickup; sleep-over options; what the host family will provide in terms of food and drinks; limits on television and movies; and how to handle emergencies.

You may decide that this type of setup is all you need in terms of your sitting requirements or you may explore more elaborate co-ops.

Finding Member Families

Families who come together to share babysitting responsibilities have a common denominator. They may all have children in the preschool or play group. They may live in the same neighborhood or attend the same church or temple. With a common bond, there is a sense in which you know something about the other families—maybe not specific details about specific families, but a general sense of what their day-to-day lives are about. Remember that these parents will be caring for your child, so take time to form a group of parents who are compatible, reliable, and responsible.

Not all families have the right temperament for co-op life. You must have a willingness to allow children in your home, for instance. Some parents may have a harder time with this than others, even if it's only once every week or two. In families that adhere to strict time schedules and routines, a child staying up past bedtime may be too disruptive. Other families may welcome a break from routine and enjoy a different kind of evening once in a while.

Co-ops range from a few families to thirty or forty. In very large co-ops, it is difficult to know all the families well. A small group gives a sense of extended family, while a large group offers what seems like a limitless supply of sitters.

Of course, different families will have different needs. Some parents like to use sitter time to go out to Saturday night dinners or movies. Others work occasional weeknights or want to sign up for a night class. Still others would like to find sitters for occasional weekend getaways. A successful co-op has families with compatible, but not necessarily identical needs. If every family liked to go out on Saturday nights, who would sit? If some like to stay at home on weekend nights, all the better. As long as they all use the co-op at some point. What better arrangement than to have readily available babysitters every Saturday night if all you have to do in return is babysit on Sunday afternoons or Wednesday nights?

It's also important that families live reasonably close to one another. When one family lives a distance from the core group, the parents are not called upon to sit very much. Conversely, they may not find it convenient to drop off their children, either. Set some geographical boundaries that make sense for every member family.

Children need not all be the same age for the group to work well. However, the more easily the kids are able to play with the sitter's children, the more they enjoy the experience. Very young children accept your choice of co-op families more readily than older ones, who often demand veto power over the choice of sitters. Co-ops usually lose their appeal, for the kids, anyway, when they reach ten or eleven.

Bookkeeping

One approach to co-op bookkeeping is to select a secretary who keeps a tally of every family's hours. Members decide how many points to assign each hour or half hour of sitting. When a family needs a sitter, it calls the secretary to find out who's done the least babysitting, and calls that family. Co-ops that use the secretary method usually "pay" in points or credits. In one co-op we know of, the secretary receives two points each month for each family as compensation for the bookkeeping.

Another method of keeping records is to use a ticket system to pay and collect for services.

In our co-op, we first met to cut up tickets from poster paper (and to get to know each other better). Each family was given seventy-

five tickets to spend as needed. Charges were set up to meet the group's needs. Members paid one ticket per half hour for one child; one and a half tickets for two children. On overnighters, the clock stopped at midnight and resumed at eight in the morning with a four-ticket surcharge (six for two kids). It took a few meetings before this final, and most workable, arrangement came to light.

After the initial meeting to decide the rules of the co-op, the group needs to hold periodic meetings to fine-tune the agreed-upon process, consider new members, and socialize.

Calling a Family to Sit

When it's time to call on a family to sit for your child, it's exciting to look at a roster of twelve names and know that you have choices—and an excellent chance of finding someone available. Whom you ask can depend on several factors. The best choice may live on the way downtown, making for smooth logistics. Or you may have heard that the family needs tickets. Perhaps your kids play well together. It doesn't matter if the families within the group tend to rely on one or two closer families, as long as everyone is participating at a level that meets their needs.

While it might seem, at first, that a family that sits all the time and doesn't request return sitting is a dream come true, it can actually work against the system. When a few families start to collect the tickets and don't circulate them, the whole system bogs down. Other parents start to hoard their remaining tickets. One solution is to freeze tickets at a maximum number. In a co-op that begins with seventy-five tickets, parents might agree to freeze at one hundred. When they reach a hundred, they cannot sit again until they work down the pile.

It's important to seek out families who are really interested in using the co-op for sitting on a fairly regular basis. Some parents may be drawn to the group more for its social benefits. One or two half-hearted, but sociable, members are workable. Invite them to the group's family get-together but, for the organization to remain vital, keep the core sitting pool clearly defined. One solution is to make rules for minimum participation: Families can be dropped from the co-op if they miss two consecutive meetings or don't spend any tickets in three or four months.

To put everyone at ease, all families should be provided with a packet of information when the co-op starts, then provide copies to new families as they join. First, put together a roster with all the families, addresses, and phone numbers; second, have each family complete a medical release form; third, have each family complete an information sheet:

- Child's name, address, and phone
- Parents' names and work numbers (after all, you may want or need to make babysitting arrangements during the day)
- Doctor's name and number; medical-plan information
- Medical conditions; routine medications
- Height and weight (necessary for correct dosage of medications)
- Allergies
- Food quirks and preferences
- Special needs (e.g., sleeps with teddy bear)
- Medical release forms

Every family should have a copy of every other child's information.

Depending on how formal or informal your group is, you might want to develop a list of guidelines that keeps things running smoothly and avoids misunderstandings. It's important for the parents to discuss how they set limits for behavior. There are different ways to handle situations, but all methods must be acceptable.

Beyond its purpose of providing free, reliable babysitting, a co-op offers families a chance to get together socially. It's the ideal group in many ways: Everyone has children about the same age; the children all know each other; and many adult friendships are formed there. There are numerous opportunities for get-togethers, including picnics in the park, Halloween parties, and Easter egg hunts.

A final word
Being a working parent is hard work. It requires long hours. Lots of responsibility. But now—armed with new ideas—we hope you're up to the Herculean dual tasks ahead of you.

Appendix A: Leaves of Absence

Excerpts from the UCLA service employees union agreement (AF-SCME: American Federation of State, County, and Municipal Employees).

Article 22: Leaves of Absence

A. General Provisions

In accordance with the provisions of this Article, leaves of absence, with or without pay, may be approved by the University.

1. BENEFIT ELIGIBILITY: Approved leave without pay shall not be considered a break in service. An eligible employee on approved leave without pay may elect to continue University-sponsored benefit plans for the period of the leave by remitting to the University the entire premium amount due for the period of the approved leave. Regulations of the retirement systems determine the effects of the leave without pay or retirement benefits.

2. PERIODS ON LEAVE in a without-loss-of-straight-time pay status shall be considered time worked.

3. REQUESTS FOR LEAVE: Requests for leaves of absence shall be submitted in writing to the University. Such requests shall be submitted sufficiently in advance of the requested leave date to provide the University time to assess the operational impact of granting the request. If the employee learns of the event giving rise to the need for the leave more than thirty days in advance, the employee shall provide the University with notice as soon as the employee learns of the need for leave, and, at a minimum, with thirty days advance, written notice, the employee shall provide the University with as much advance, written notice as possible, and, at a minimum, with such notice no more than five working days after learning of the event.

4. RETURN TO WORK: Except as provided in Section C, Medical Leave of Absence, Section D, Family Care Leave, and Section K, Leave of Absence for Union Business, an employee who has been granted an approved leave with or without pay shall be returned to the same or a similar position in the same department/division when the duration of the leave is six calendar months or less, or twelve months, if extended. If the position held has been abolished or affected by layoff during the leave, the employee shall be afforded the same considerations which would have been afforded had that employee been on pay status when the position was abolished or affected by the layoff. The date of return to work is determined when the leave is granted.

B. Personal Leave

1. A NONPROBATIONARY CAREER EMPLOYEE may be granted a personal leave of absence without pay at the sole, nongrievable discretion of the University. Such leave shall not exceed six calendar months.

2. IF AN EMPLOYEE'S REQUEST for a personal leave of absence without pay is denied, such denial may, upon the employee's written request, be reviewed by the Department/Division Head. The results of such a review shall not be subject to Article 6—Grievance Procedure or Article 7—Arbitration Procedure of this Agreement.

3. THE UNIVERSITY at its sole nongrievable discretion may approve extension of a personal leave of absence without pay for a total leave of not normally more than twelve months.

C. Medical Leaves of Absence

A Medical Leave of Absence is the period(s) an eligible employee is granted leave from work for medical reason in accordance with Section C, Eligibility, below. This leave includes the combined use of accrued sick leave and the medical leave of absence without pay in accordance with the provisions of this Article and Article 21—Sick Leave. In the event that an employee's accumulated sick-leave credit is exhausted, an employee may be placed on a Medical Leave of Absence without pay in accordance with the provisions of this Article. Medical leaves of absence without pay are provided for leaves due to nonwork-related illness or injuries. . . .

1. b A FEMALE EMPLOYEE disabled on account of pregnancy, childbirth, or related medical conditions is entitled to a medical leave of absence in accordance with the provisions of this Article. . . .

3. c VERIFICATION OF MEDICAL DISABILITY for pregnancy-related purposes additionally includes a physician's statement regarding the estimated date of delivery and the anticipated date of the employee's ability to perform the essential assigned functions of her job. . . .

4. b DURING THE PERIOD of verified pregnancy-related/childbearing disability, a female employee is entitled to and the University shall grant a medical leave of absence of up to four months. If the pregnancy-related/childbearing medical disability continues beyond four months, a medical leave of absence may be granted in accordance with Section C 4 a above, for, a total medical absence not to exceed six months. Additionally, the employee may be eligible for a parental leave to care for a newly born or adopted child following the pregnancy-related/childbearing disability leave(s) of absence. The total of parental leave and pregnancy-related/childbearing disability leave, when taken in conjunction, shall not exceed six months. This parental leave of absence is granted under the provisions of Section D, Family Care Leave, of this article.

4. c. AFTER ACCRUED SICK LEAVE is exhausted, an eligible employee may be required to use accrued vacation and compensatory time off prior to taking medical leave without pay, but not to exceed a total medical absence from work of six months. In the event that the employee's accrued sick leave is greater than six months, a medical leave of absence without pay, in addition to the use of all accrued sick leave, shall not be granted.

5. a RETURN FROM A MEDICAL LEAVE OF ABSENCE: An employee who has been granted a medical leave of absence for pregnancy-related/childbearing disability purposes shall be returned to the same job provided the employee returns to work immediately upon termination of the pregnancy-related/childbearing disability and provided such return is within four months of the day on which the pregnancy-related/childbearing disability medical leave commenced. If the same job is not available, a similar job will be offered. If a similar job is not available, the employee shall be afforded the same considerations which would have been afforded had the employee been on pay status when the position was abolished or affected by layoff. A female employee who is also granted Parental Leave shall be returned to work in accordance with Section D 3 g, of this Article.

D. Family Care Leave

1. PARENTAL LEAVE: Parental leave is to care for the employee's newborn or newly adopted child. Parental Leave shall be initiated within one year of the birth or placement of the child. The total of Pregnancy Disability Leave and Parental Leave, when taken in conjunction, shall not exceed six months pursuant to Section C 4 b of this Article.

Chapter 1: The Time to Plan: Before Your Baby Is Born

THE DEPENDENT CARE CONNECTION
P.O. Box 2783
Westport, CT 06880
(800) 873-4636
Offers nationwide resources and referrals for child care and elder care for companies.

FAMILY AND WORK INSTITUTE
330 Seventh Avenue, 14th Floor
New York, NY 10001
(212) 465-2004
Researches family/work/child-care/corporate issues. Catalog available.

9 TO 5, NATIONAL ASSOCIATION OF WORKING WOMEN
238 W. Wisconsin Avenue, Suite 700
Milwaukee, WI 53203
(414) 274-0926
Job Problem Hotline: (800) 522-0925
The national organization, which has chapters in all fifty states, promotes the rights of, and respect for, office workers. Many issues they address involve working parents. Newsletter published five times a year.

NOW/National Organization for Women
Legal Defense and Education Fund
99 Hudson Street
New York, NY 10013-2815
(212) 925-6635
Legal resource kit, $5, includes information on Family and Medical Leave Act, rights of pregnant workers, Q & A on maternity and paternal leaves, and fact sheet on fetal protection policy.

Women's Bureau
U.S. Department of Labor
200 Constitution Avenue, NW
Washington, DC 20210
(202) 219-6652
Free publications on many aspects of women in the workforce. Topics include job rights, flexible work styles, employers, and child care.

Work/Family Directions, Inc.
930 Commonwealth Avenue West
Boston, MA 02215
(617) 278-4000
This national information company provides resource and referral services to both large and small companies for child care and elder care.

Chapter 2: The New Working Mom: The Fourth Trimester

America Online—AOL
(800) 827-6364
Through the Parents' Information Network, parents with computer and modem can browse through pertinent articles. The chat lines offer parents a chance to discuss their own issues and solicit advice from other parents. Specialized forums include work-at-home moms, stay-at-home dads, breast-feeding moms.

PRODIGY SERVICES
(800) 776-3449
The HomeLife Bulletin Board offers members a forum to discuss parenting issues. Special forums for adoption issues and parenting children with special needs.

UCLA WORKING PARENTS NEWSLETTER
Bellagio Site, Box 951785
Los Angeles, CA 90095-1785
Subscriptions available for companies, child-care providers, and others. Write for rates.

WORKING MOTHER MAGAZINE
P.O. Box 5240
Harlan, IA 51593-2740
Focuses on both workplace and parenting issues

Chapter 3: Finding Child Care: It Takes Time to Make the Right Match

BANANAS
5232 Claremont Avenue
Oakland, CA 94618
(510) 658-7101
Many wonderful handouts available in exchange for a first-class stamp. Send for list (also costs one stamp). Includes "Preparing Your Child for a Visit Away from Home"; "Planning for Summer or Holiday Custody"; and other titles.

CHILD CARE ACTION CAMPAIGN
330 Seventh Avenue, 17th Floor
New York, NY 10001
(212) 239-0138
Child-care advocacy group working for better regulation and work conditions in the field.

CHILD CARE AWARE HOTLINE
National Association of Child Care Resource and Referral Agencies
(800) 424-2246
The hotline operator will give you the name of your local R&R agency.

NANNY NEWS
P.O. Box 277
Hopewell, NJ 08525
(800) 634-6266
This bimonthly newsletter is aimed at a readership of both in-home caregivers and their employers. Thoughtful articles; readers' comments encouraged. One-year subscription, $14.95. Also publishes the monthly *In-Home Childcare Resource Guide* with ideas and information for in-home caregivers. One-year subscription, $12.

NATIONAL ASSOCIATION FOR THE EDUCATION OF YOUNG CHILDREN
1509 16th Street, NW
Washington, DC 20036-1426
(202) 232-8777
(800) 424-2460
Free catalog of publications about child care and the education of young children. Bimonthly journal, *Young Children*, features scholarly but readable articles.

NATIONAL CENTER FOR THE EARLY CHILDHOOD WORK FORCE (NCECW)
733 15th Street, NW, Suite 1037
Washington, DC 20005-2112
(800) 879-6784
Advocacy group for child-care workers. Sponsors annual Worthy Wages Day.

NOBODY'S PERFECT: LIVING & GROWING WITH CHILDREN WHO HAVE SPECIAL NEEDS
by Nancy B. Miller (Paul H. Brookes Publishing)
A comprehensive look at the challenges facing parents of children with disabilities or chronic illnesses

U.S. INFORMATION AGENCY
Exchange Visitor Services
Washington, DC 20547-0001
(202) 619-4700
Free list of approved agencies that provide au pairs.

Chapter 4: Let the Caring Begin

GOING TO MY NURSERY SCHOOL
by Susan Kuklin (Bradbury Press).
In color photographs, young children see what to expect in a typical preschool day.

MAMA, DO YOU LOVE ME?
by Barbara Joosse,
illustrated by Barbara Lavallee (Chronicle Books).
Beautifully illustrated story about separation.

RUNAWAY BUNNY
by Margaret Wise Brown (HarperCollins).
Our favorite book to ease separation anxiety—for both children and parents.

YOU GO AWAY
by Dorothy Corey,
illustrated by Lois Axeman (Albert Whitman & Co.).
This story shows how parents *always* return, just like they said they would.

Chapter 6: Nine to Five for Children Under Five

THE GOODBYE BOOK
by Judith Viorst,
illustrated by Kay Chorao (Aladdin Books/Macmillan Publishing)

MOMMIES AT WORK
DADDIES AT WORK
by Eve Merriam,
illustrations by Eugenie Fernandes (Gryphon House).
Two separate books show children all kinds of jobs that parents have—
and can do.

WILL YOU COME BACK FOR ME?
by Ann Tompert,
illustrated by Robin Kramer (Albert Whitman & Co.).
For preschoolers, a comforting story about separation.

Chapter 8: Before and After Work

BOB KEESHAN'S FAMILY FUN ACTIVITY BOOKS (Deaconess Press).
Captain Kangaroo has suggestions for warm summer night and cold
winter night activities, both quiet and energetic.

Chapter 9: Juggling Time, Space, and Sanity

AMERICAN CHILDCARE, INC.
505 North Lake Shore Drive, Suite 203
Chicago, IL 60611
(312) 644-7300
(312) 644-7423, fax
Specializes in same kind of care as KiddieCorp.
Chicago and San Francisco only.

BOOKS ON TAPE
(800) 626-3333
The largest audio book rental company with over three thousand titles. These full-length books (5-15 cassettes each) rent for $8.50 to
$19.50, plus postage, for 30 days.

THE COMPLETE BOOK OF CHILDREN'S PARTIES
by Clare Beaton (Kingfisher Books).
Fun, cheap, and clever theme parties. Teddy bear parties with home-made masks. Black Jell-O at the monster bash.

KIDDIECORP
5665 Oberlin Drive, Suite 102
San Diego, CA 92121
(619) 455-1718
(619) 455-5841, fax
Specializes in temporary, on-site child care at conventions, infant through teens. Available all over the United States. Bonded, licensed, insured.

KIDS' PARTY GAMES AND ACTIVITIES
by Penny Warner (Meadowlark Press).
A good range of things to do arranged by age and type of activity: traditional and contemporary games, group activities.

THE PENNY WHISTLE BIRTHDAY PARTY BOOK
by Meredith Brokaw and Annie Gilbar
illustrations by Jill Weber (Simon and Schuster).
Packed with clever ideas for toddlers to preteens. Many projects that parents and birthday child can do together.

"POSITIVE PARENTING GUIDE FOR BUSINESS TRAVELERS"
MCI
(800) KID-TIPS (543-8477)
Free brochure with tips for parents who travel on business.

Chapter 10: As Times Goes By

CARETAKERS OF WONDER
by Cooper Edens (Green Tiger Press).
Fanciful but comforting ideas of what happens when we are asleep.

CHARLOTTE'S WEB
by E. B. White (HarperCollins).
Classic story of friendship, on a farm, of a little girl, a pig, and a spider.

FROG IN THE MIDDLE
by Susanna Gertz (Four Winds Press).
A gentle tale that examines the problems of three friends playing together.

THE GEORGE AND MARTHA SERIES
by James Marshall (Houghton Mifflin).
Each of the five books has five stories about the friendship between these two hippopotami, emphasizing the importance of sharing, listening, and sensitivity.

GOODNIGHT MOON
by Margaret Wise Brown (HarperCollins).
Great falling-asleep book.

LET'S BE ENEMIES
by Janice May Udry,
illustrated by Maurice Sendak (Harper & Row).
This very early Sendak (1961) depicts the ups and downs of friendship as two little boys grapple with issues of grabbing the best toys and taking all the crayons.

Chapter 11: Time Off: Holidays and Vacations

AMERICAN CAMPING ASSOCIATION
(800) 428-2267
A $12.95 guidebook includes listings on all ACA-accredited day and sleep-away camps.

Chapter 12: Working-Family Issues

CENTER FOR MEDIA EDUCATION
(202) 628-2620
Publications include *Parents' Guide to Television*.
Call for list.

THE FATHERHOOD PROJECT
at the Family and Work Institute
330 Seventh Avenue, 14th Floor
New York, NY 10001
(212) 465-2044
Research and publications materials on fatherhood issues. Free bibliography of books on fatherhood.

FATHERS AND BABIES
by Jean Marzallo (Poseidon Press).
Short, one-page sections explain the basics of babyhood (teething, safe toys, bath time, etc.) to fathers. Humorous illustrations.

THE SECOND SHIFT
by Arlie Hochschild (Viking).
Readable discussion of the issues in families when both parents work outside the home.

Chapter 13: Difficult Times: Worries and Fears

SAFETYBELTSAFEUSA
(310) 673-2666
Detailed information on car seats, belts, and harnesses; recalls; installation tips.

Index

art museums, 192–94
   activities for children at, 193–94
arts and crafts projects, 217
   family get-togethers and, 226
   for parent-led summer camp,
      229–30
AT&T, 25
attention-deficit disorder, *see* special-
   needs children
attention seeking, nonstop chatter as,
   161
au pairs, 78–79, 81, 293

babysitters:
   at conventions, 183, 184
   family vacations and, 235
   for school holidays, 121
   see also caregivers; child care
babysitting co-ops, 279–84
   bookkeeping for, 282–83
   calling family to sit from, 283–84
   finding member families for,
      281–82
   friendships formed through, 280–81
Bananas (R&R), 60, 291
Beaton, Clare, 295
beds, infant sharing with parents, 201
bedtime rituals, 178, 200–204
   feeding and, 202, 204
   nighttime-naptime distinction
      and, 203–4
   sharing responsibility for, 242
   teaching child to be self-soothing
      and, 202–3
beepers, 116, 208
before-school care, 138
beggars, 263
Bencivengo, Judy, 56
benefits:
   company-paid, during parental
      leave, 24–27
   differing needs of employees and,
      32
   for in-home caregivers, 82
   for part-time employees, 31

bilingualism, caregivers who speak
   another language and, 127–29
bill paying, finding time for, 275
birth, *see* childbirth
birthday parties, 194–99
   activities for, 196–97, 198
   for first birthday, 195
   gifts at, 197–98
   invitations to, 197
   number of guests at, 196
   party favors for, 198
   planning of, 197
   for preschoolers, 195–96
   resources for, 295
   for school-age children, 196
   specialness of, 194–95
   themes for, 194, 197
*Bob Keeshan's Family Fun Activity
   Books*, 294
body language, 213
Books on Tape, 294
bookstores:
   libraries vs., 189
   story hours at, 188
booster seats, 267–68
bottle feeding:
   combining nursing and, 47–48
   in crib, 202
brainstorming, 218–19
breastfeeding, *see* nursing
breast pumps, 47–48
bribing:
   for creative acts, 217
   with sweets or toys, 177
Brokaw, Meredith, 295
Brown, Margaret Wise, 293, 296
brunch, on Sunday, 189
budgeting, teaching children about,
   250
business travel, 122, 178–82
   bending of rules and routines dur-
      ing, 181–82
   best time of day to leave for, 179–80
   child sent to stay with relatives
      during, 179, 182

generational differences and, 36–37, 87
  holiday meals at home of, 224
  older, caring for, 244–45
  responses of, to pregnancy, 36
  unsolicited advice from, 36–37
  see also relatives
green cards, 83
greeting rituals, 98
grocery shopping, 187
  with kids, 169–71
  lists for, 170
Grumman Corporation, 32
guilt:
  business travel and, 180
  returning to work and, 45

health concerns:
  at child care, 73, 74–75
  see also sick children
health insurance:
  duplication of, 32
  for in-home caregivers, 82
  during parental leave, 24–27
  for part-time employees, 31
health maintenance organizations (HMOs), 175–76
Hewlett-Packard, 32
hiking, as family outing, 187–88
Hochschild, Arlie, 240, 297
holidays, 220–26
  child care for, 120–21, 220–21
  family get-togethers and, 224–26
  resources for, 296
  from Thanksgiving until early January, 222–23
  see also vacations
home:
  arriving at, after workday, 161–62
  child care in, *see* in-home care; live-in caregivers
  leaving child alone at, 206–10; *see also* latchkey children
  working at, 32, 41, 42, 122–24, 176–78
  see also chores

homelessness, 263
homeowner's insurance, 82, 86
homework:
  after-school care and, 137, 139, 166
  developing routine for, 166
  doing at library, 191
  helping with, 165–68
  latchkey children and, 208
  long-term assignments, 167
  problems with, 146
  while watching TV, 258–59
Honeywell, 33
hospital pediatric wings, sick-care rooms in, 108
hotels, for family vacations, 233–35
housekeeping styles, at home vs. child care, 54–55
housework:
  for in-home caregivers, 80–81
  see also chores

IBM, 24, 30
Illinois, law regarding children left home alone in, 206–7
illness:
  canceling plans because of, 42–43
  of caregivers, 62–63, 70
  of child, 114
  child care and, 75, 92, 105–9
  of family day-care providers, 62–63
  parental or family leave and, 25
  sick-child days and, 32
  sick days and, 114
  see also sick children
Immigration and Naturalization Service, 83
independence, learned in preschool, 53
infants:
  adaptability of, 97
  center-based care for, 69, 70
  creativity of, 217
  determining child-care needs of, 54–55

infants *(cont.)*
    evaluating care of, 126–27
    friendships of, 211–12
    newborn, car travel with, 268
    non-parents' reactions to, 278
    nursing of, 42, 43, 47–48
    in restaurants, 172
    safety seats for, 267
    separation anxiety in, 202–3
    shared care for, 85
    sleeping of, 42
    sleeping in parents' bed, 202
    sleep patterns of, 123
    sleep problems in, 201, 202–4
    taking to work, 118–19
    temperament of, 54
    working at home with, 123
in-home care, 35, 70, 76–85
    agreements for, 83–84
    checking references for, 79, 81
    with child of caregiver's own, 76
    classes for, 84–85
    cost of, 76
    driving and, 82–83
    holidays and, 221
    housework requirements and,
        80–81
    immigration status and, 83
    insurance and, 82–83
    interviews for, 80–81
    leaving instructions and important
        information for, 89–92
    with live-in caregiver, 76–79
    scheduling day for, 84
    searching for, 79–80
    shared care and, 85–86
    tax matters and, 82
    working at home and, 123–24
In-Home Childcare Resource Guide, 292
insurance:
    car, 83
    homeowner's, 82, 86
    in-home care and, 82–83
    see also health insurance
IRS (Internal Revenue Service), 34, 82

jealousy:
    of caregiver, 99–101
    spouse's feelings of, 43
job changes, making changes in child
    care due to, 132
job sharing, 31
Joosse, Barbara, 293

Keeshan, Bob, 294
KiddieCorp, 295
Kids' Party Games and Activities
    (Warner), 295
kindergarten, 53
    after-school care and, 139
    see also preschools
kitchen, family time together in,
    162–63
Kuklin, Susan, 293

language skills, caregivers who speak
    another language and, 127–29
latchkey children, 138, 206–10
    answering door or phone, 208–9
    emergency plans for, 207–8
    estimating your return time for, 208
    legal issues and, 206–7
    number of siblings and, 210
    preparation of, 207
    setting firm rules for, 209, 210
late nights, *see* working late
laundry, 186, 187, 275
    during family vacations, 235
leaves of absence:
    for elder care, 245
    sample union agreement on,
        285–88
    see also parental leave
legal issues:
    immigration policies and, 83
    leaving child home alone and,
        206–7
    parental leave and, 24–27
    pregnancy in workplace and, 24
    tax matters related to child care
        and, 34, 82

last few days before, 38
law and, 24–27
negotiation of, 27–28
paid days in, 23–24
planning, 20–23
receiving work calls at home during, 38
recovery process during, 41, 43
relationship with spouse during, 49–50
researching policies on, 26, 27
returning early from, 23, 27
returning to work after, 16, 21, 23, 26–27, 44–49, 92–94, 111
sample union agreement on, 285–88
technical definition of, 24
temporary replacements during, 20, 21, 23, 28
when to start, 22–24
work crises during, 43
work taken home during, 41, 42
Parenthood, 129
parenting seminars, 31
Parents' Guide to Television, 297
parks, docent- and ranger-led walks in, 187–88
parties:
    resources for, 295
    see also birthday parties
part-time work, 31
pediatricians, scheduling child's appointments with, 115, 175–76
peer pressure, 259–61
Penny Whistle Birthday Party Book, The (Brokaw and Gilbar), 295
phone calls:
    answered by child home alone, 208–9
    answering machines and, 116, 162, 209
    beepers and, 116, 208
    during business travel, 178, 180
    cellular phones and, 116, 208
    to child at child care, 101

to home or caregiver during workday, 45, 115–16
interviewing caregivers in, 64–65, 71
during lunch breaks, 116
phone numbers, for emergencies, 90–91, 208, 209
phone trees, for schools, 148
photographs:
    of baby, kept at workplace, 112–13
    of birthday parties, 195, 198
    of caregivers and other children in child care, 135
    of family get-togethers, 226
    of first birthdays, 195
    of parents, kept at child care, 98
physical disabilities, *see* special-needs children
picking up children:
    after child care or after-school programs, 97–98, 100, 157–58
    greeting rituals for, 98
plane travel, 236–38
    ear discomfort and, 238
    fear of, 236
    food and drink in, 237
    naptime and, 237–38
    preparing children for, 237
    seating arrangements for, 237–38
    what to take along for, 237
playing:
    in preschools, 129, 131–32
    preteens' attitude toward, 139–40
    by twosomes vs. threesomes, 214–16
popularity, friendship vs., 211
"Positive Parenting Guide for Business Travelers," 295
postpartum blues, 50
postpartum period, 39–52
    feeling like mere caretaker in, 48–49
    meeting other new parents in, 50–52

breast-pumping at, 47–48

commuting to and from, 155–56, 158–59, 275

done at home, 32, 41, 42, 122–24, 176–78

flexible workplace and, 32

leave from, *see* parental leave

missing your baby at, 110–13

networking with other parents at, 117–18

phone calls from, during parental leave, 38

pregnancy at, 15–20

returning to, after childbirth, 16, 21, 23, 26–27, 44–49, 92–94, 111

taking child to, 118–20

talking with other working parents at, 21–22

when to leave, during pregnancy, 22–24

see also coworkers; employers

workdays:

being a parent during, 114–16

for children under five, 125–36

child's appointments during, 115, 175–76

morning routine for, 150–52

picking up child after, 157–58

ride home at end of, 158–61

taking break at end of, 158

for working parents, 110–24

workers' compensation, 82

work/family committees, 30

Work/Family Directions, Inc., 33, 290

working hours:

flexibility in scheduling of, 31, 114–15

long, creative handling of, 122

working late, 121–22

alternatives to, 115

Working Mother, 53, 291

working mothers, attitudes toward, 15

worrying, about child care, 113

You Go Away (Corey), 293

Young Children, 292